BBC

DOCTOR WHO

EMPIRE OF THE WOLF

"These time-travelling tales are mysterious and are quite the story!"
The GWW

"Houser once again skilfully blends together different aspects of the Doctor Who universe."
Blogtor Who

"This is the perfect comic for all Doctor Who fans, old or new."
DC Comics News

"Definitely leaves you wanting more."
Warped Factor

"A fan combo with lots of potential."
TM Smash

"Jody Houser 100% nails her characters every time and Missy is no different."
Geek Culture Reviews

"A treat for fans."
CBR

"Highly recommended to all Whovians."
Kabooom

"The story & plot is presented in such an exciting manner!"
Reading With a Flight Ring

"Delivers a multiple Doctor story, but with a difference."
DC Comic News

"The art captures the look and feel of the actors while remaining organic to the comic medium"
Comical Opinion

"A masterpiece of characterization."
Bleeding Cool

"An entertaining ride."
Screenrant

"A radical romp through time and space!"
Nerdist

Doctor Who Backlist

See Reader's Guide (page 110) for full list of titles

TENTH DOCTOR:
YEAR ONE
Hardback: 9781785863998

ELEVENTH DOCTOR:
YEAR ONE
Hardback: 9781785864001

TWELFTH DOCTOR:
YEAR ONE
Hardback: 9781785864018

Group Editor
Jake Devine

Art Director
Oz Browne

Titan Comics

Editorial Assistant
Calum Collins

Production Manager
Jackie Flook

Digital & Marketing Manager
Jo Teather

Publishing Director
John Dziewiatkowski

Editor
Phoebe Hedges

Sales & Circulation Manager
Steve Tothill

Head Of Rights
Jenny Boyce

Operations Director
Leigh Baulch

Senior Creative Editor
David Leach

Marketing Coordinator
Lauren Noding

Acquisitions Editor
Duncan Baizley

Publishers
Vivian Cheung & Nick Landau

Production Controllers
Caterina Falqui & Kelly Fenlon

Publicist
Phoebe Trillo

Publishing Director
Ricky Claydon

For rights information contact Jenny Boyce
jenny.boyce@titanemail.com

Special thanks to Chris Chibnall, Matt Strevens, Mandy Thwaites, Suzy L. Raia, Gabby De Matteis, Ross McGlinchey, David Wilson-Nunn, Kirsty Mullan and Kate Bush for their invaluable assistance.

BBC Studios

Chair, Editorial Review Boards **Nicholas Brett** | Managing Director, Consumer Products and Licensing **Stephen Davies**
Director, Magazines **Mandy Thwaites** | Compliance Manager **Cameron McEwan** | UK Publishing Co-Ordinator **Eva Abramik**

DOCTOR WHO: EMPIRE OF THE WOLF
ISBN: 9781787736436

Published by Titan Comics, a division of Titan Publishing Group, Ltd. 144 Southwark Street, London, SE1 0UP.
Titan Comics is a registered trademark. All rights reserved.

A CIP catalogue record for this title is available from the British Library.
First edition: May 2022.

10 9 8 7 6 5 4 3 2 1

Printed in Spain

Titan Comics does not read or accept unsolicited DOCTOR WHO submissions of ideas, stories or artwork.

BBC

DOCTOR WHO

EMPIRE OF THE WOLF

WRITER
JODY HOUSER

ARTIST
ROBERTA INGRANATA

COLORIST
WARNIA K. SAHADEWA

LETTERER
RICHARD STARKINGS OF
COMICRAFT

TITAN
COMICS

BBC

BBC

DOCTOR WHO

EMPIRE OF THE WOLF

PREVIOUSLY...

Dashing across time and space, the Eighth Doctor has had many adventures, but his greatest challenge – the Time War – is yet to come. Reeling from the loss of his dear friends Amy and Rory, the Eleventh Doctor is looking to escape reality and just have a bit of fun. Neither Doctor expects what's about to happen next...

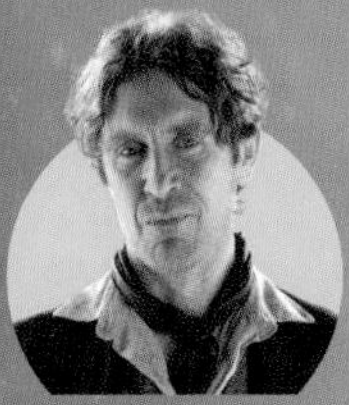

Eighth Doctor

The last incarnation before the terrible Time War, the Eighth Doctor is a suave gentleman, sporting an excitable sensibility behind a tough exterior.

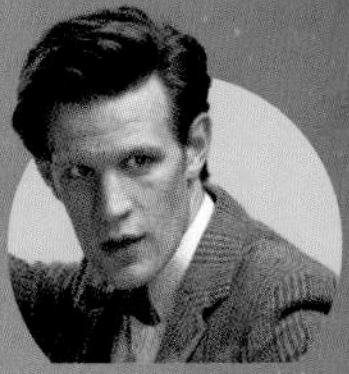

Eleventh Doctor

Last of the Time Lords of Gallifrey. Never cruel or cowardly, he is a gangly boy professor with an old soul. He has made many mistakes, but owns all of them.

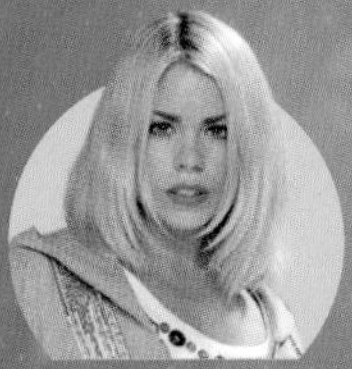

Rose

Abandoned in a universe not entirely unlike our own, Rose Tyler settled down with the human regeneration of the Tenth Doctor, known as John Smith. Her temporal travels will never be forgotten.

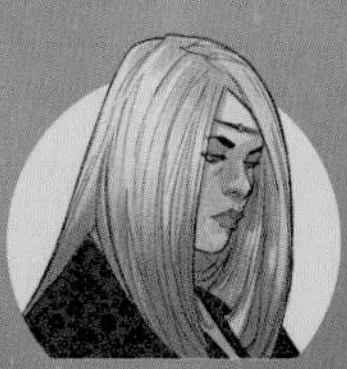

Empress Rose

Determined to right wrongs across the universe, this Rose Tyler from an alternate timeline has been glorified as the Bad Wolf Empress by her devoted followers.

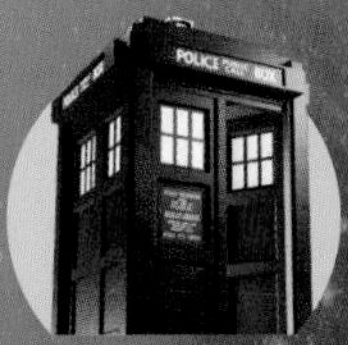
POLICE BOX

The **TARDIS**

'Time and Relative Dimension in Space'. Bigger on the inside, this unassuming blue police box is your ticket to amazing adventures across time and space!

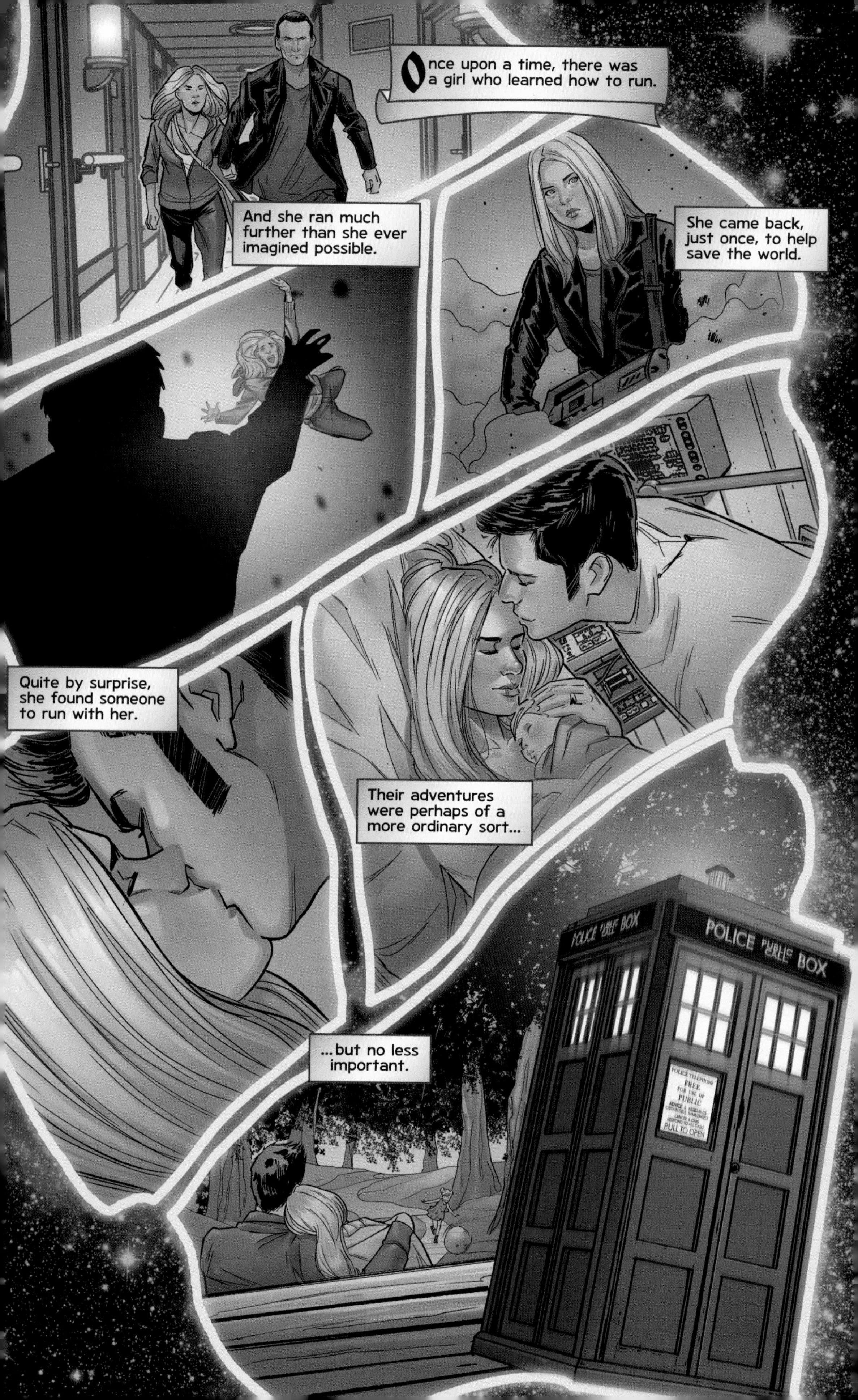
Once upon a time, there was a girl who learned how to run.
And she ran much further than she ever imagined possible.
She came back, just once, to help save the world.
Quite by surprise, she found someone to run with her.
Their adventures were perhaps of a more ordinary sort...
...but no less important.
POLICE PUBLIC CALL BOX
POLICE PUBLIC CALL BOX
PULL TO OPEN

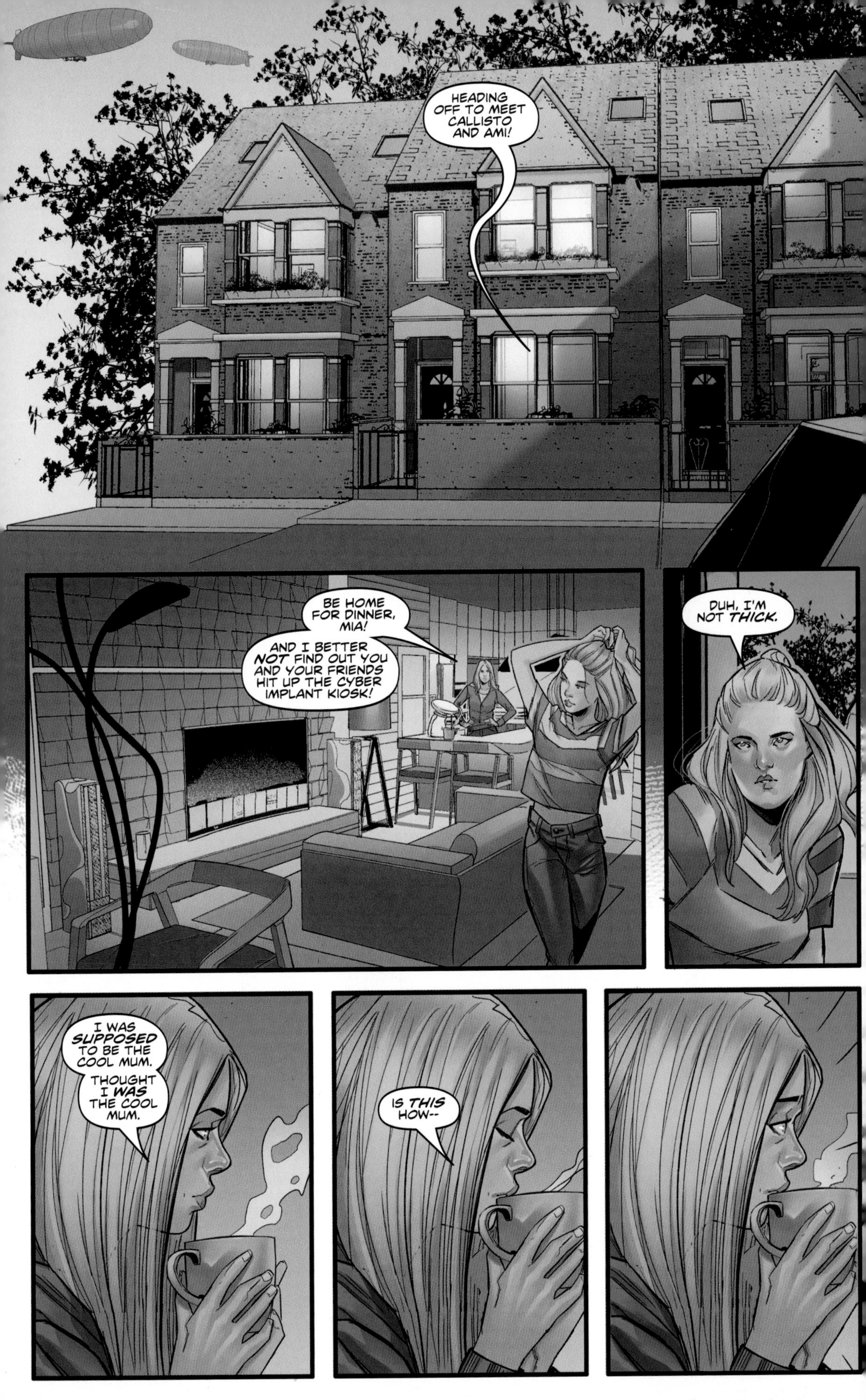
HEADING OFF TO MEET CALLISTO AND AMI!
BE HOME FOR DINNER, MIA!
AND I BETTER *NOT* FIND OUT YOU AND YOUR FRIENDS HIT UP THE CYBER IMPLANT KIOSK!
DUH, I'M NOT *THICK*.
I WAS *SUPPOSED* TO BE THE COOL MUM.
THOUGHT I *WAS* THE COOL MUM.
IS *THIS* HOW--

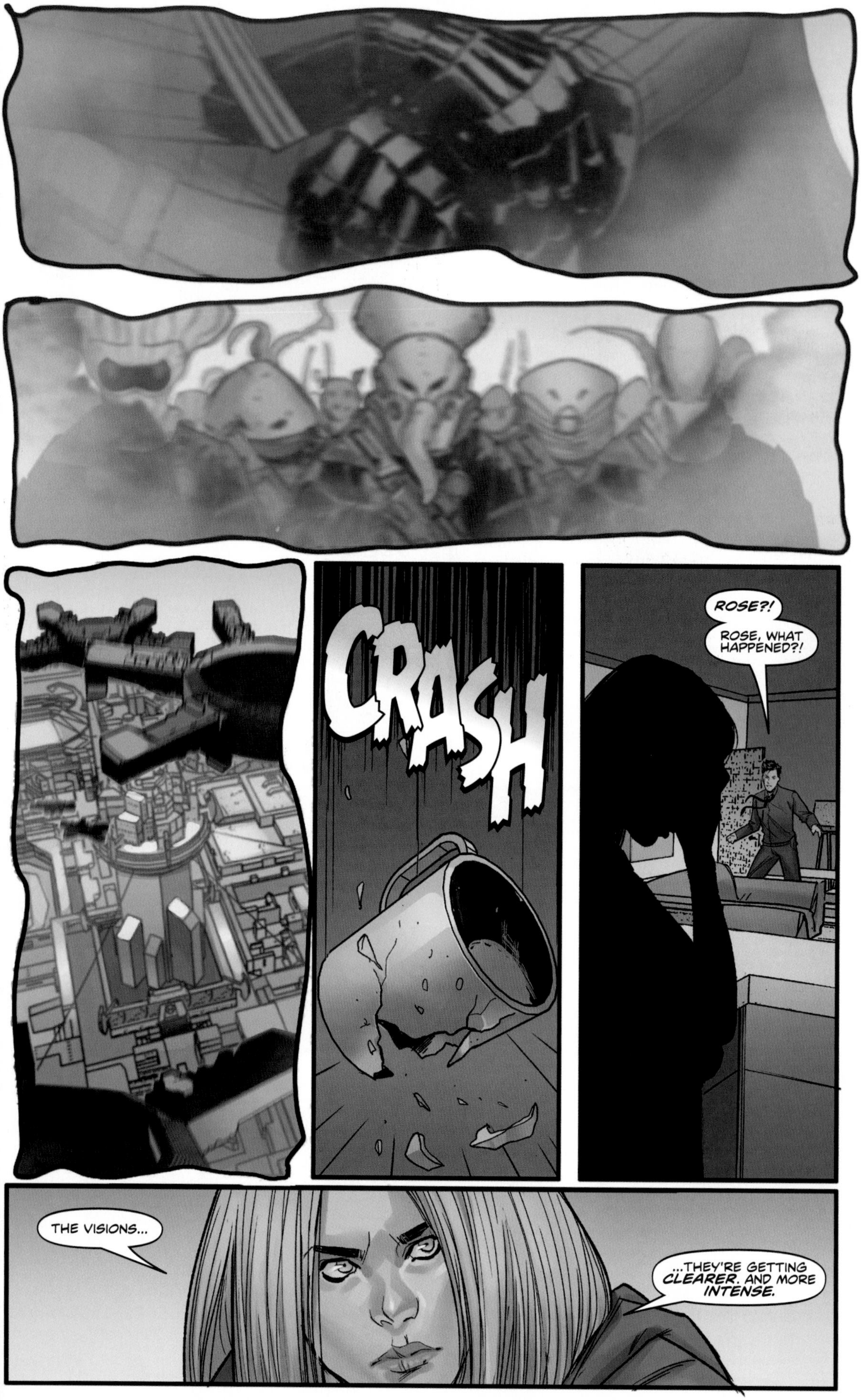
CRASH
ROSE?!
ROSE, WHAT HAPPENED?!
THE VISIONS...
...THEY'RE GETTING CLEARER. AND MORE INTENSE.

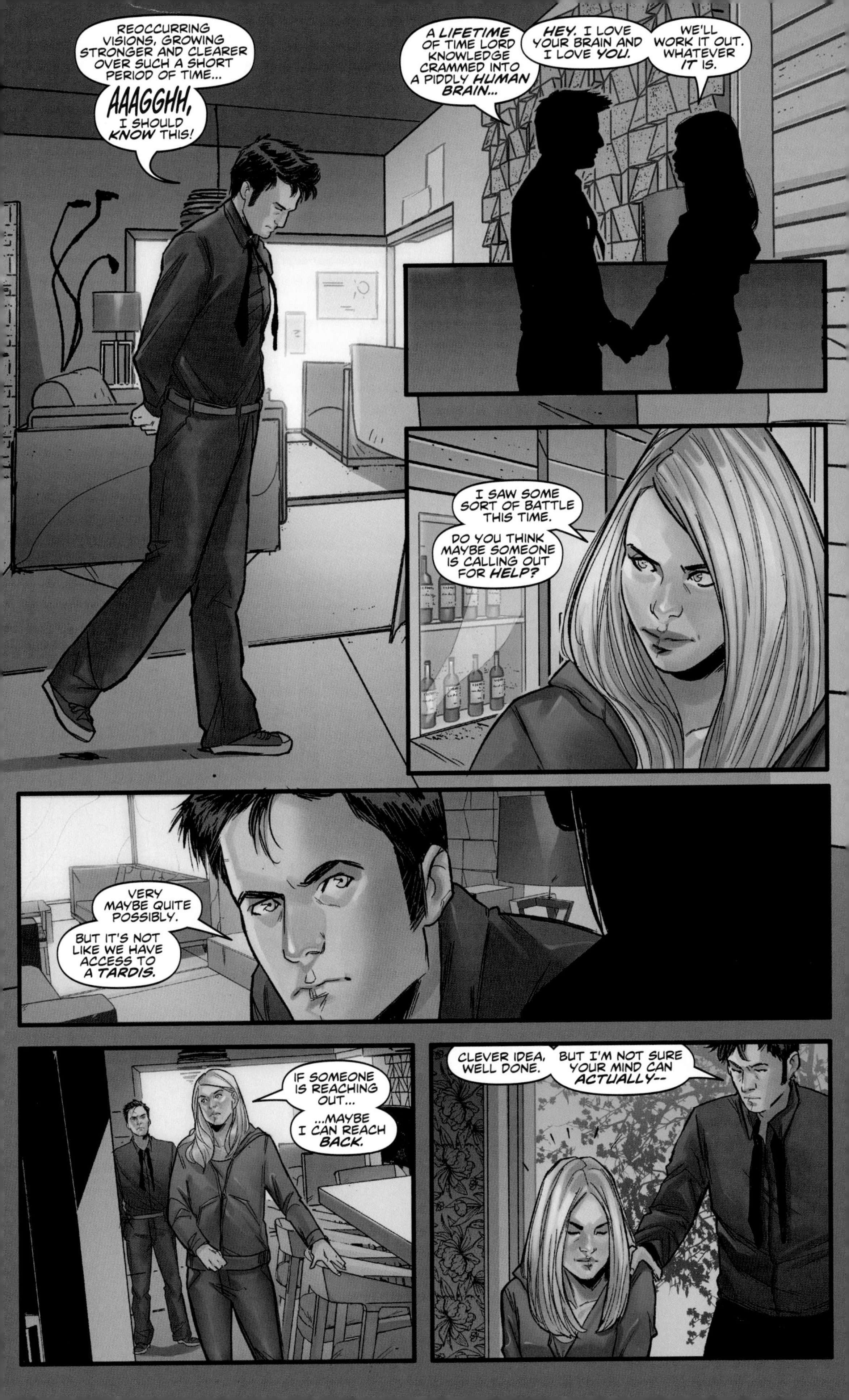
REOCCURRING VISIONS, GROWING STRONGER AND CLEARER OVER SUCH A SHORT PERIOD OF TIME...
AAAGGHH, I SHOULD KNOW THIS!
A LIFETIME OF TIME LORD KNOWLEDGE CRAMMED INTO A PIDDLY HUMAN BRAIN...
HEY. I LOVE YOUR BRAIN AND I LOVE YOU.
WE'LL WORK IT OUT. WHATEVER IT IS.
I SAW SOME SORT OF BATTLE THIS TIME.
DO YOU THINK MAYBE SOMEONE IS CALLING OUT FOR HELP?
VERY MAYBE QUITE POSSIBLY.
BUT IT'S NOT LIKE WE HAVE ACCESS TO A TARDIS.
IF SOMEONE IS REACHING OUT...
...MAYBE I CAN REACH BACK.
CLEVER IDEA, WELL DONE.
BUT I'M NOT SURE YOUR MIND CAN ACTUALLY--

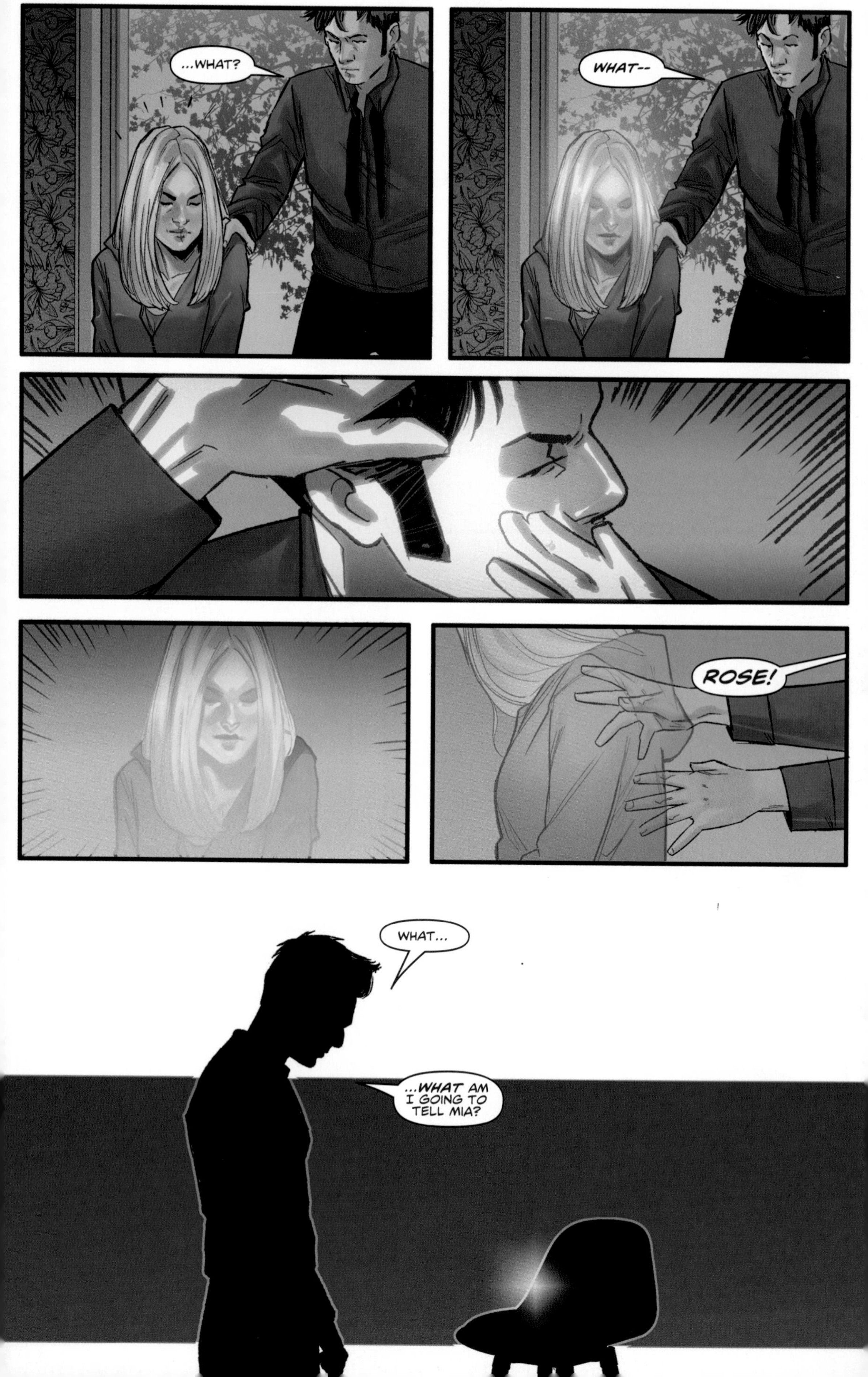
...WHAT?
WHAT--
ROSE!
WHAT...
...WHAT AM I GOING TO TELL MIA?

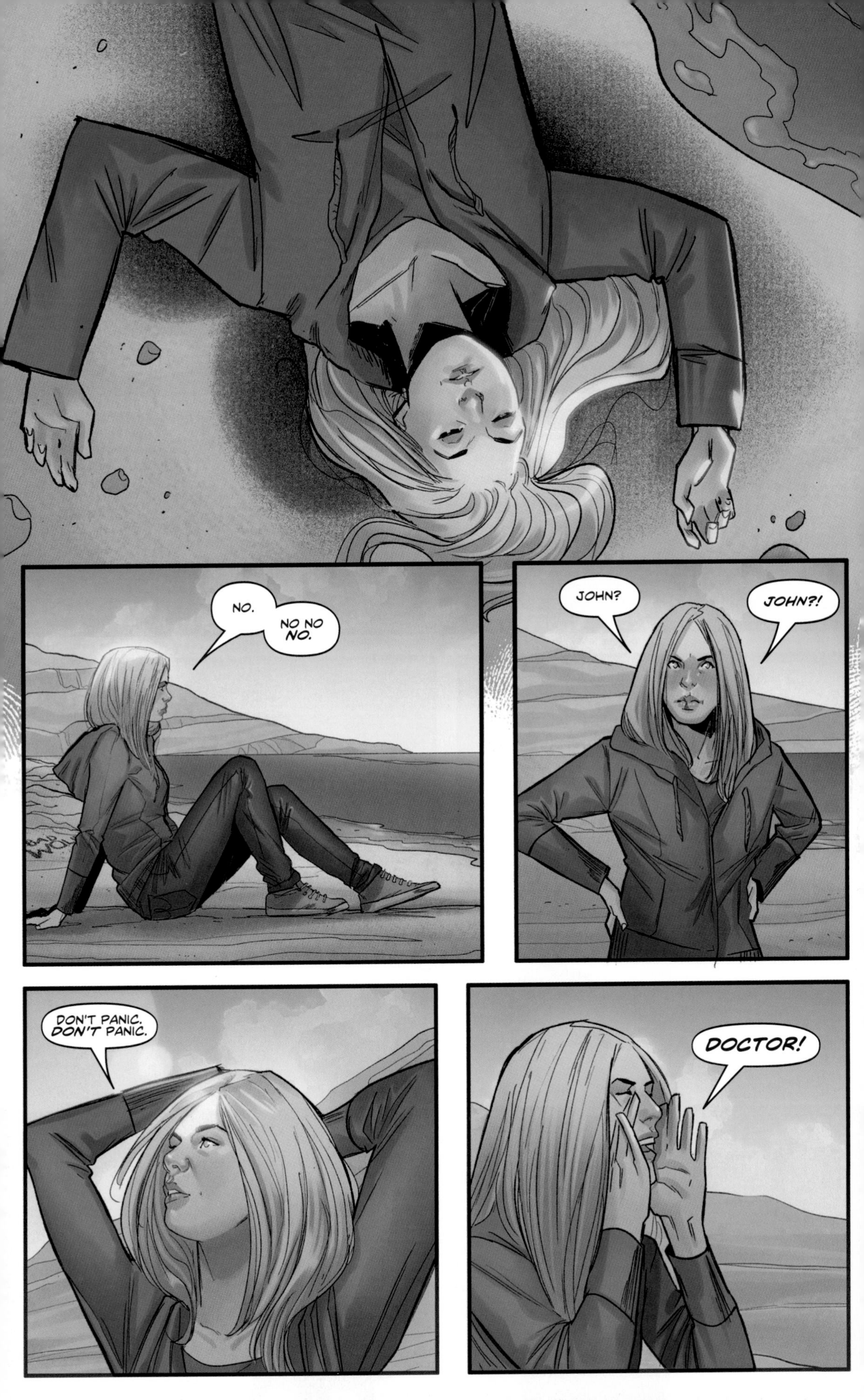
NO.
NO NO *NO.*
JOHN?
JOHN?!
DON'T PANIC.
DON'T PANIC.
DOCTOR!

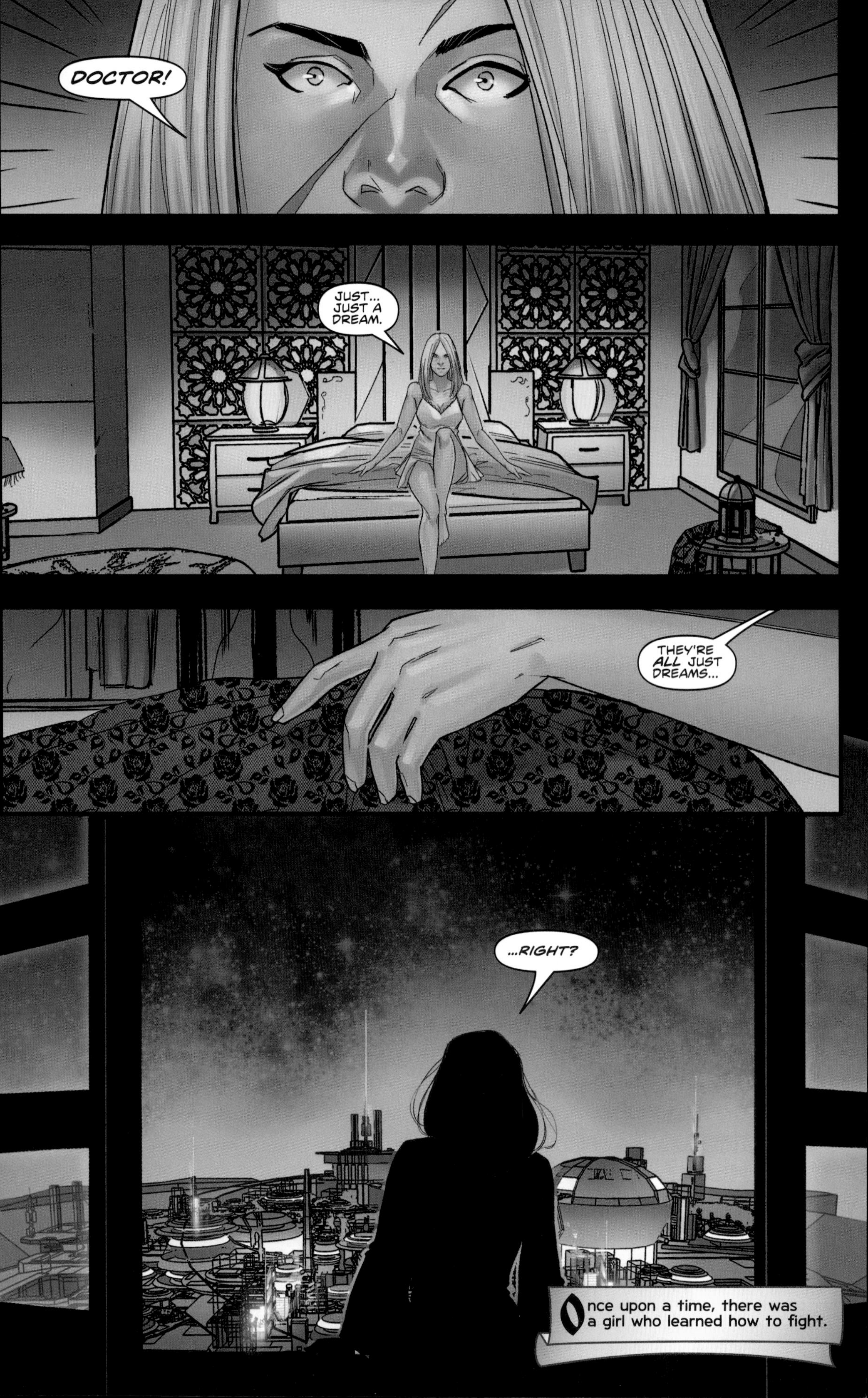
DOCTOR!
JUST... JUST A DREAM.
THEY'RE ALL JUST DREAMS...
...RIGHT?
Once upon a time, there was a girl who learned how to fight.

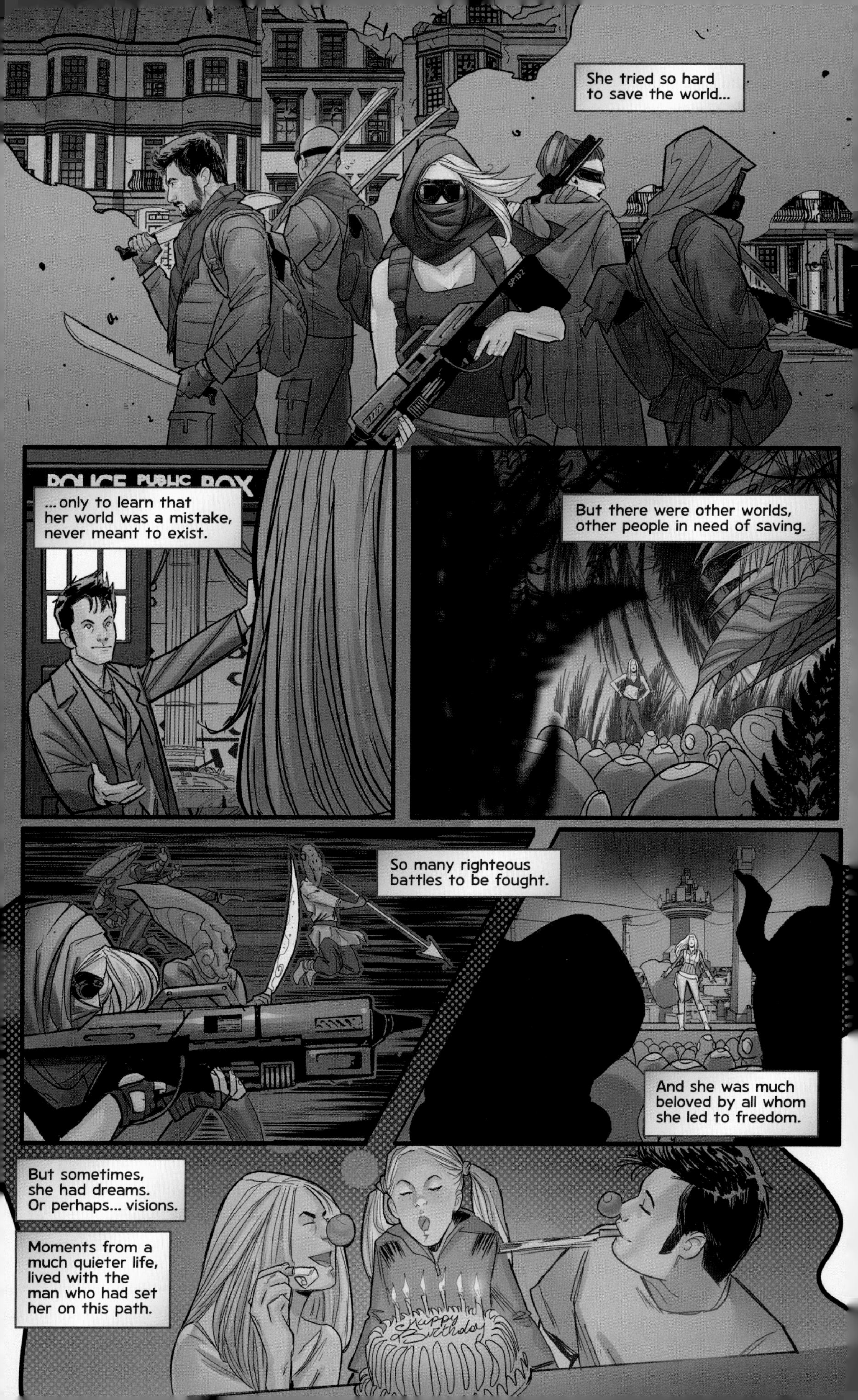
She tried so hard to save the world...
POLICE PUBLIC BOX
...only to learn that her world was a mistake, never meant to exist.
But there were other worlds, other people in need of saving.
So many righteous battles to be fought.
And she was much beloved by all whom she led to freedom.
But sometimes, she had dreams. Or perhaps... visions.
Moments from a much quieter life, lived with the man who had set her on this path.
Happy Birthday

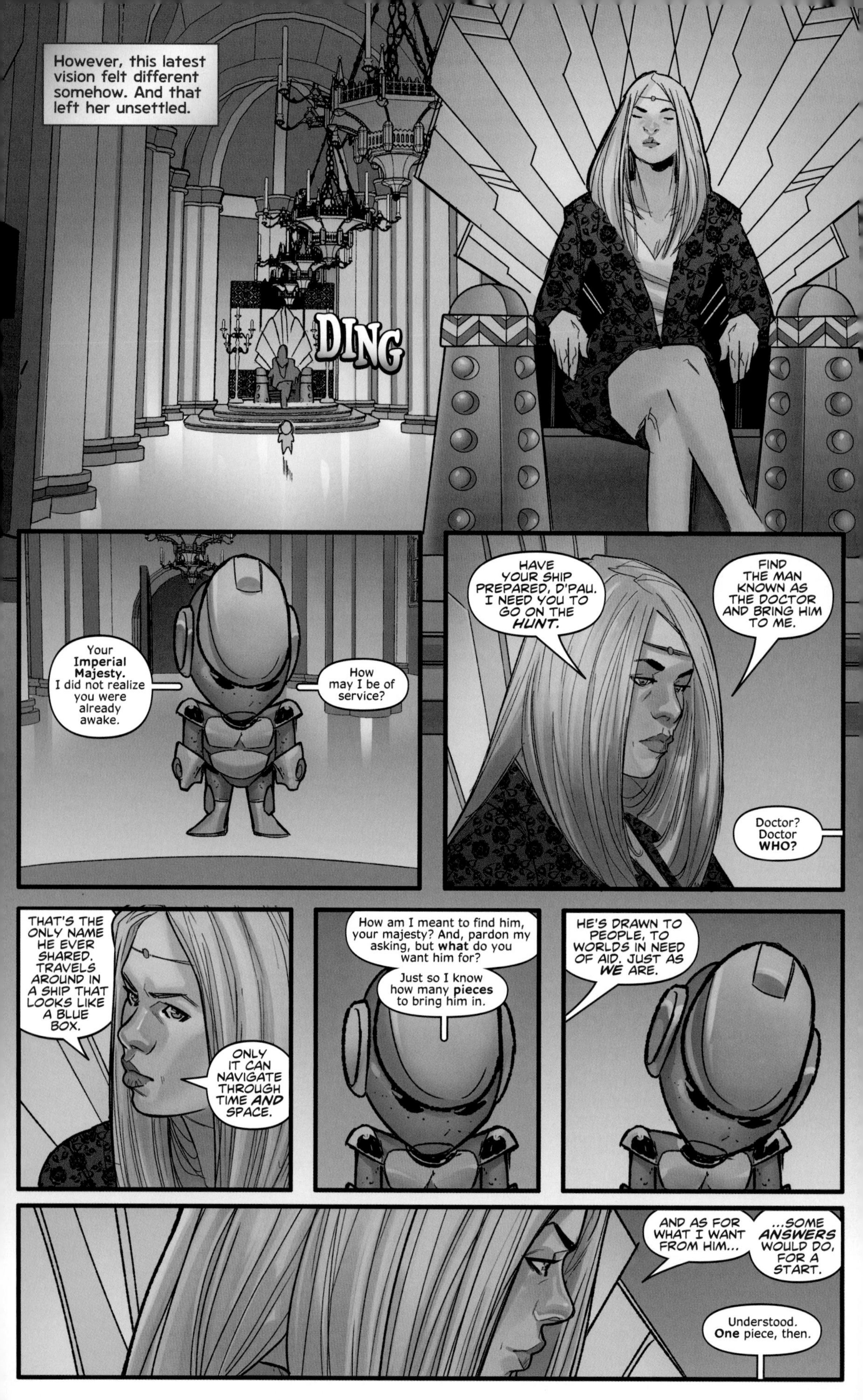
However, this latest vision felt different somehow. And that left her unsettled.
DING
Your **Imperial Majesty.** I did not realize you were already awake.
How may I be of service?
HAVE YOUR SHIP PREPARED, D'PAU. I NEED YOU TO GO ON THE ***HUNT.***
FIND THE MAN KNOWN AS THE DOCTOR AND BRING HIM TO ME.
Doctor? Doctor **WHO?**
THAT'S THE ONLY NAME HE EVER SHARED. TRAVELS AROUND IN A SHIP THAT LOOKS LIKE A BLUE BOX.
ONLY IT CAN NAVIGATE THROUGH TIME ***AND*** SPACE.
How am I meant to find him, your majesty? And, pardon my asking, but **what** do you want him for?
Just so I know how many **pieces** to bring him in.
HE'S DRAWN TO PEOPLE, TO WORLDS IN NEED OF AID. JUST AS ***WE*** ARE.
AND AS FOR WHAT I WANT FROM HIM...
...SOME ***ANSWERS*** WOULD DO, FOR A START.
Understood. **One** piece, then.

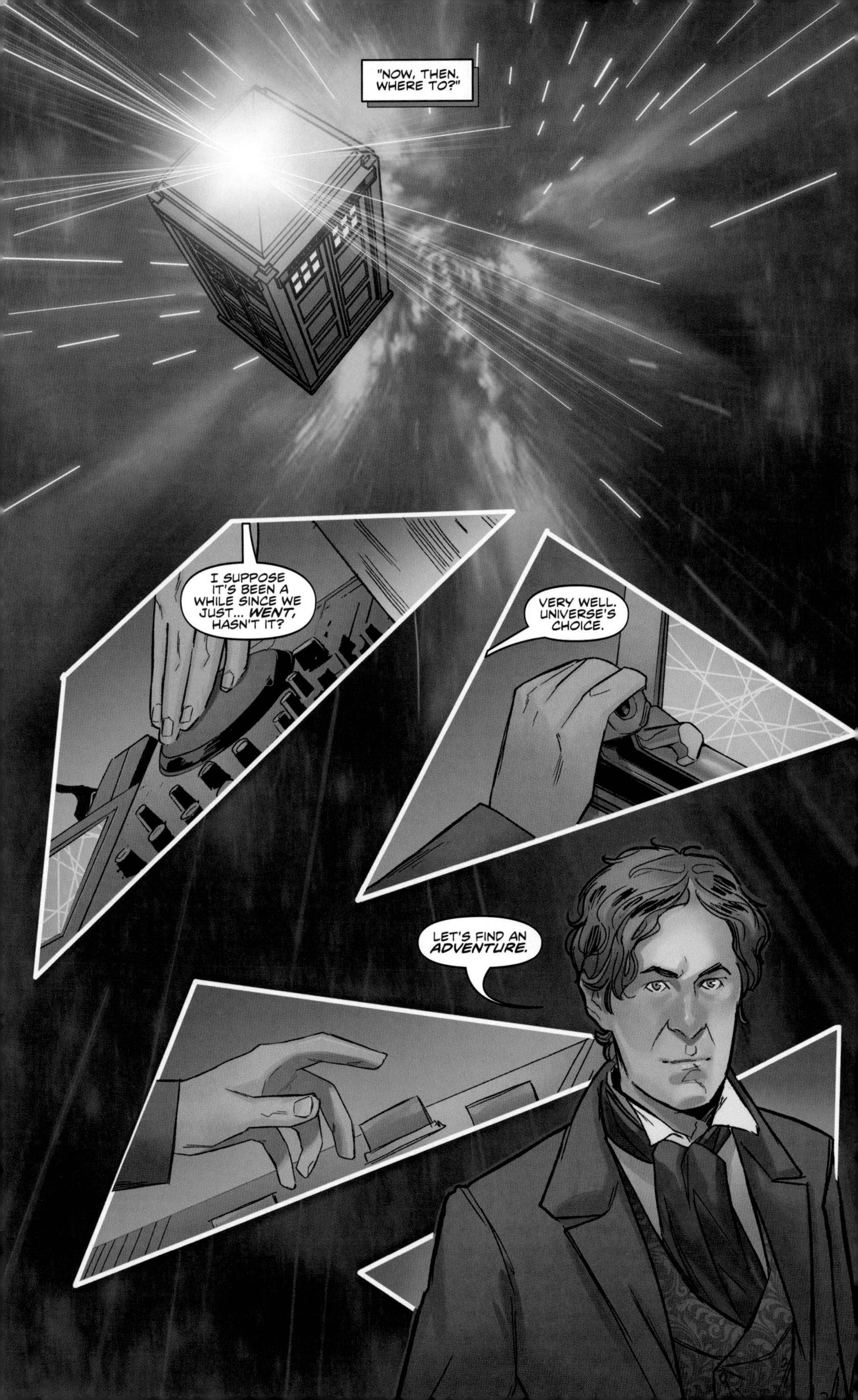
"NOW, THEN. WHERE TO?"
I SUPPOSE IT'S BEEN A WHILE SINCE WE JUST... *WENT,* HASN'T IT?
VERY WELL. UNIVERSE'S CHOICE.
LET'S FIND AN *ADVENTURE.*

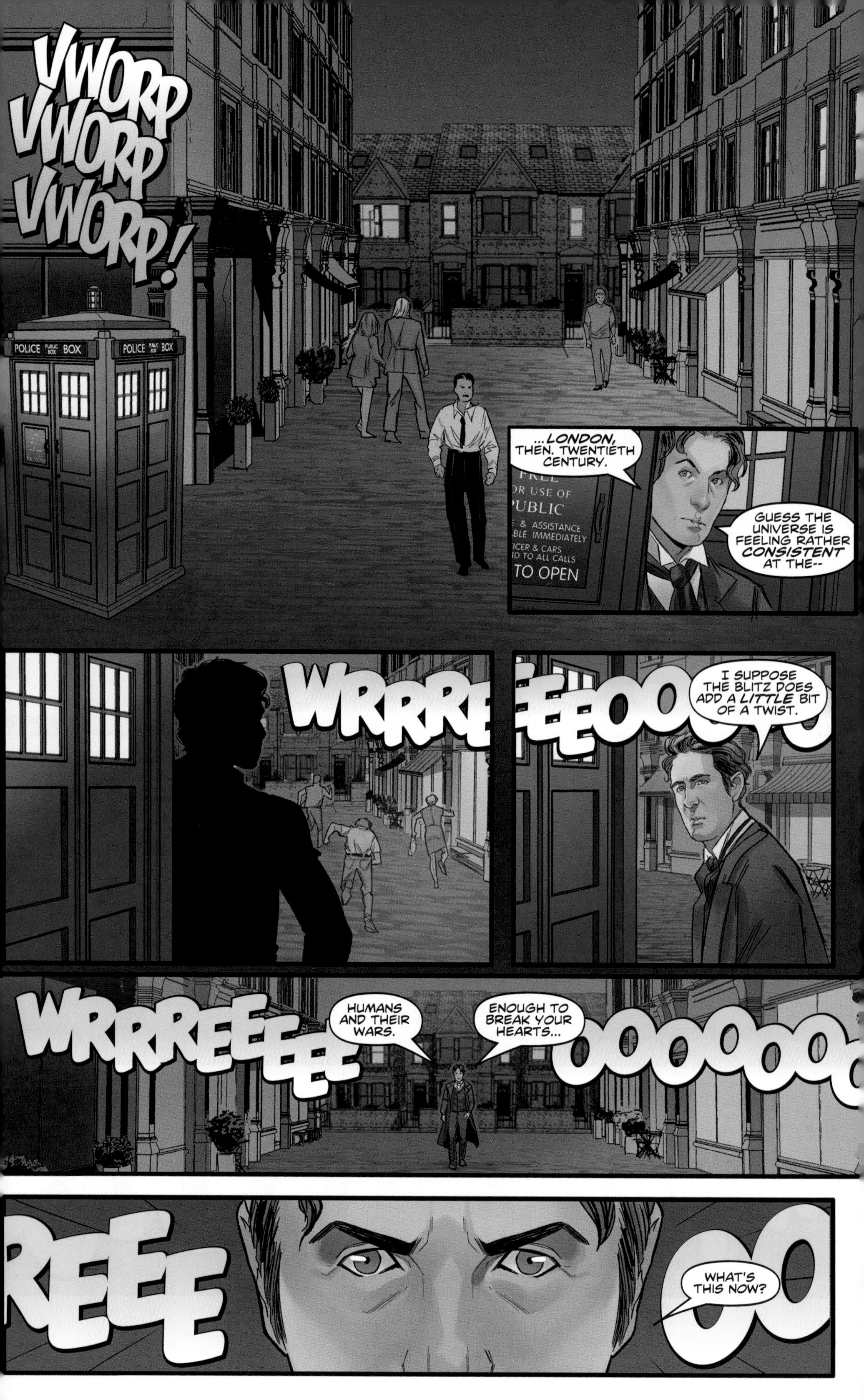
VWORP
VWORP
VWORP!
POLICE PUBLIC BOX
POLICE PUBLIC BOX
...*LONDON*, THEN. TWENTIETH CENTURY.
GUESS THE UNIVERSE IS FEELING RATHER *CONSISTENT* AT THE--
WRRREEEOOO
I SUPPOSE THE BLITZ DOES ADD A *LITTLE* BIT OF A TWIST.
WRRREEEEE
HUMANS AND THEIR WARS.
ENOUGH TO BREAK YOUR HEARTS...
OOOOOO
REEE
OO
WHAT'S THIS NOW?

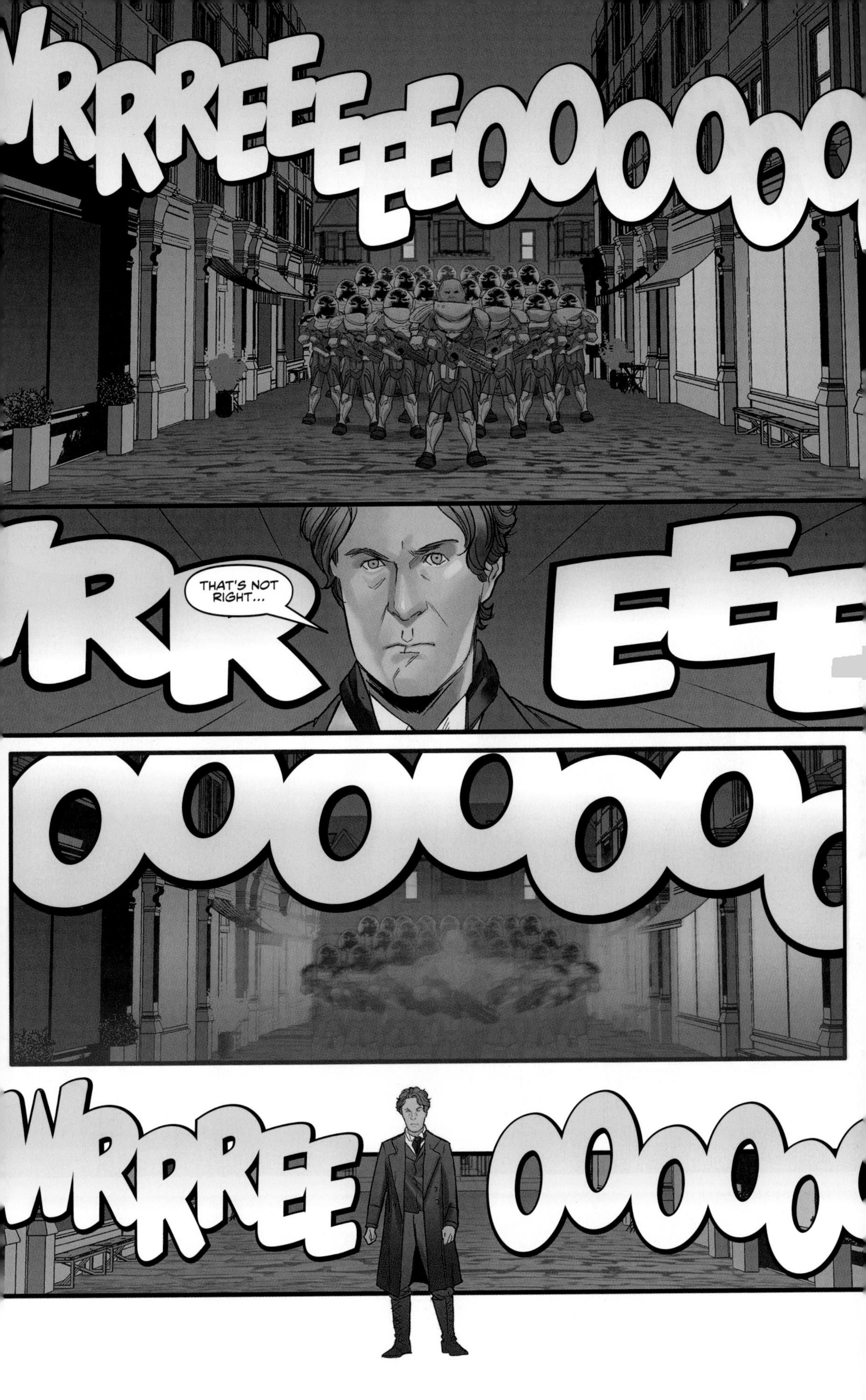
VRRREEEEOOOOOO
RR
THAT'S NOT RIGHT...
EEE
OOOOOO
WRRREE
OOOOOO

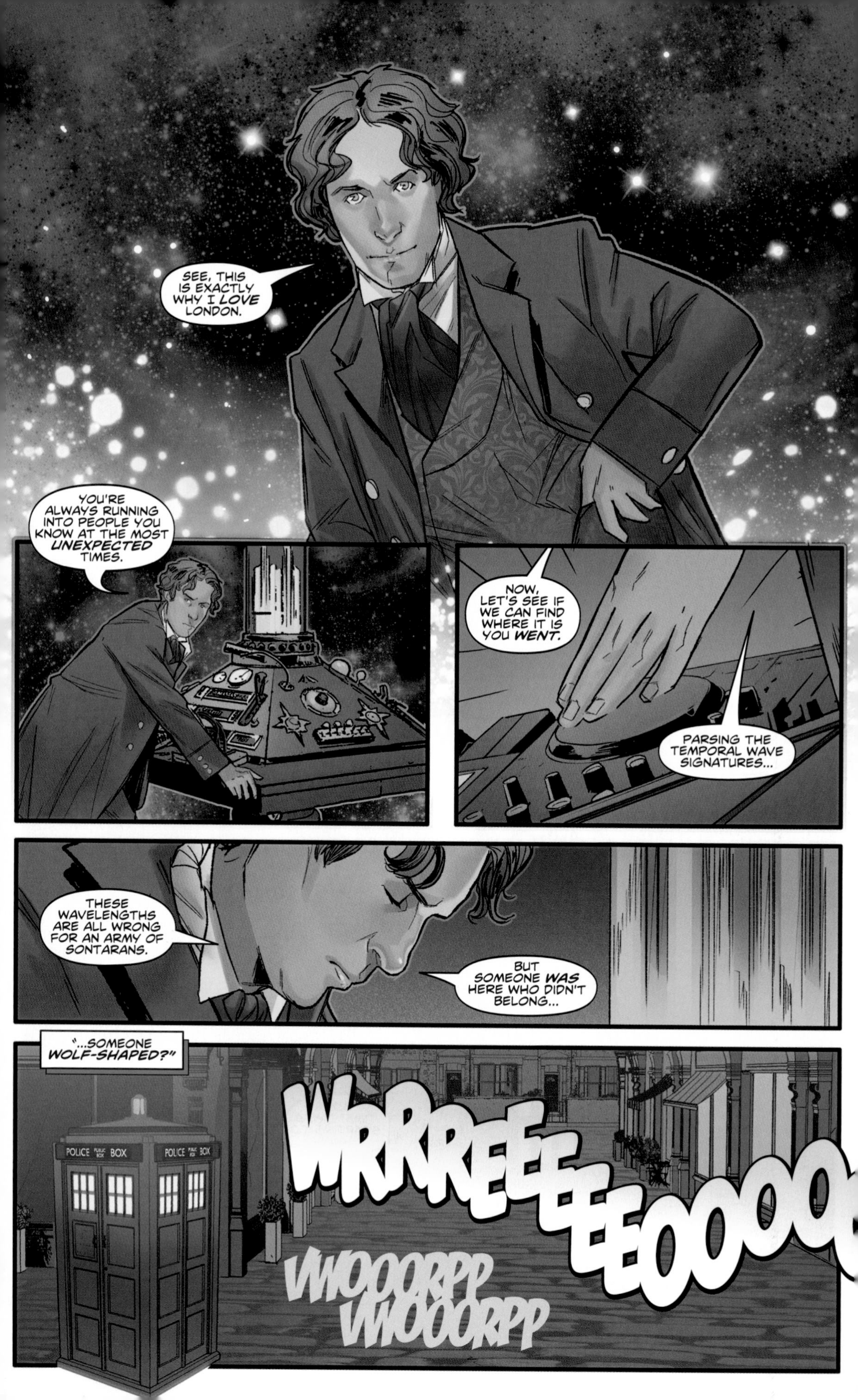
SEE, THIS IS EXACTLY WHY I *LOVE* LONDON.
YOU'RE ALWAYS RUNNING INTO PEOPLE YOU KNOW AT THE MOST *UNEXPECTED* TIMES.
NOW, LET'S SEE IF WE CAN FIND WHERE IT IS YOU *WENT*.
PARSING THE TEMPORAL WAVE SIGNATURES...
THESE WAVELENGTHS ARE ALL WRONG FOR AN ARMY OF SONTARANS.
BUT SOMEONE *WAS* HERE WHO DIDN'T BELONG...
"...SOMEONE *WOLF-SHAPED?*"
POLICE PUBLIC BOX BOX
POLICE PUBLIC BOX BOX
WRRREEEEEOOOO
VWOOORPP VWOOORPP

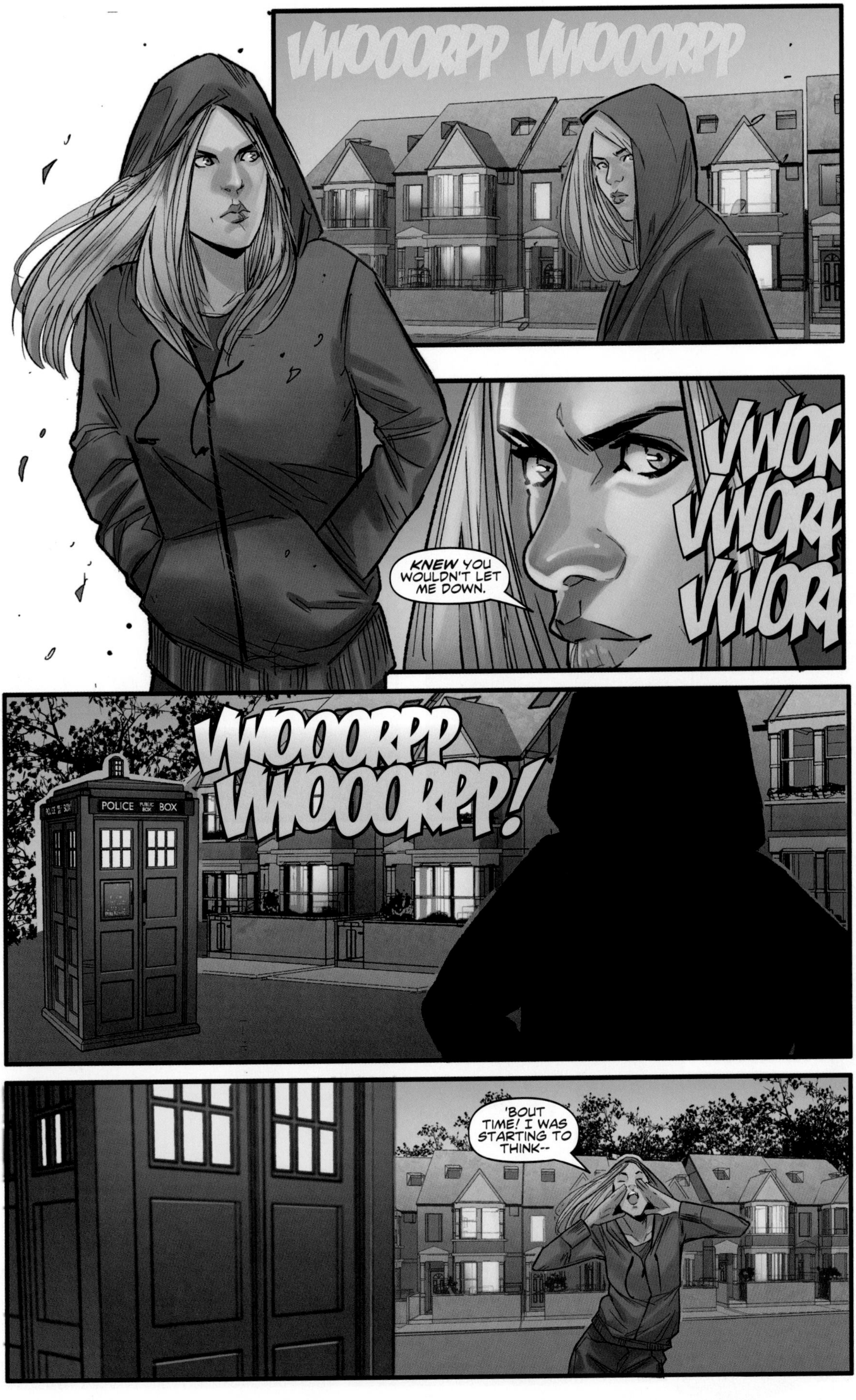
VWOOORPP VWOOORPP
KNEW YOU WOULDN'T LET ME DOWN.
VWORP VWORP VWORP
POLICE PUBLIC BOX CALL BOX
VWOOORPP VWOOORPP!
'BOUT TIME! I WAS STARTING TO THINK--

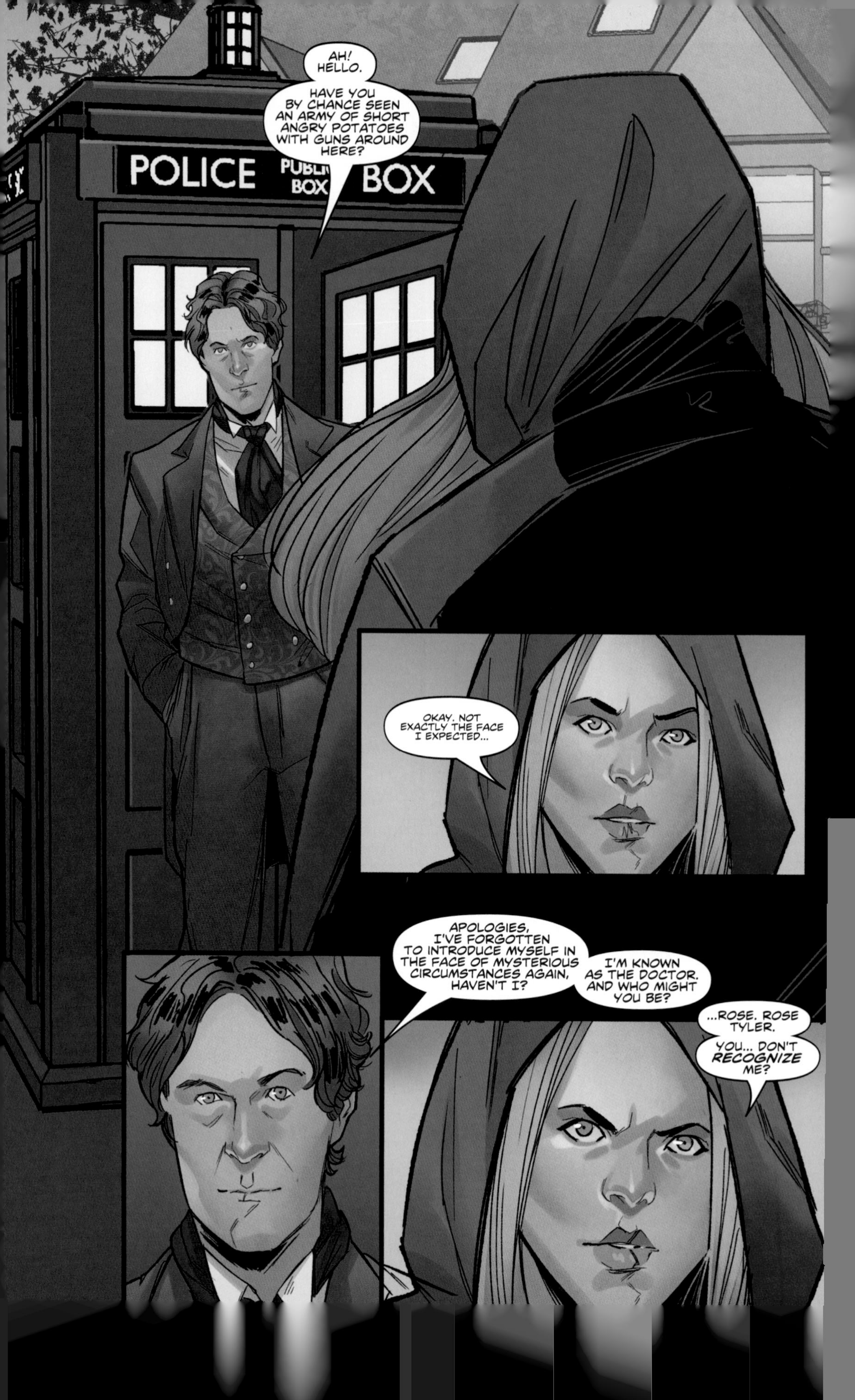
POLICE PUBLIC BOX BOX
AH! HELLO.
HAVE YOU BY CHANCE SEEN AN ARMY OF SHORT ANGRY POTATOES WITH GUNS AROUND HERE?
OKAY. NOT EXACTLY THE FACE I EXPECTED...
APOLOGIES, I'VE FORGOTTEN TO INTRODUCE MYSELF IN THE FACE OF MYSTERIOUS CIRCUMSTANCES AGAIN, HAVEN'T I?
I'M KNOWN AS THE DOCTOR. AND WHO MIGHT YOU BE?
...ROSE. ROSE TYLER.
YOU... DON'T *RECOGNIZE* ME?

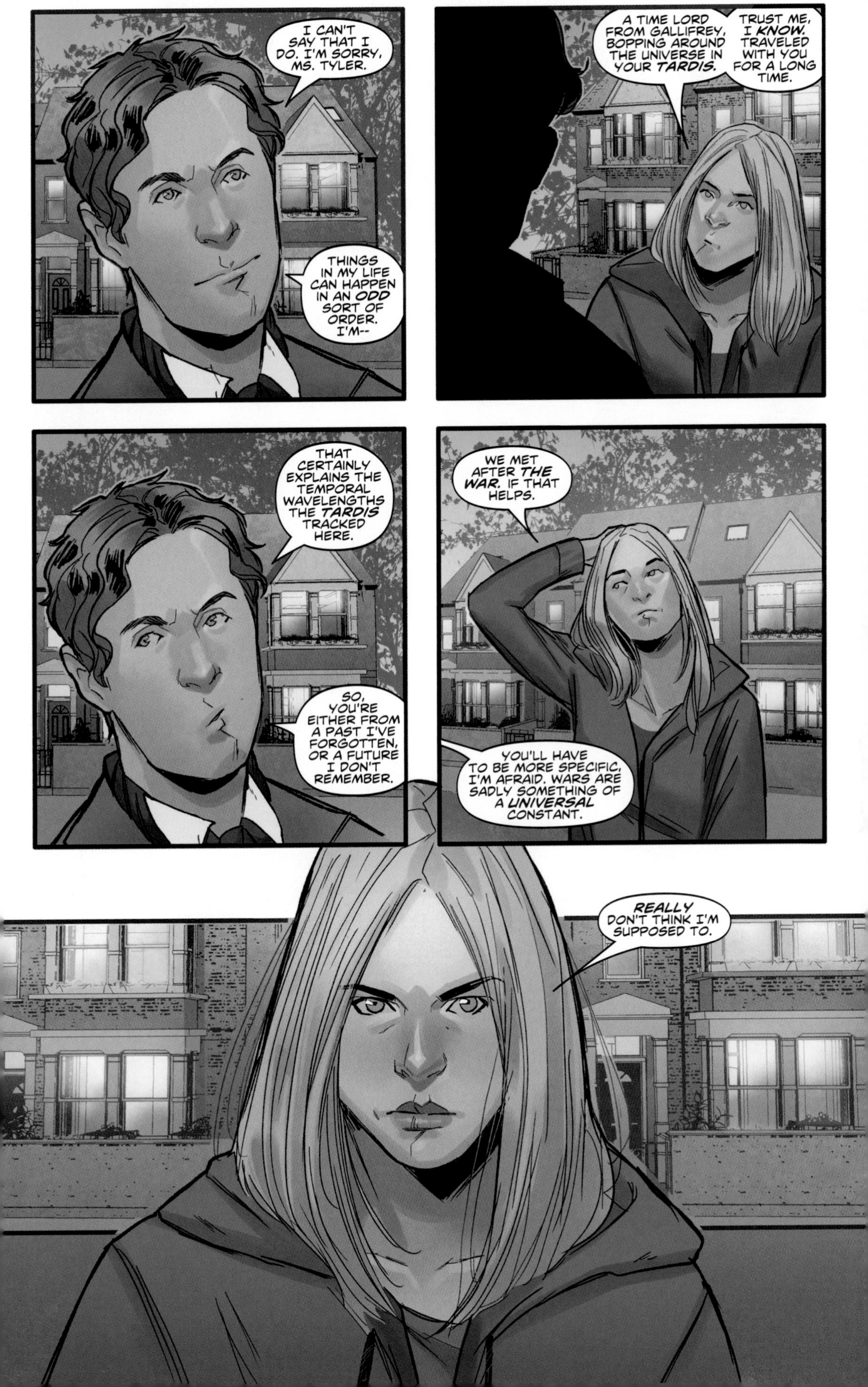
I CAN'T SAY THAT I DO. I'M SORRY, MS. TYLER.
THINGS IN MY LIFE CAN HAPPEN IN AN *ODD* SORT OF ORDER. I'M--
A TIME LORD FROM GALLIFREY, BOPPING AROUND THE UNIVERSE IN YOUR *TARDIS.*
TRUST ME, I *KNOW.* TRAVELED WITH YOU FOR A LONG TIME.
THAT CERTAINLY EXPLAINS THE TEMPORAL WAVELENGTHS THE *TARDIS* TRACKED HERE.
SO, YOU'RE EITHER FROM A PAST I'VE FORGOTTEN, OR A FUTURE I DON'T REMEMBER.
WE MET AFTER *THE WAR.* IF THAT HELPS.
YOU'LL HAVE TO BE MORE SPECIFIC, I'M AFRAID. WARS ARE SADLY SOMETHING OF A *UNIVERSAL* CONSTANT.
REALLY DON'T THINK I'M SUPPOSED TO.

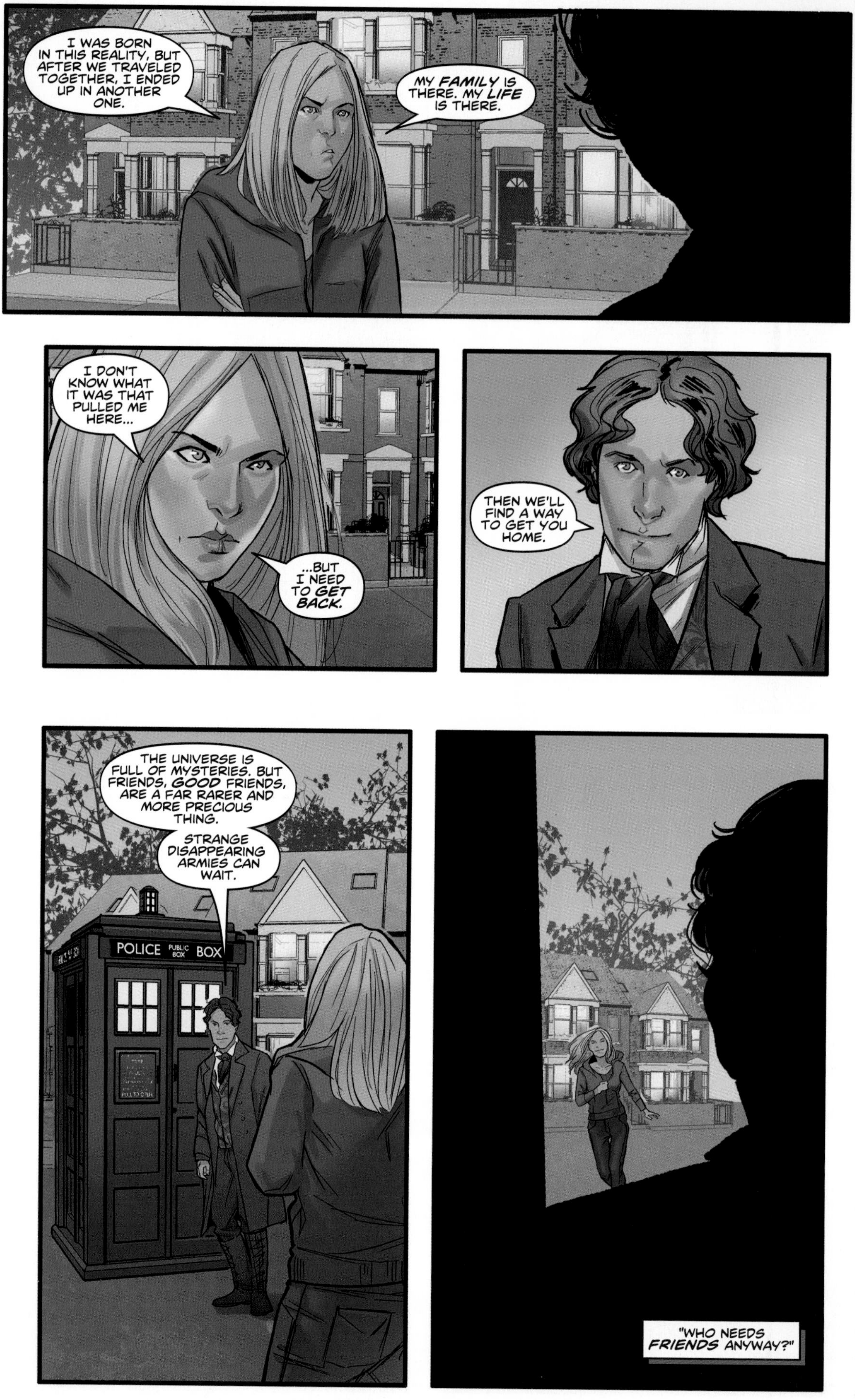
I WAS BORN IN THIS REALITY, BUT AFTER WE TRAVELED TOGETHER, I ENDED UP IN ANOTHER ONE.
MY *FAMILY* IS THERE. MY *LIFE* IS THERE.
I DON'T KNOW WHAT IT WAS THAT PULLED ME HERE...
...BUT I NEED TO *GET BACK.*
THEN WE'LL FIND A WAY TO GET YOU HOME.
THE UNIVERSE IS FULL OF MYSTERIES. BUT FRIENDS, *GOOD* FRIENDS, ARE A FAR RARER AND MORE PRECIOUS THING.
STRANGE DISAPPEARING ARMIES CAN WAIT.
POLICE PUBLIC BOX BOX
"WHO NEEDS *FRIENDS* ANYWAY?"

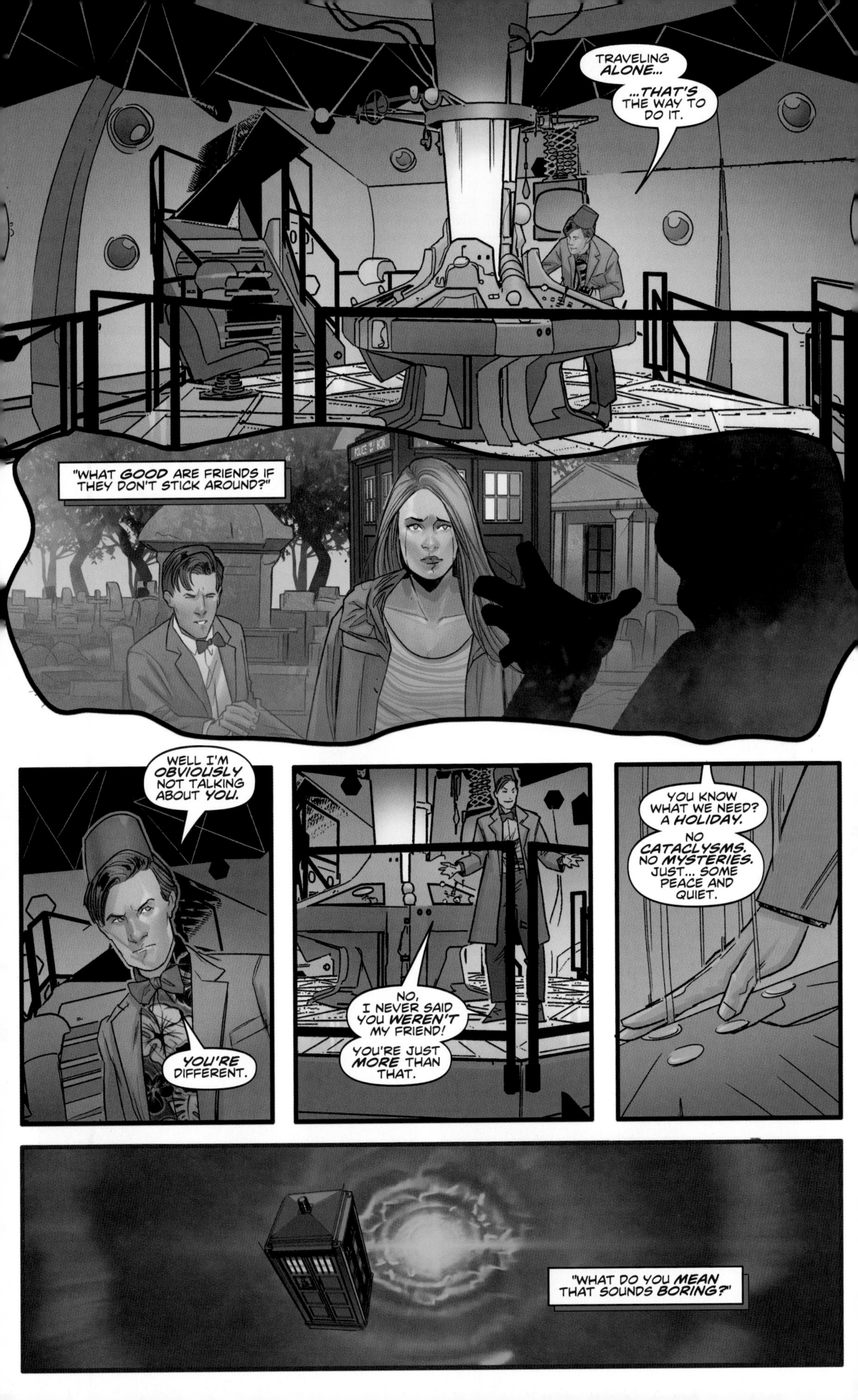
TRAVELING ALONE... ...THAT'S THE WAY TO DO IT.
"WHAT GOOD ARE FRIENDS IF THEY DON'T STICK AROUND?"
WELL I'M OBVIOUSLY NOT TALKING ABOUT YOU.
YOU'RE DIFFERENT.
NO, I NEVER SAID YOU WEREN'T MY FRIEND!
YOU'RE JUST MORE THAN THAT.
YOU KNOW WHAT WE NEED? A HOLIDAY.
NO CATACLYSMS. NO MYSTERIES. JUST... SOME PEACE AND QUIET.
"WHAT DO YOU MEAN THAT SOUNDS BORING?"

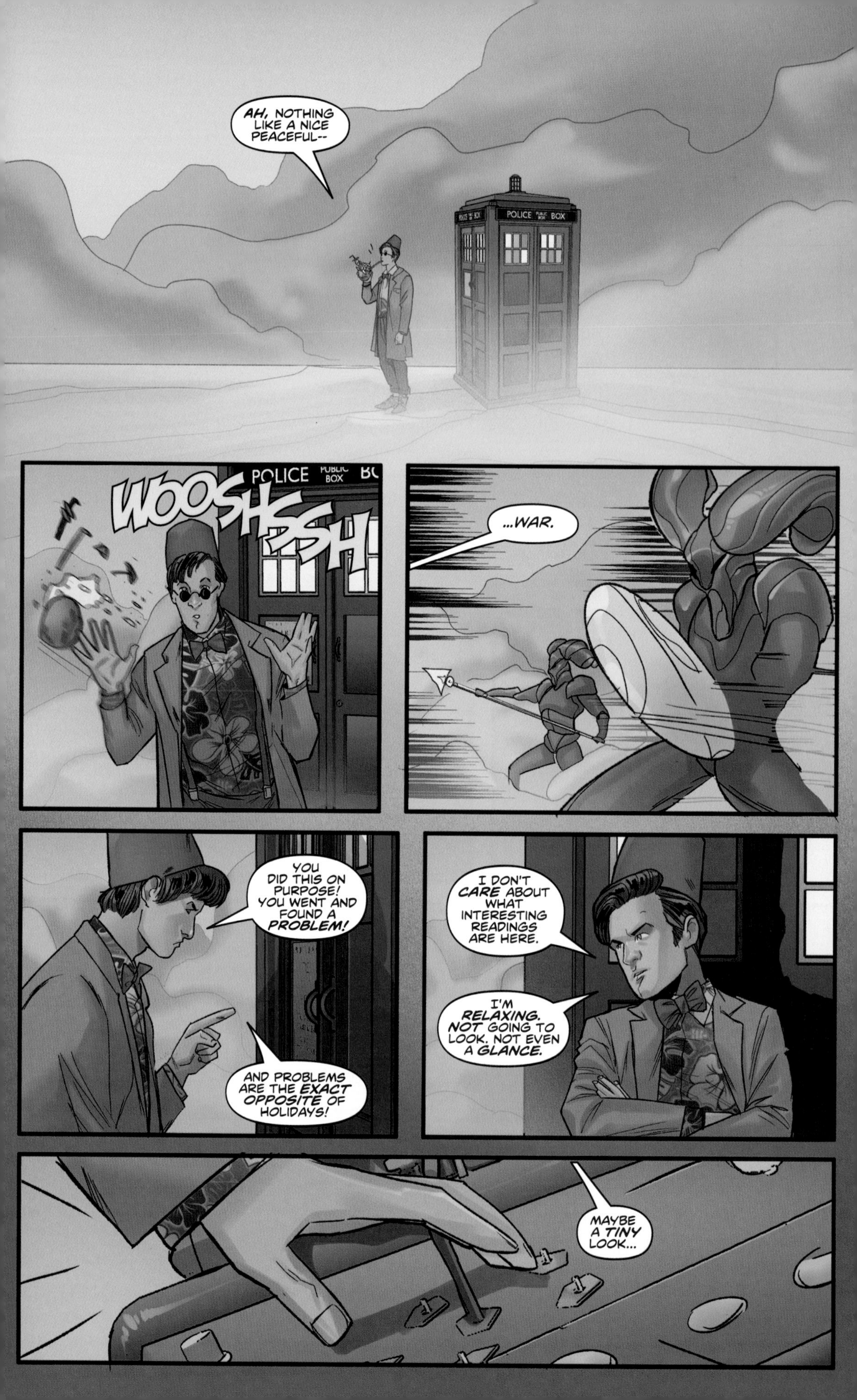
AH, NOTHING LIKE A NICE PEACEFUL--
POLICE PUBLIC BOX
POLICE PUBLIC BOX
WOOSHSSH!
...WAR.
YOU DID THIS ON PURPOSE! YOU WENT AND FOUND A PROBLEM!
AND PROBLEMS ARE THE EXACT OPPOSITE OF HOLIDAYS!
I DON'T CARE ABOUT WHAT INTERESTING READINGS ARE HERE.
I'M RELAXING. NOT GOING TO LOOK. NOT EVEN A GLANCE.
MAYBE A TINY LOOK...

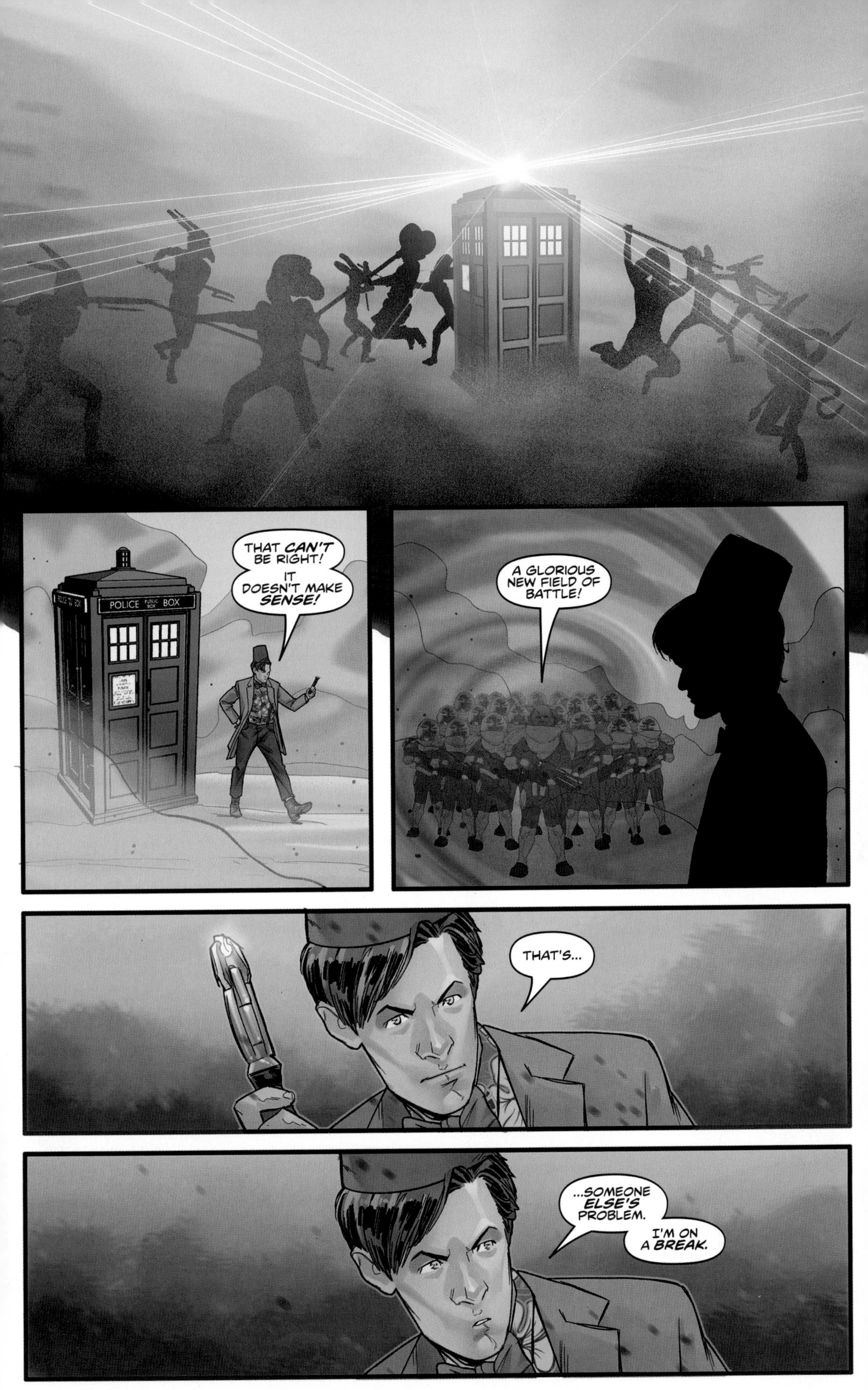

POLICE PUBLIC BOX BOX
THAT CAN'T BE RIGHT! IT DOESN'T MAKE SENSE!
A GLORIOUS NEW FIELD OF BATTLE!
THAT'S...
...SOMEONE ELSE'S PROBLEM.
I'M ON A BREAK.

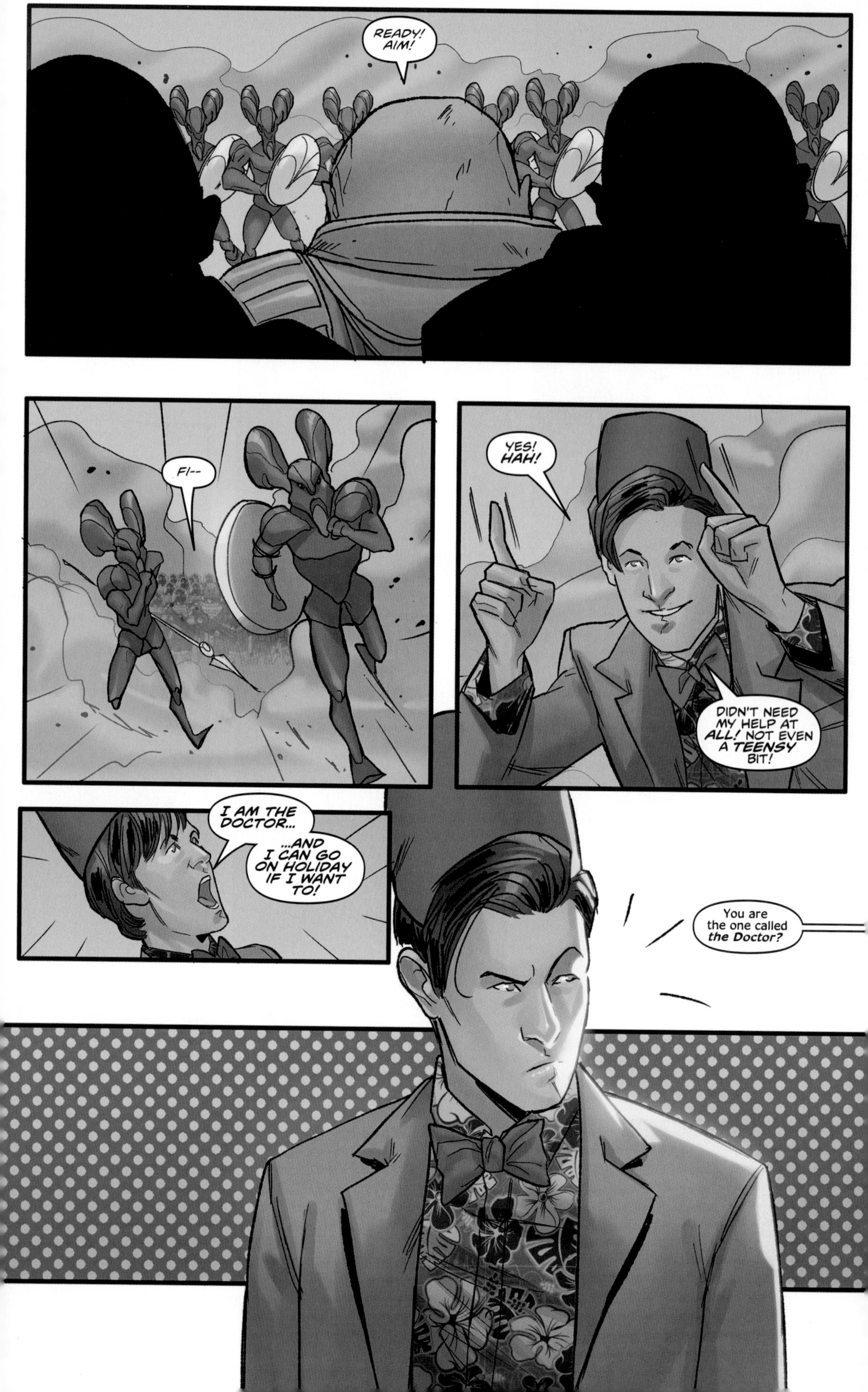
READY! AIM!
FI--
YES! HAH!
DIDN'T NEED MY HELP AT ALL! NOT EVEN A TEENSY BIT!
I AM THE DOCTOR...
...AND I CAN GO ON HOLIDAY IF I WANT TO!
You are the one called the Doctor?

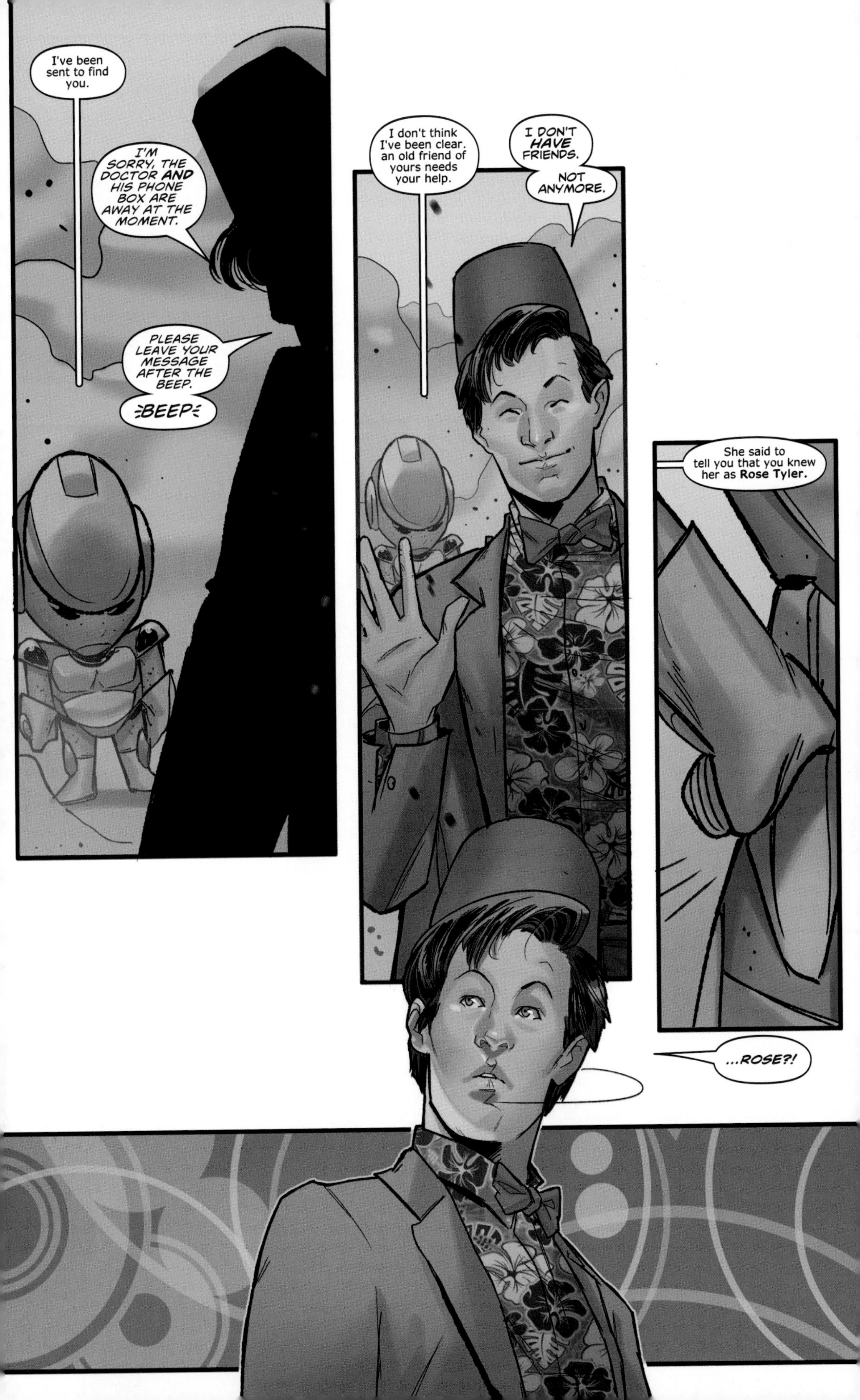
I've been sent to find you.
I'M SORRY, THE DOCTOR AND HIS PHONE BOX ARE AWAY AT THE MOMENT.
PLEASE LEAVE YOUR MESSAGE AFTER THE BEEP.
BEEP
I don't think I've been clear. an old friend of yours needs your help.
I DON'T HAVE FRIENDS.
NOT ANYMORE.
She said to tell you that you knew her as Rose Tyler.
...ROSE?!

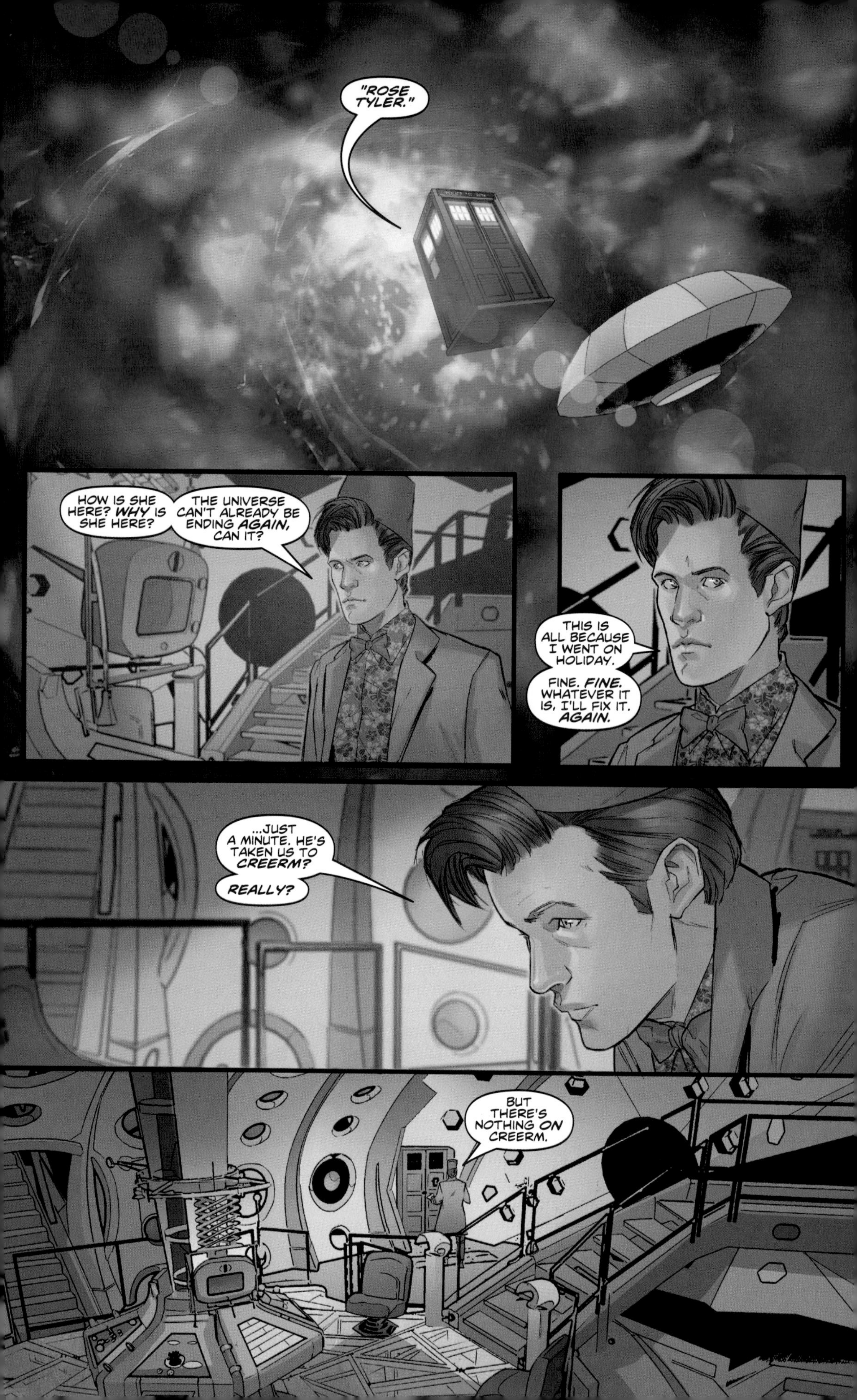
"ROSE TYLER."
HOW IS SHE HERE? WHY IS SHE HERE?
THE UNIVERSE CAN'T ALREADY BE ENDING AGAIN, CAN IT?
THIS IS ALL BECAUSE I WENT ON HOLIDAY.
FINE. FINE. WHATEVER IT IS, I'LL FIX IT. AGAIN.
...JUST A MINUTE. HE'S TAKEN US TO CREERM?
REALLY?
BUT THERE'S NOTHING ON CREERM.

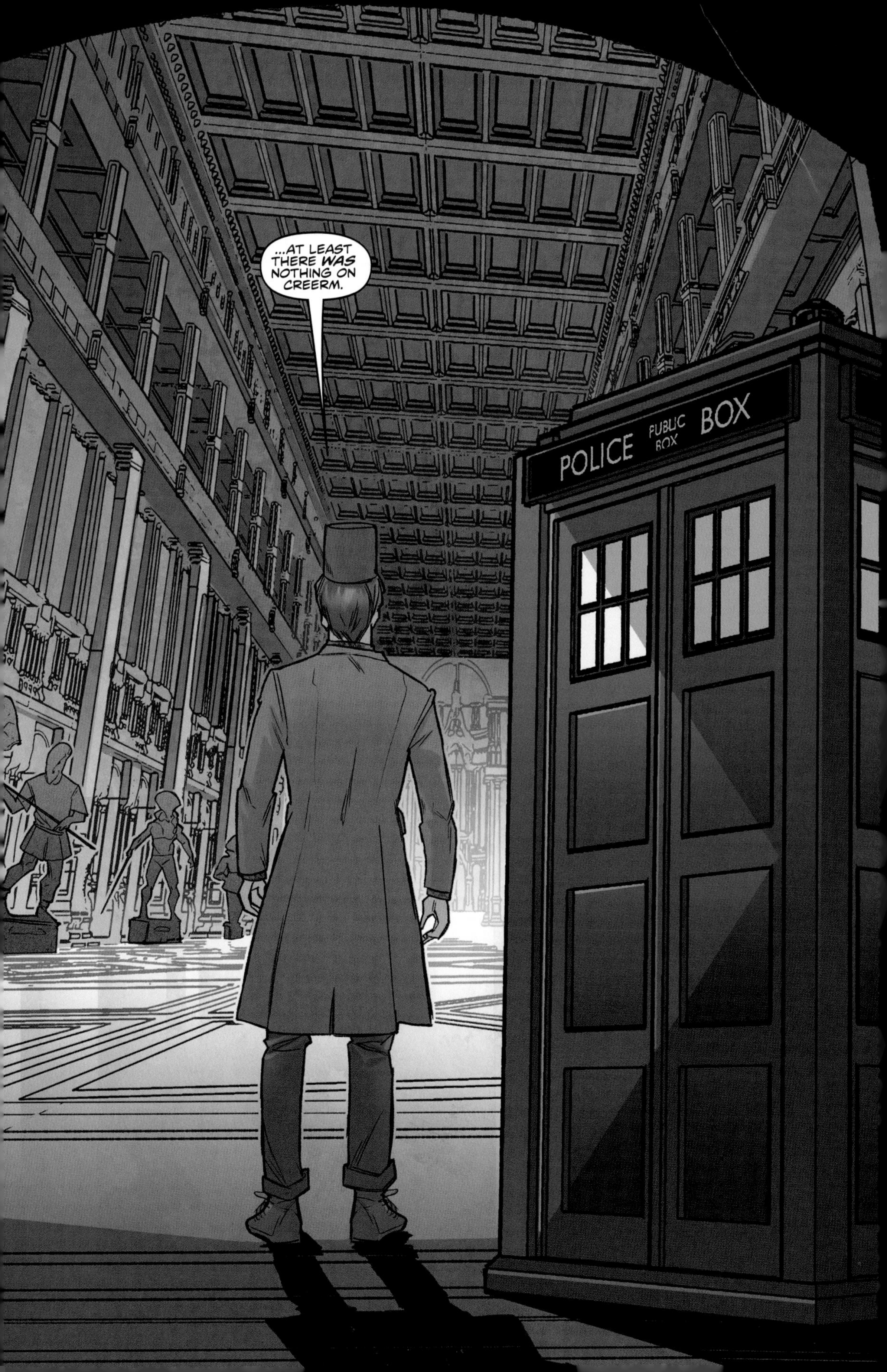
...AT LEAST THERE WAS NOTHING ON CREERM.
POLICE PUBLIC BOX BOX

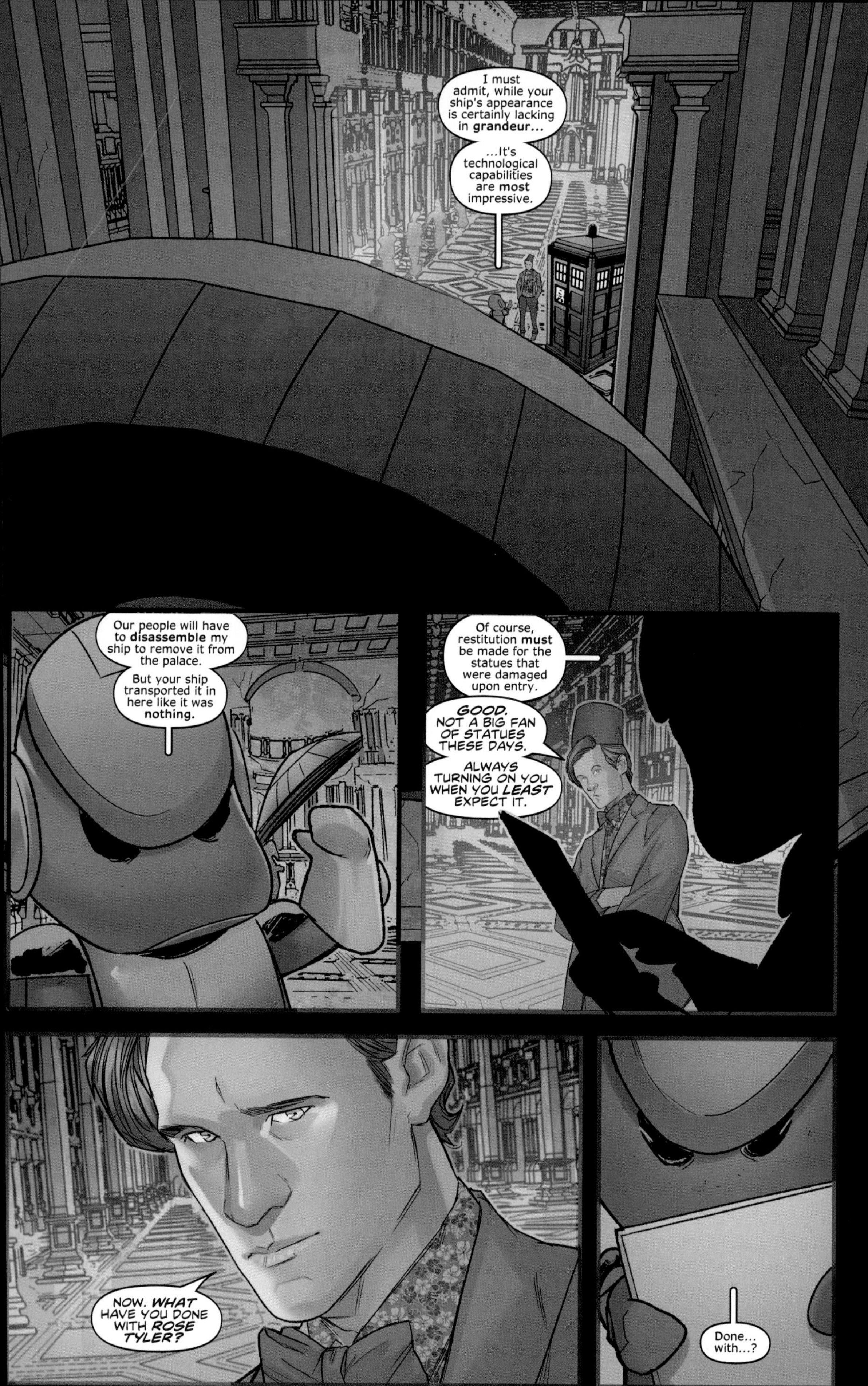
I must admit, while your ship's appearance is certainly lacking in **grandeur...**
...It's technological capabilities are **most** impressive.
Our people will have to **disassemble** my ship to remove it from the palace.
But your ship transported it in here like it was **nothing.**
Of course, restitution **must** be made for the statues that were damaged upon entry.
GOOD. NOT A BIG FAN OF STATUES THESE DAYS.
ALWAYS TURNING ON YOU WHEN YOU *LEAST* EXPECT IT.
NOW. *WHAT* HAVE YOU DONE WITH *ROSE TYLER?*
Done... with...?

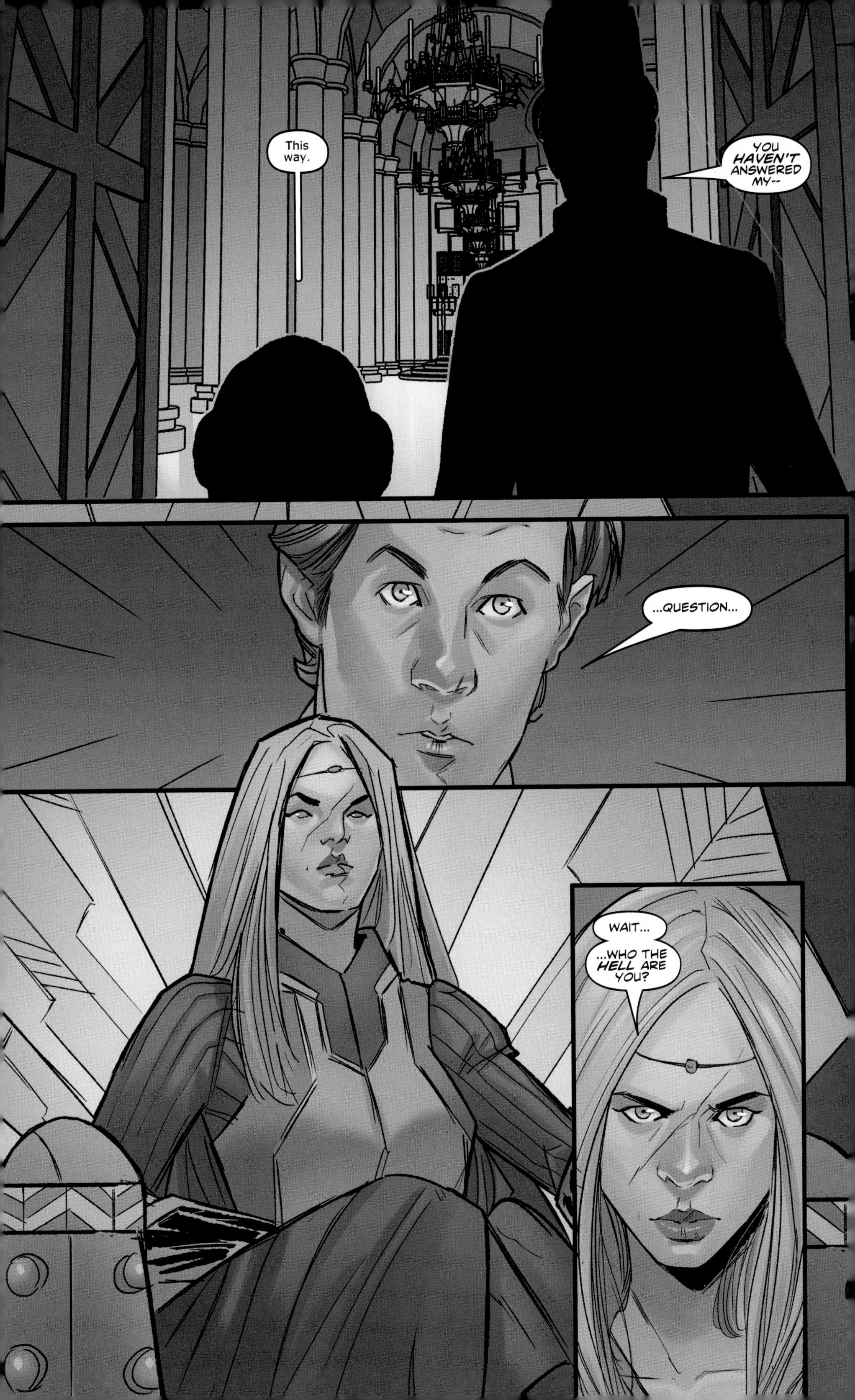
This way.
YOU HAVEN'T ANSWERED MY--
...QUESTION...
WAIT...
...WHO THE HELL ARE YOU?

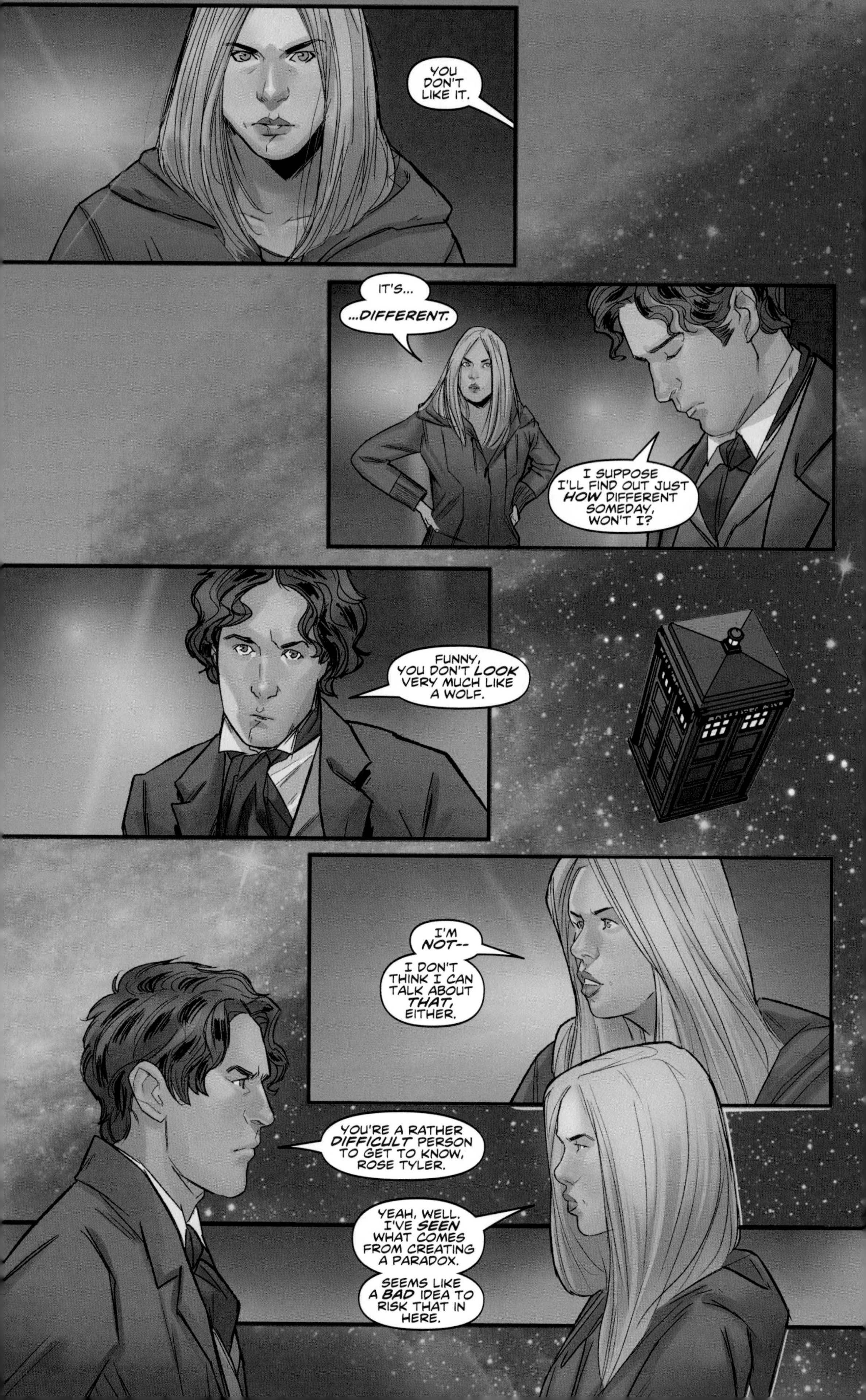
YOU DON'T LIKE IT.
IT'S...
...DIFFERENT.
I SUPPOSE I'LL FIND OUT JUST HOW DIFFERENT SOMEDAY, WON'T I?
FUNNY, YOU DON'T LOOK VERY MUCH LIKE A WOLF.
I'M NOT--
I DON'T THINK I CAN TALK ABOUT THAT, EITHER.
YOU'RE A RATHER DIFFICULT PERSON TO GET TO KNOW, ROSE TYLER.
YEAH, WELL. I'VE SEEN WHAT COMES FROM CREATING A PARADOX.
SEEMS LIKE A BAD IDEA TO RISK THAT IN HERE.

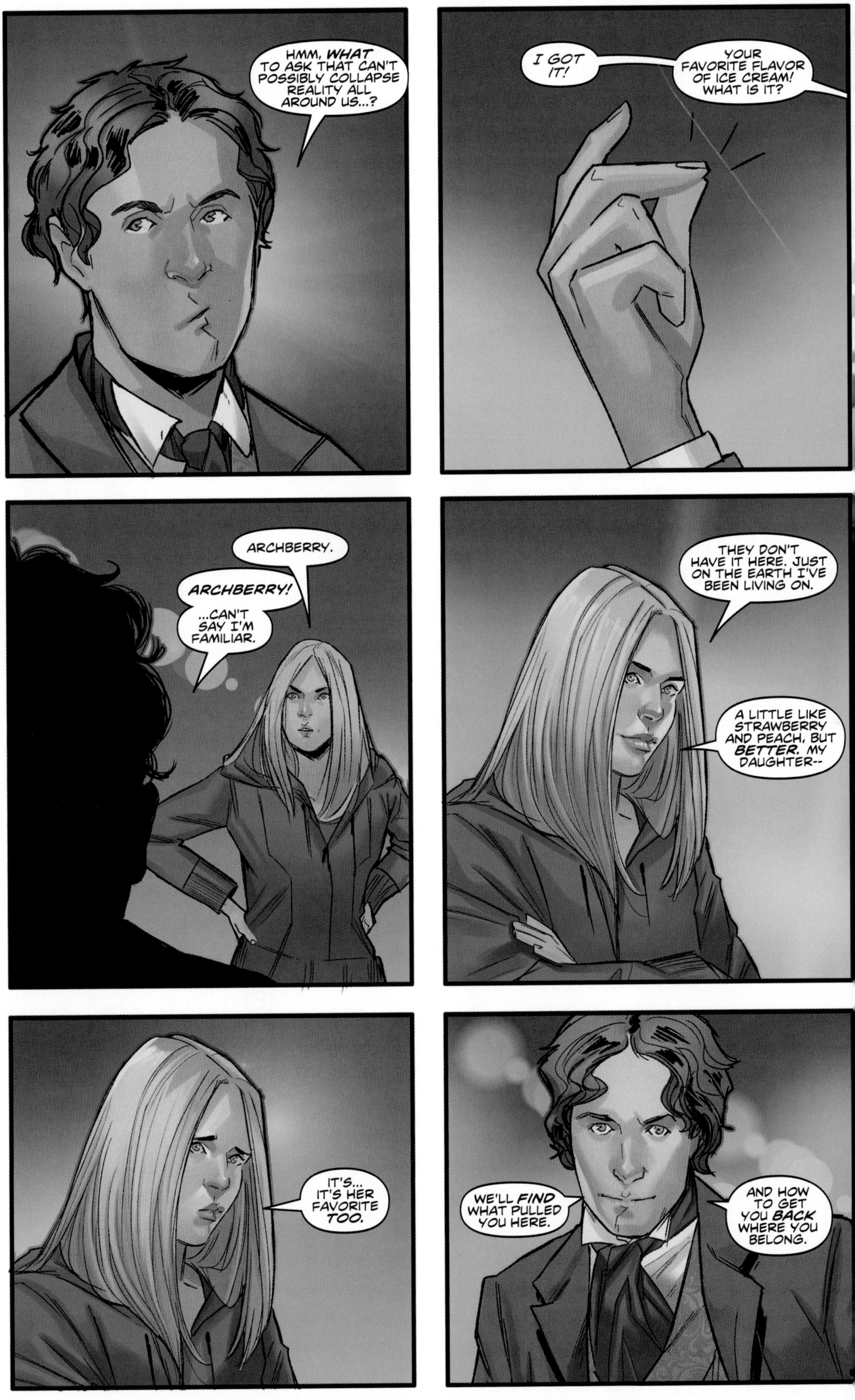
HMM, WHAT TO ASK THAT CAN'T POSSIBLY COLLAPSE REALITY ALL AROUND US...?
I GOT IT!
YOUR FAVORITE FLAVOR OF ICE CREAM! WHAT IS IT?
ARCHBERRY.
ARCHBERRY!
...CAN'T SAY I'M FAMILIAR.
THEY DON'T HAVE IT HERE. JUST ON THE EARTH I'VE BEEN LIVING ON.
A LITTLE LIKE STRAWBERRY AND PEACH, BUT BETTER. MY DAUGHTER--
IT'S... IT'S HER FAVORITE TOO.
WE'LL FIND WHAT PULLED YOU HERE.
AND HOW TO GET YOU BACK WHERE YOU BELONG.

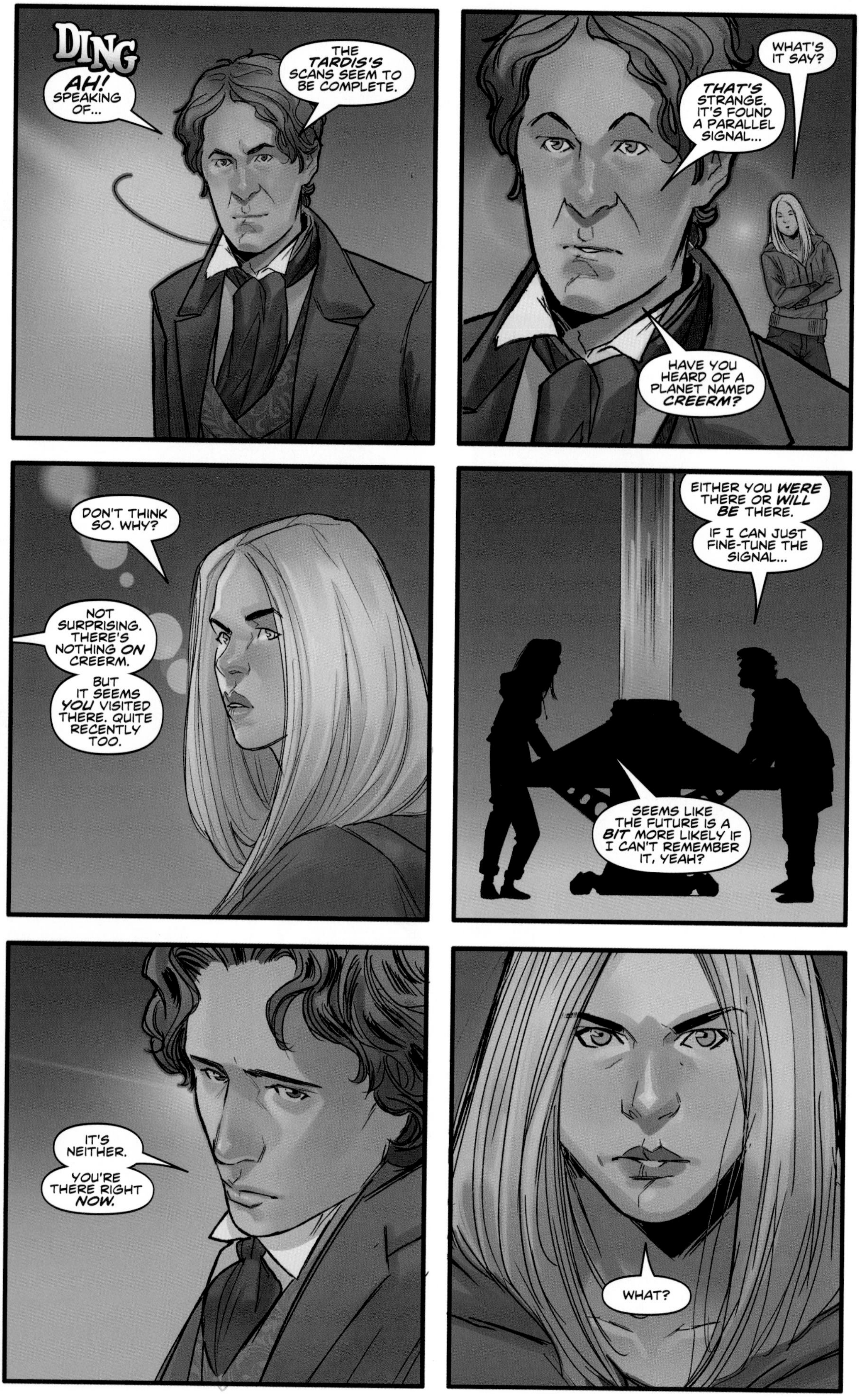
DING
AH! SPEAKING OF...
THE TARDIS'S SCANS SEEM TO BE COMPLETE.
WHAT'S IT SAY?
THAT'S STRANGE. IT'S FOUND A PARALLEL SIGNAL...
HAVE YOU HEARD OF A PLANET NAMED CREERM?
DON'T THINK SO. WHY?
NOT SURPRISING. THERE'S NOTHING ON CREERM.
BUT IT SEEMS YOU VISITED THERE. QUITE RECENTLY TOO.
EITHER YOU WERE THERE OR WILL BE THERE.
IF I CAN JUST FINE-TUNE THE SIGNAL...
SEEMS LIKE THE FUTURE IS A BIT MORE LIKELY IF I CAN'T REMEMBER IT, YEAH?
IT'S NEITHER.
YOU'RE THERE RIGHT NOW.
WHAT?

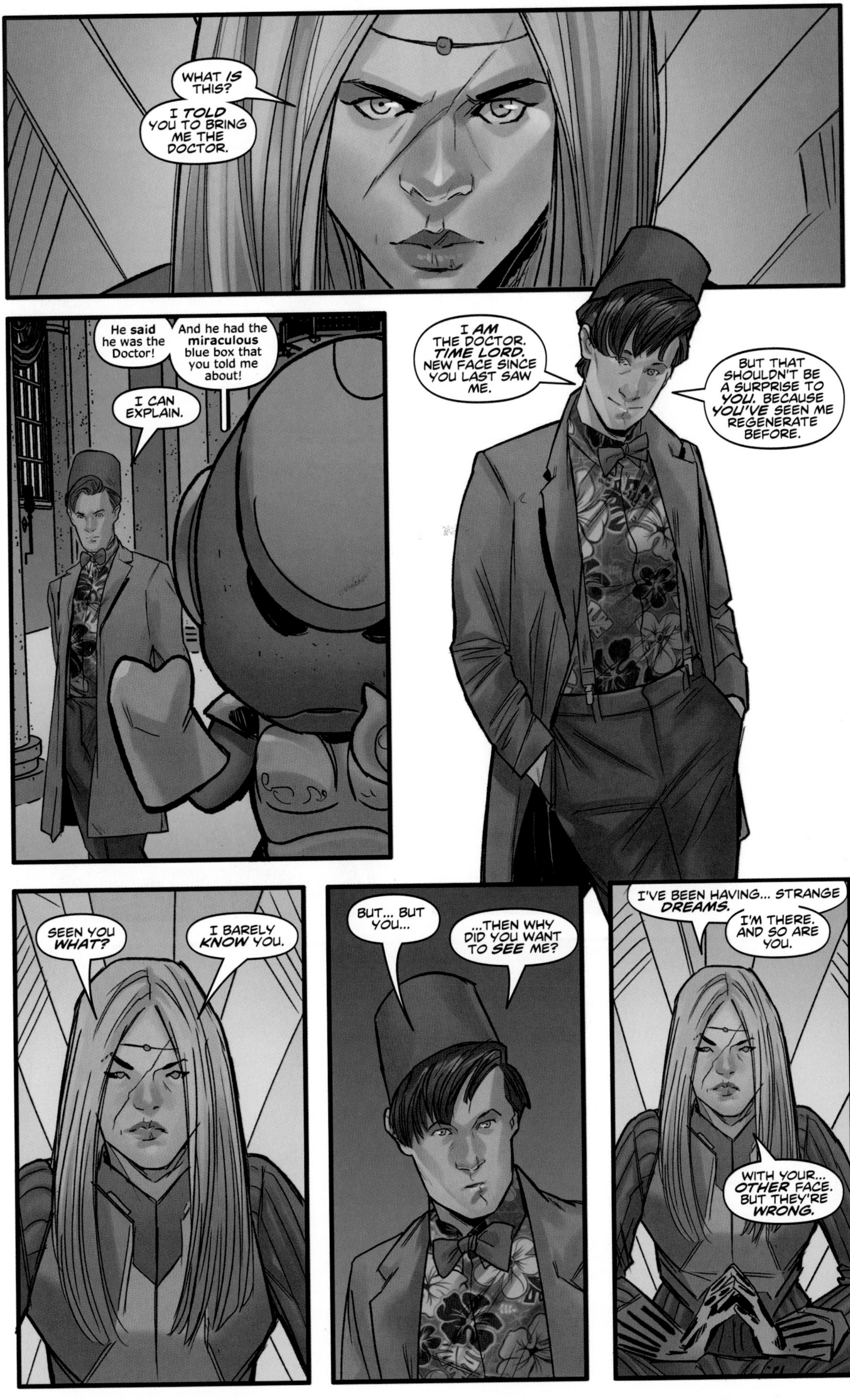
WHAT IS THIS?
I TOLD YOU TO BRING ME THE DOCTOR.
He said he was the Doctor!
And he had the miraculous blue box that you told me about!
I CAN EXPLAIN.
I AM THE DOCTOR. TIME LORD. NEW FACE SINCE YOU LAST SAW ME.
BUT THAT SHOULDN'T BE A SURPRISE TO YOU. BECAUSE YOU'VE SEEN ME REGENERATE BEFORE.
SEEN YOU WHAT?
I BARELY KNOW YOU.
BUT... BUT YOU...
...THEN WHY DID YOU WANT TO SEE ME?
I'VE BEEN HAVING... STRANGE DREAMS.
I'M THERE. AND SO ARE YOU.
WITH YOUR... OTHER FACE. BUT THEY'RE WRONG.

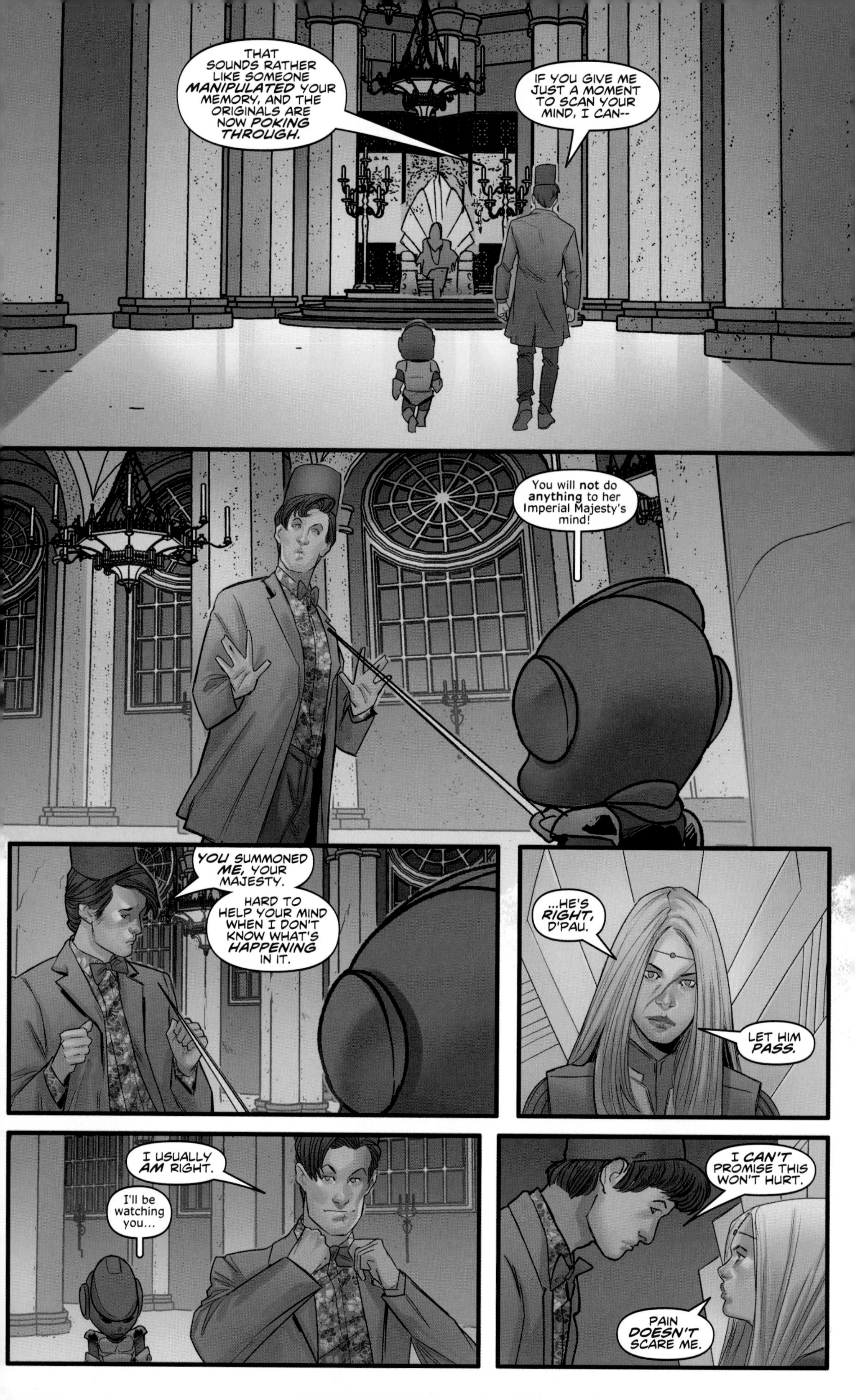
THAT SOUNDS RATHER LIKE SOMEONE MANIPULATED YOUR MEMORY, AND THE ORIGINALS ARE NOW POKING THROUGH.
IF YOU GIVE ME JUST A MOMENT TO SCAN YOUR MIND, I CAN--
You will not do anything to her Imperial Majesty's mind!
YOU SUMMONED ME, YOUR MAJESTY.
HARD TO HELP YOUR MIND WHEN I DON'T KNOW WHAT'S HAPPENING IN IT.
...HE'S RIGHT, D'PAU.
LET HIM PASS.
I USUALLY AM RIGHT.
I'll be watching you...
I CAN'T PROMISE THIS WON'T HURT.
PAIN DOESN'T SCARE ME.

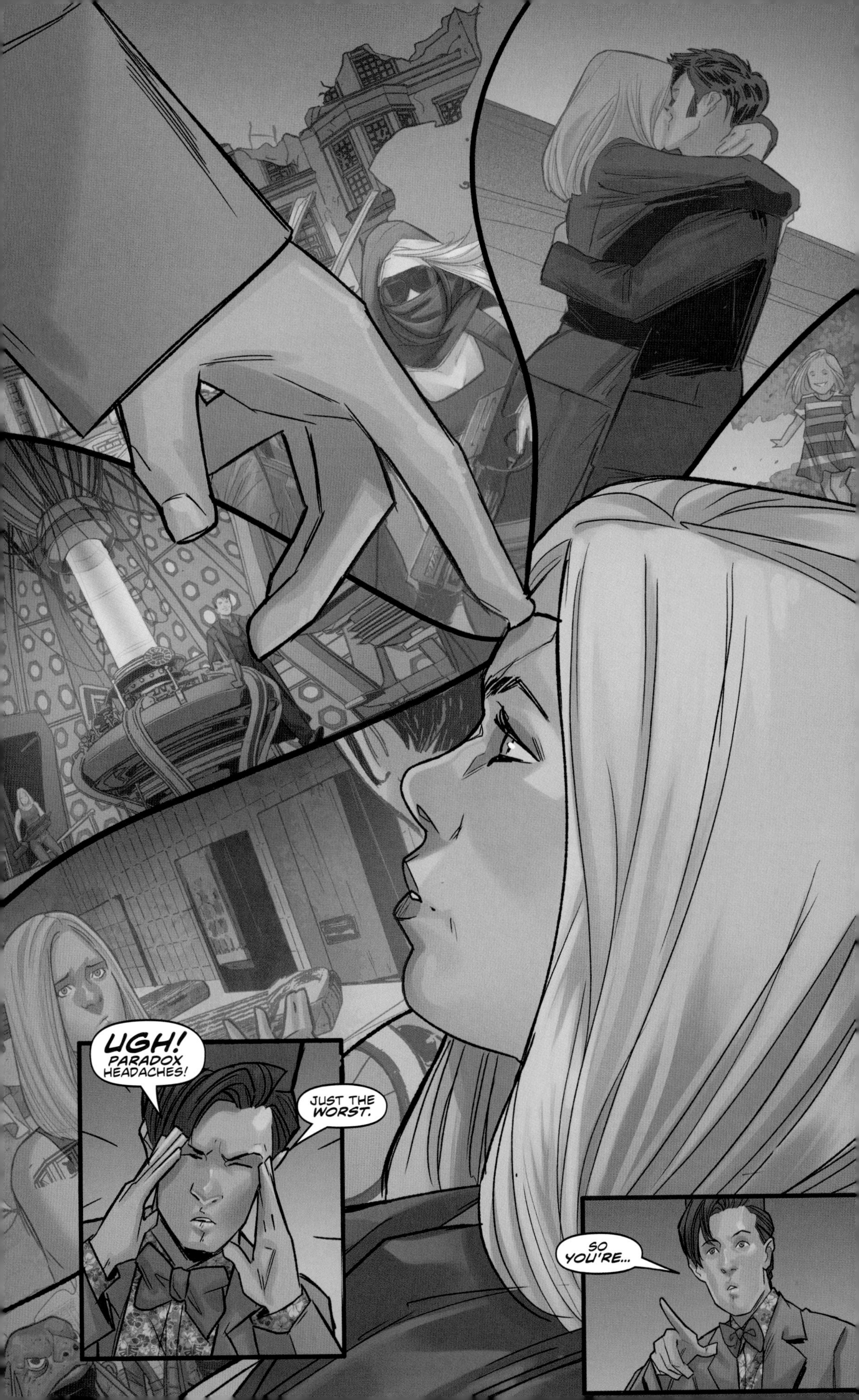
UGH! PARADOX HEADACHES!
JUST THE WORST.
SO YOU'RE...

MY WORLD MAY BE *GONE.* AND *YOU* MAY HAVE FORGOTTEN ME.

BUT I HAVE DONE *GREAT* THINGS. HELPED SO *MANY PEOPLE.* BECAUSE OF THE PATH *YOU* SET ME ON.

THAT'S WHY *I* NEED YOU TO *FIX* WHATEVER IS WRONG. SAVING PEOPLE IS YOUR WHOLE *DEAL,* YEAH? SO HELP ME GET BACK TO IT.

BUT... WHERE DOES IT *END?*

WHEN... WHEN THERE'S NO ONE LEFT WHO NEEDS MY HELP, I SUPPOSE.

OR WHEN I'M *DEAD.*

AND WHAT'S ALL OF *THIS,* THEN?

MOST OF THE REVOLUTIONARIES I'VE MET BRING *DOWN* PALACES. THEY DON'T *BUILD* THEM.

I BROUGHT YOU HERE FOR YOUR *HELP.* NOT YOUR *JUDGEMENT.*

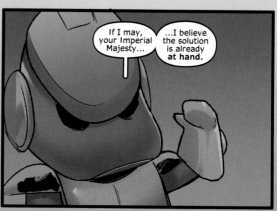

IF I MAY, YOUR IMPERIAL MAJESTY...

...I BELIEVE THE SOLUTION IS ALREADY AT HAND.

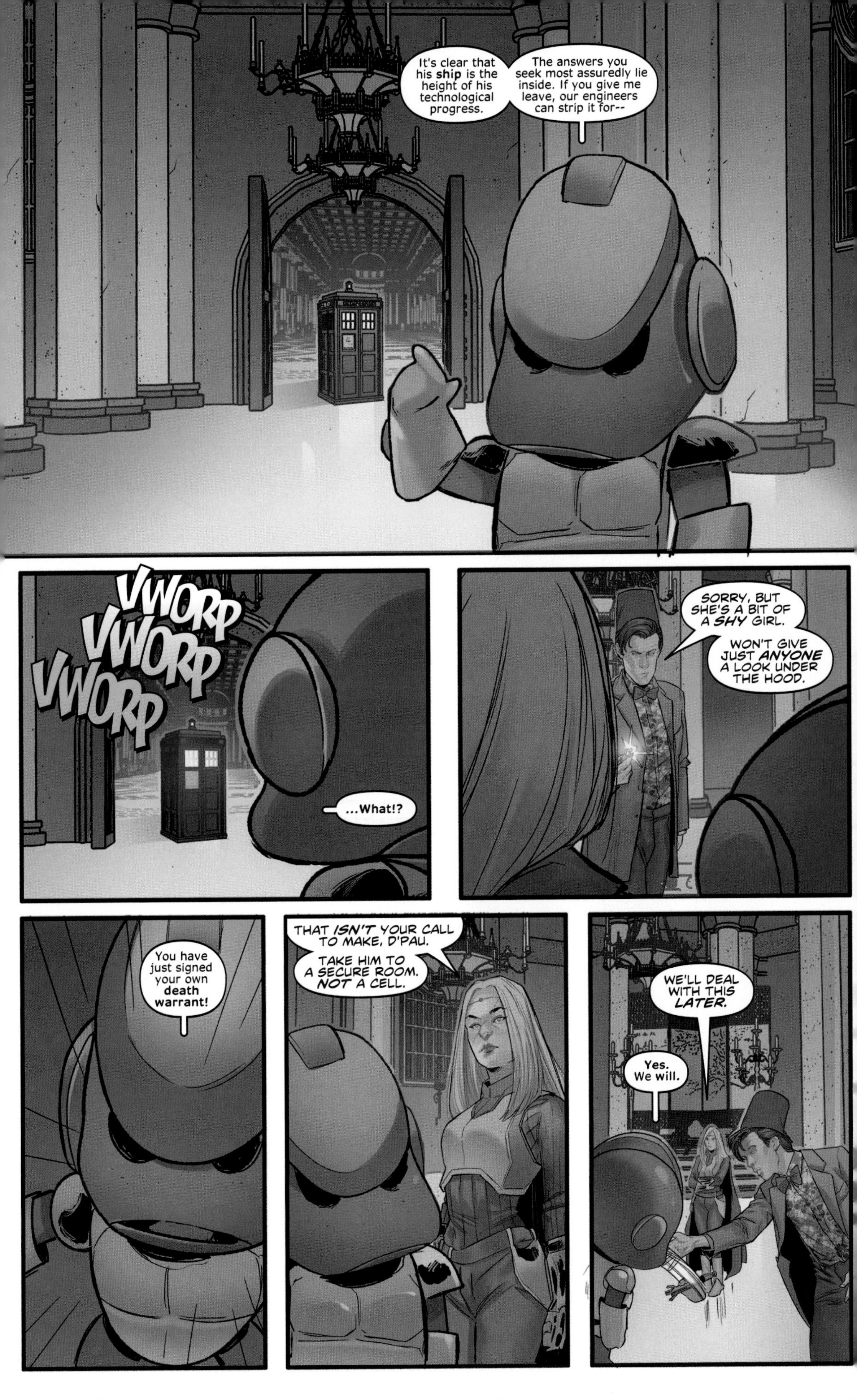
It's clear that his **ship** is the height of his technological progress.
The answers you seek most assuredly lie inside. If you give me leave, our engineers can strip it for--
VWORP VWORP VWORP
...What!?
SORRY, BUT SHE'S A BIT OF A *SHY* GIRL.
WON'T GIVE JUST ***ANYONE*** A LOOK UNDER THE HOOD.
You have just signed your own **death warrant!**
THAT *ISN'T* YOUR CALL TO MAKE, D'PAU.
TAKE HIM TO A SECURE ROOM. ***NOT*** A CELL.
WE'LL DEAL WITH THIS ***LATER.***
Yes. We will.

NOPE. DOESN'T LOOK FAMILIAR.

'COURSE, A LOT OF PLANETS I DIDN'T *EXACTLY* SEE FROM ORBIT.

THAT'S STRANGE... THERE ARE *FAR* MORE PEOPLE DOWN ON CREERM THAN THERE SHOULD BE.

INCLUDING ME, YEAH?

THE TARDIS IS PICKING UP SOME VARIATION.

BUT IT IS *A* YOU.

AND, IT APPEARS, A *ME*.

TWO DOCTORS?! WON'T THAT, YOU KNOW... ...*BREAK* SOMETHING.

I SUSPECT WE'RE RATHER *PAST* THAT POINT NOW.

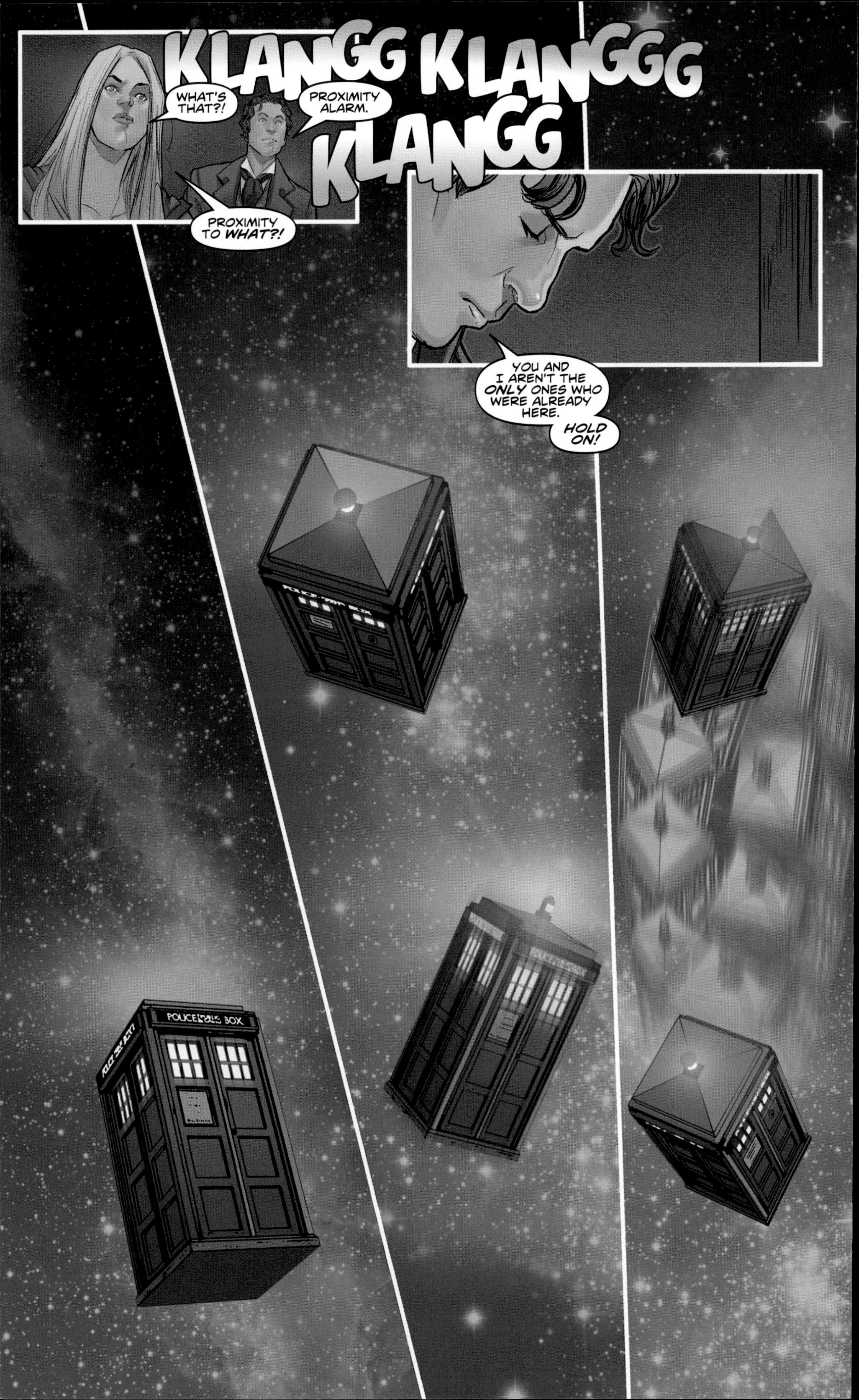
KLANGG KLANGGG
KLANGG
WHAT'S THAT?!
PROXIMITY ALARM.
PROXIMITY TO WHAT?!
YOU AND I AREN'T THE ONLY ONES WHO WERE ALREADY HERE.
HOLD ON!

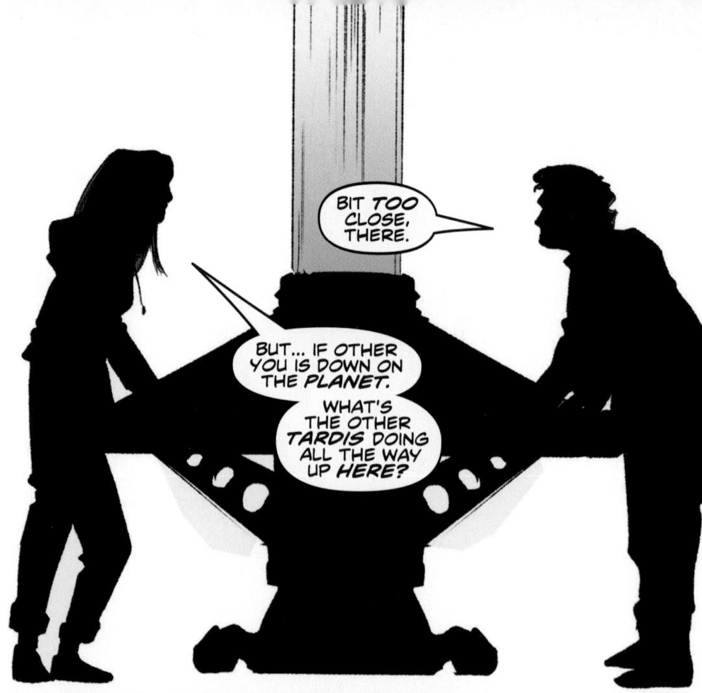
BIT TOO CLOSE, THERE.
BUT... IF OTHER YOU IS DOWN ON THE PLANET.
WHAT'S THE OTHER TARDIS DOING ALL THE WAY UP HERE?
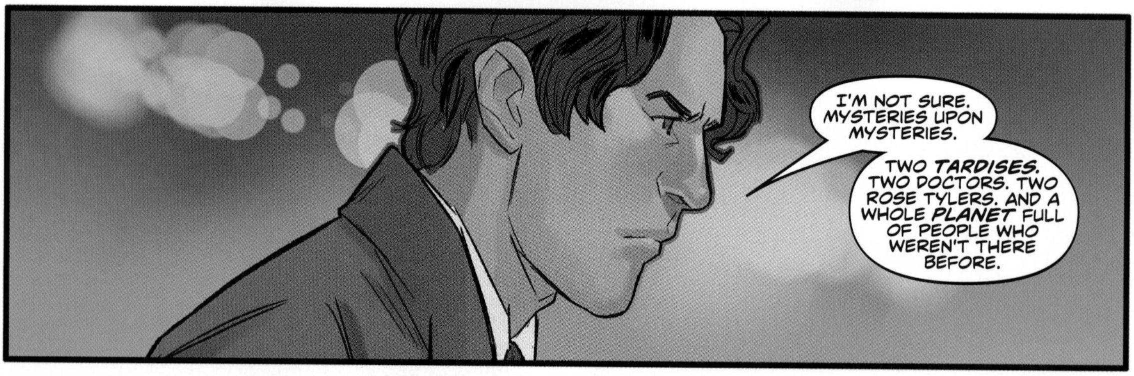
I'M NOT SURE. MYSTERIES UPON MYSTERIES.
TWO TARDISES. TWO DOCTORS. TWO ROSE TYLERS. AND A WHOLE PLANET FULL OF PEOPLE WHO WEREN'T THERE BEFORE.
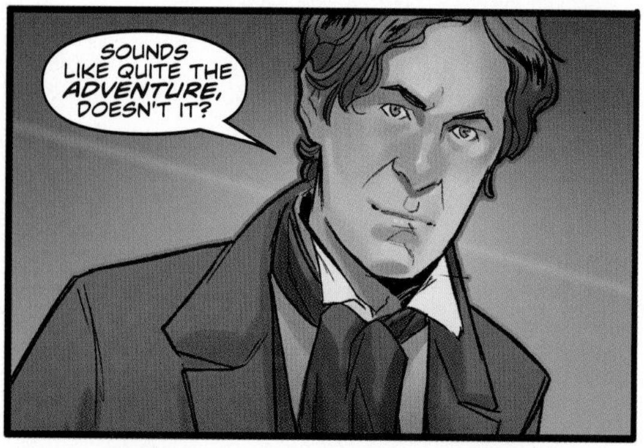
SOUNDS LIKE QUITE THE ADVENTURE, DOESN'T IT?
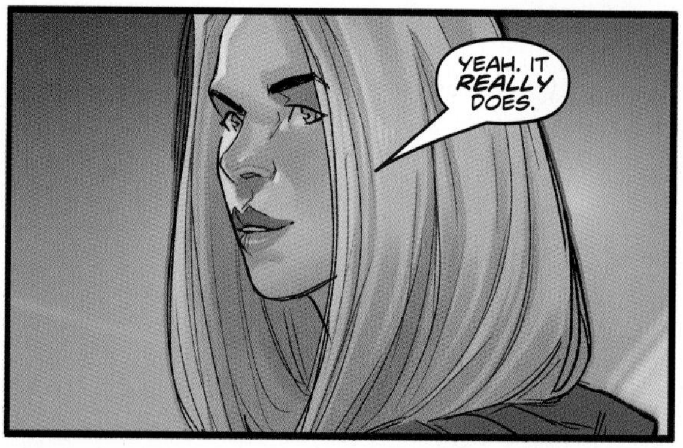
YEAH. IT REALLY DOES.
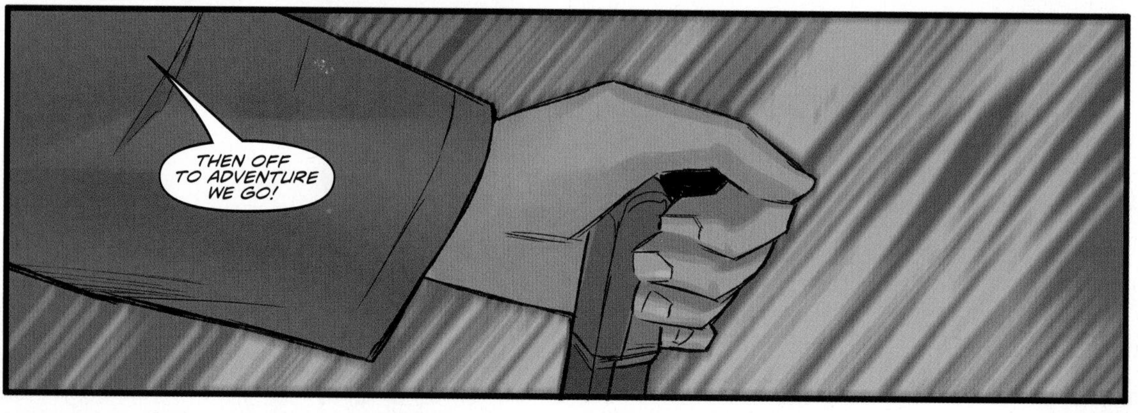
THEN OFF TO ADVENTURE WE GO!

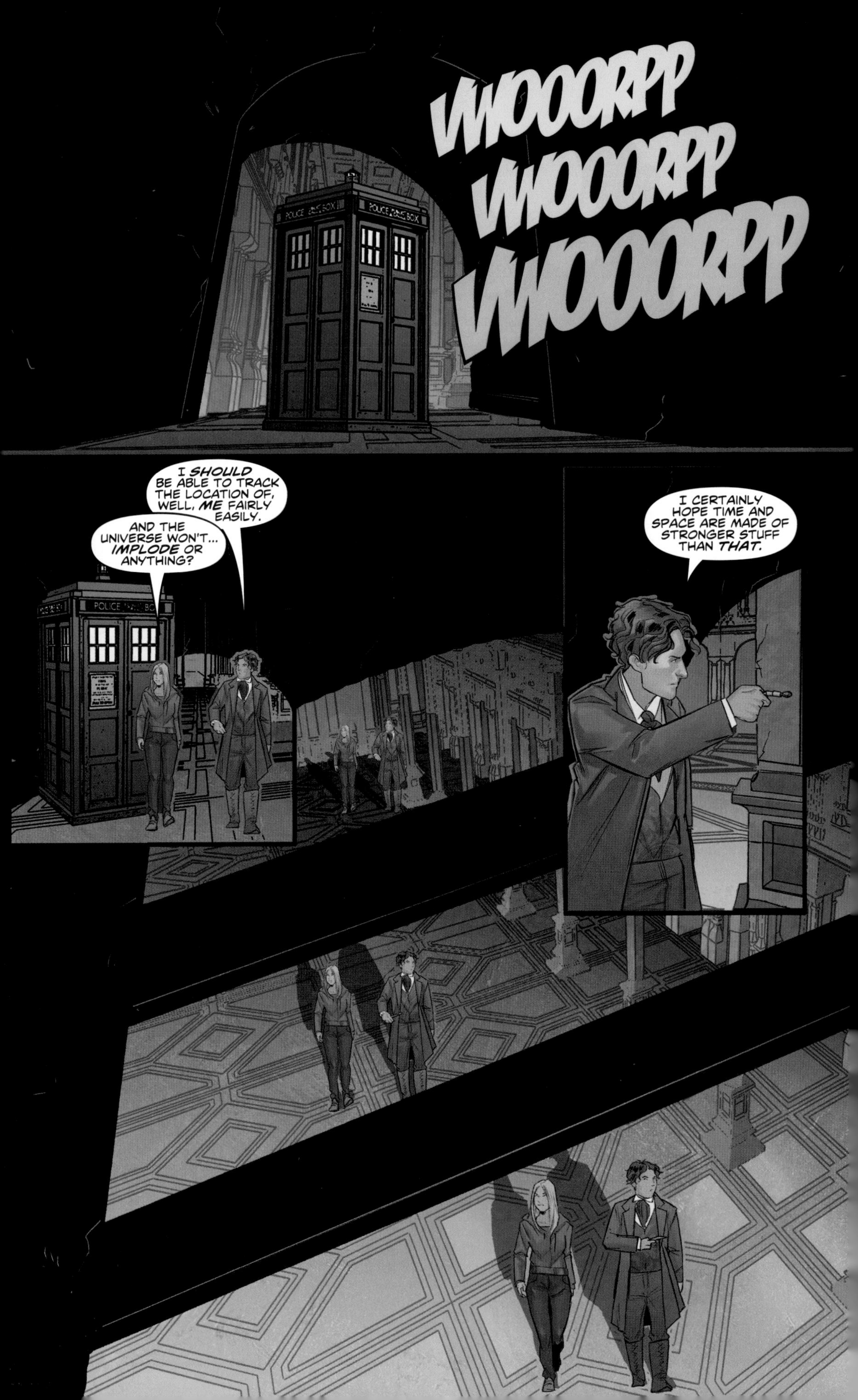
VWOOORPP
VWOOORPP
VWOOORPP
I SHOULD BE ABLE TO TRACK THE LOCATION OF, WELL, ME FAIRLY EASILY.
AND THE UNIVERSE WON'T... IMPLODE OR ANYTHING?
I CERTAINLY HOPE TIME AND SPACE ARE MADE OF STRONGER STUFF THAN THAT.

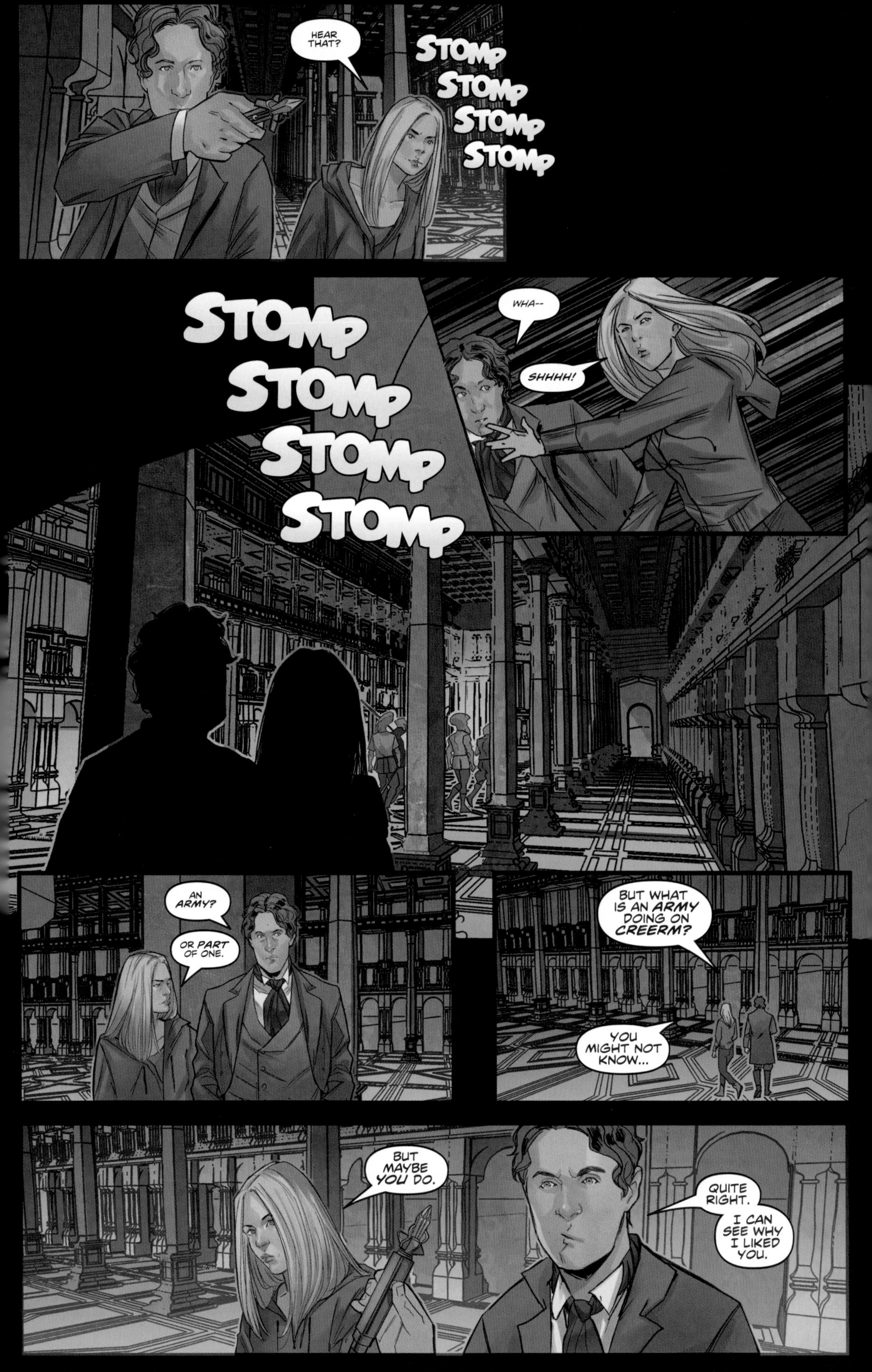
HEAR THAT?
STOMP
STOMP
STOMP
STOMP
STOMP
STOMP
STOMP
STOMP
WHA--
SHHHH!
AN ARMY?
OR PART OF ONE.
BUT WHAT IS AN ARMY DOING ON CREERM?
YOU MIGHT NOT KNOW...
BUT MAYBE YOU DO.
QUITE RIGHT.
I CAN SEE WHY I LIKED YOU.

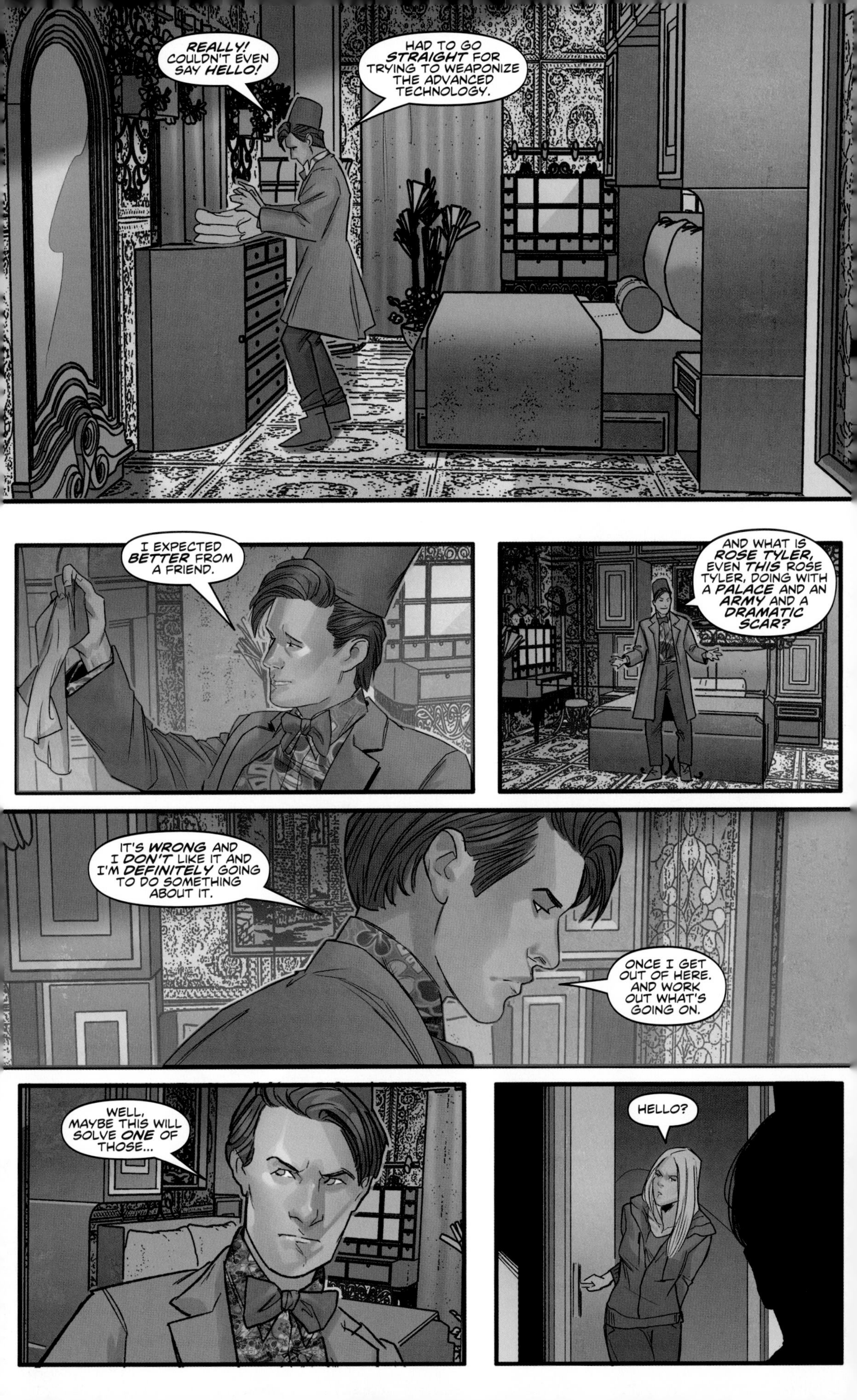
REALLY! COULDN'T EVEN SAY HELLO!
HAD TO GO STRAIGHT FOR TRYING TO WEAPONIZE THE ADVANCED TECHNOLOGY.
I EXPECTED BETTER FROM A FRIEND.
AND WHAT IS ROSE TYLER, EVEN THIS ROSE TYLER, DOING WITH A PALACE AND AN ARMY AND A DRAMATIC SCAR?
IT'S WRONG AND I DON'T LIKE IT AND I'M DEFINITELY GOING TO DO SOMETHING ABOUT IT.
ONCE I GET OUT OF HERE. AND WORK OUT WHAT'S GOING ON.
WELL, MAYBE THIS WILL SOLVE ONE OF THOSE...
HELLO?

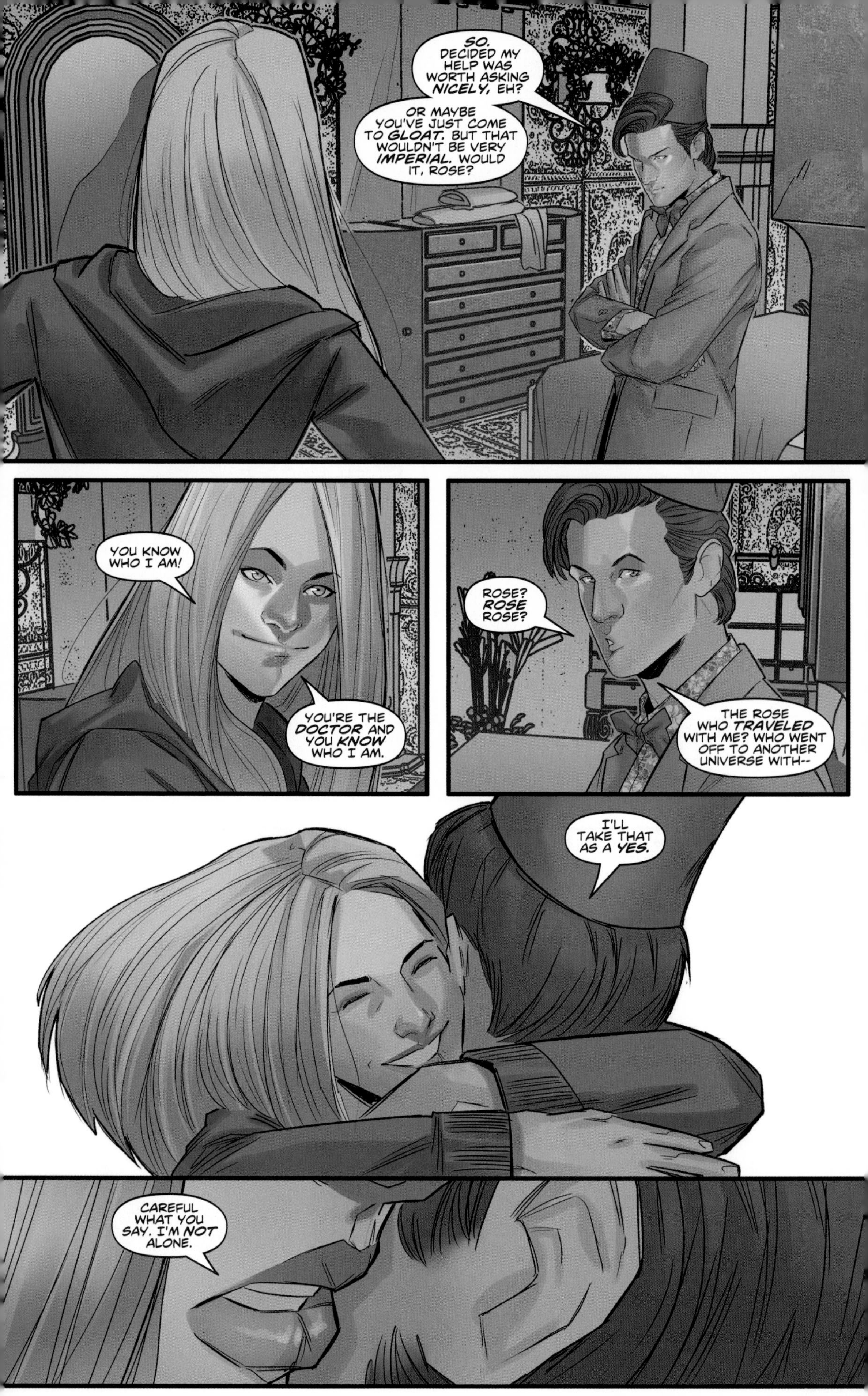
SO. DECIDED MY HELP WAS WORTH ASKING NICELY, EH?
OR MAYBE YOU'VE JUST COME TO GLOAT. BUT THAT WOULDN'T BE VERY IMPERIAL. WOULD IT, ROSE?
YOU KNOW WHO I AM!
YOU'RE THE DOCTOR AND YOU KNOW WHO I AM.
ROSE? ROSE ROSE?
THE ROSE WHO TRAVELED WITH ME? WHO WENT OFF TO ANOTHER UNIVERSE WITH--
I'LL TAKE THAT AS A YES.
CAREFUL WHAT YOU SAY. I'M NOT ALONE.

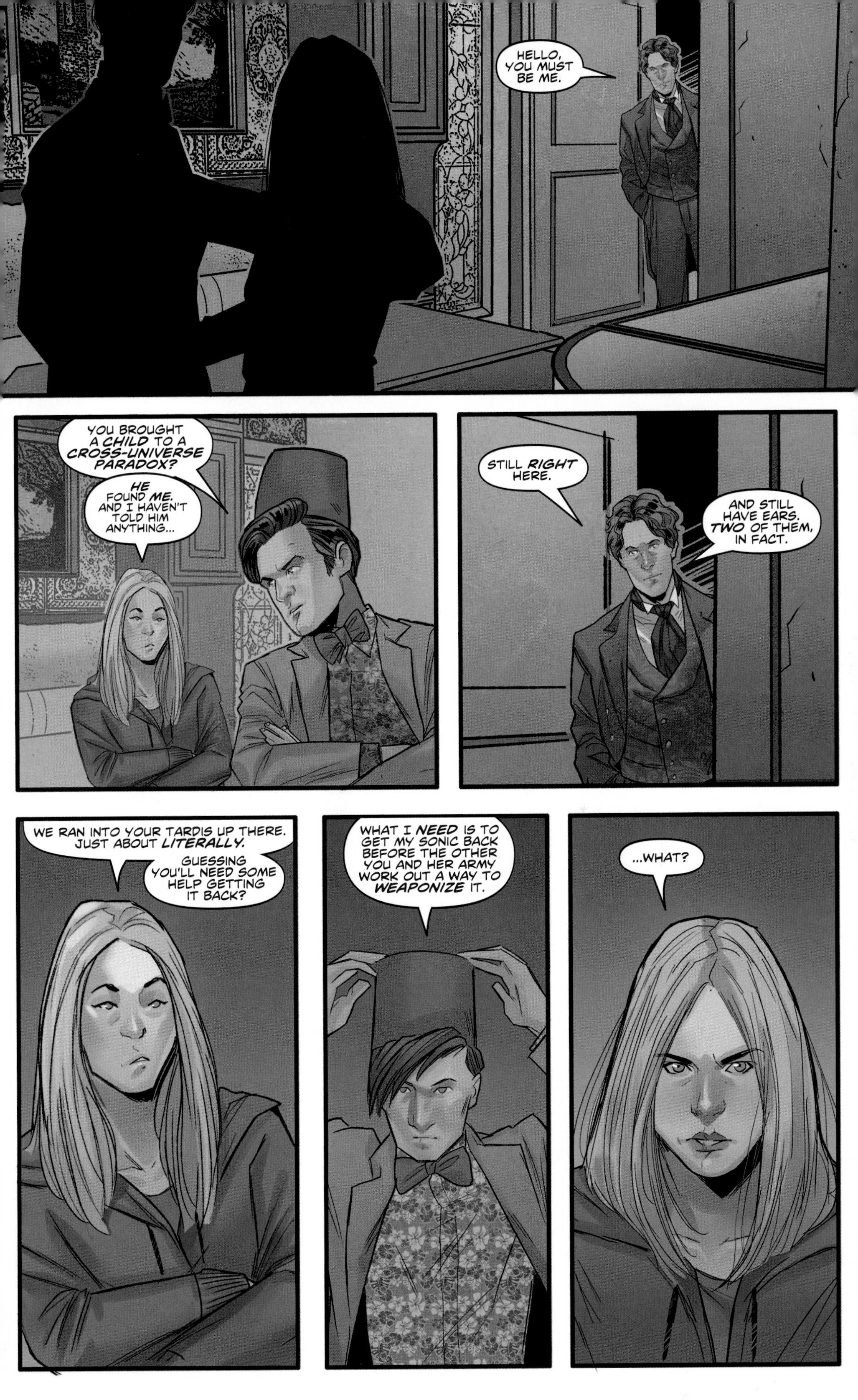
HELLO, YOU MUST BE ME.
YOU BROUGHT A *CHILD* TO A *CROSS-UNIVERSE PARADOX?*
HE FOUND *ME.* AND I HAVEN'T TOLD HIM ANYTHING...
STILL *RIGHT* HERE.
AND STILL HAVE EARS. *TWO* OF THEM, IN FACT.
WE RAN INTO YOUR TARDIS UP THERE. JUST ABOUT *LITERALLY.*
GUESSING YOU'LL NEED SOME HELP GETTING IT BACK?
WHAT I *NEED* IS TO GET MY SONIC BACK BEFORE THE OTHER YOU AND HER ARMY WORK OUT A WAY TO *WEAPONIZE* IT.
...WHAT?

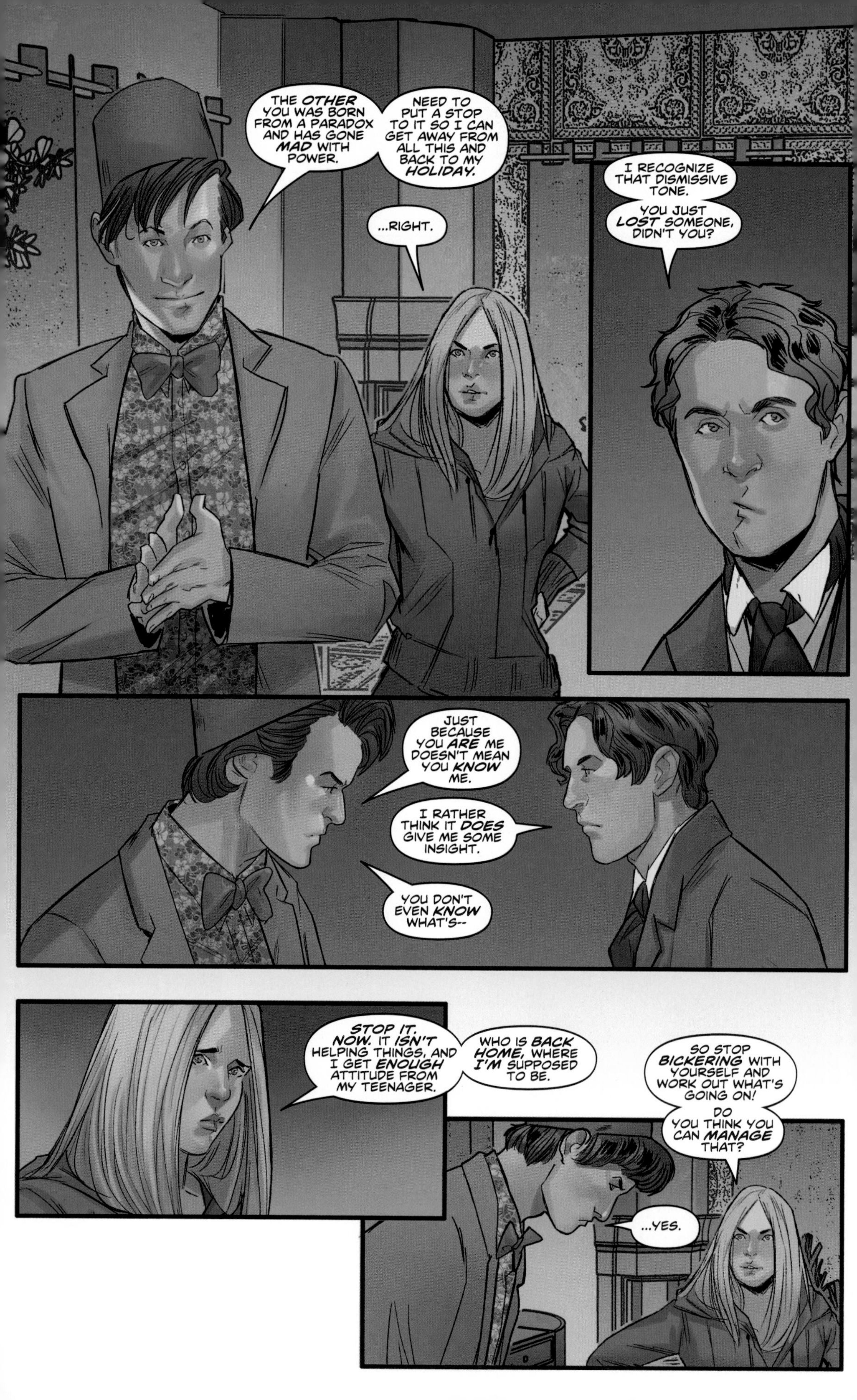
THE OTHER YOU WAS BORN FROM A PARADOX AND HAS GONE MAD WITH POWER.
NEED TO PUT A STOP TO IT SO I CAN GET AWAY FROM ALL THIS AND BACK TO MY HOLIDAY.
...RIGHT.
I RECOGNIZE THAT DISMISSIVE TONE.
YOU JUST LOST SOMEONE, DIDN'T YOU?
JUST BECAUSE YOU ARE ME DOESN'T MEAN YOU KNOW ME.
I RATHER THINK IT DOES GIVE ME SOME INSIGHT.
YOU DON'T EVEN KNOW WHAT'S--
STOP IT. NOW. IT ISN'T HELPING THINGS, AND I GET ENOUGH ATTITUDE FROM MY TEENAGER.
WHO IS BACK HOME, WHERE I'M SUPPOSED TO BE.
SO STOP BICKERING WITH YOURSELF AND WORK OUT WHAT'S GOING ON!
DO YOU THINK YOU CAN MANAGE THAT?
...YES.

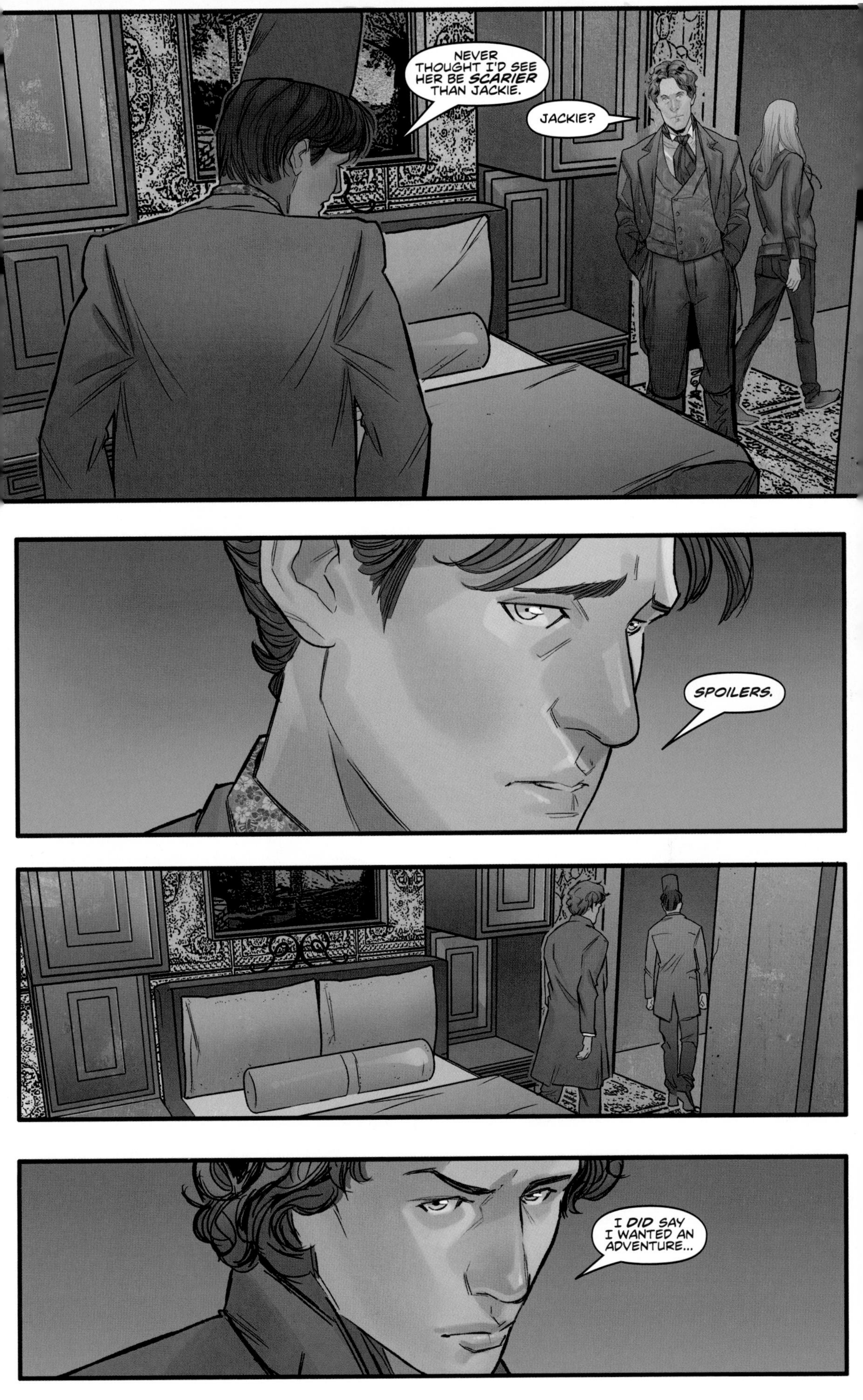
NEVER THOUGHT I'D SEE HER BE SCARIER THAN JACKIE.
JACKIE?
SPOILERS.
I DID SAY I WANTED AN ADVENTURE...

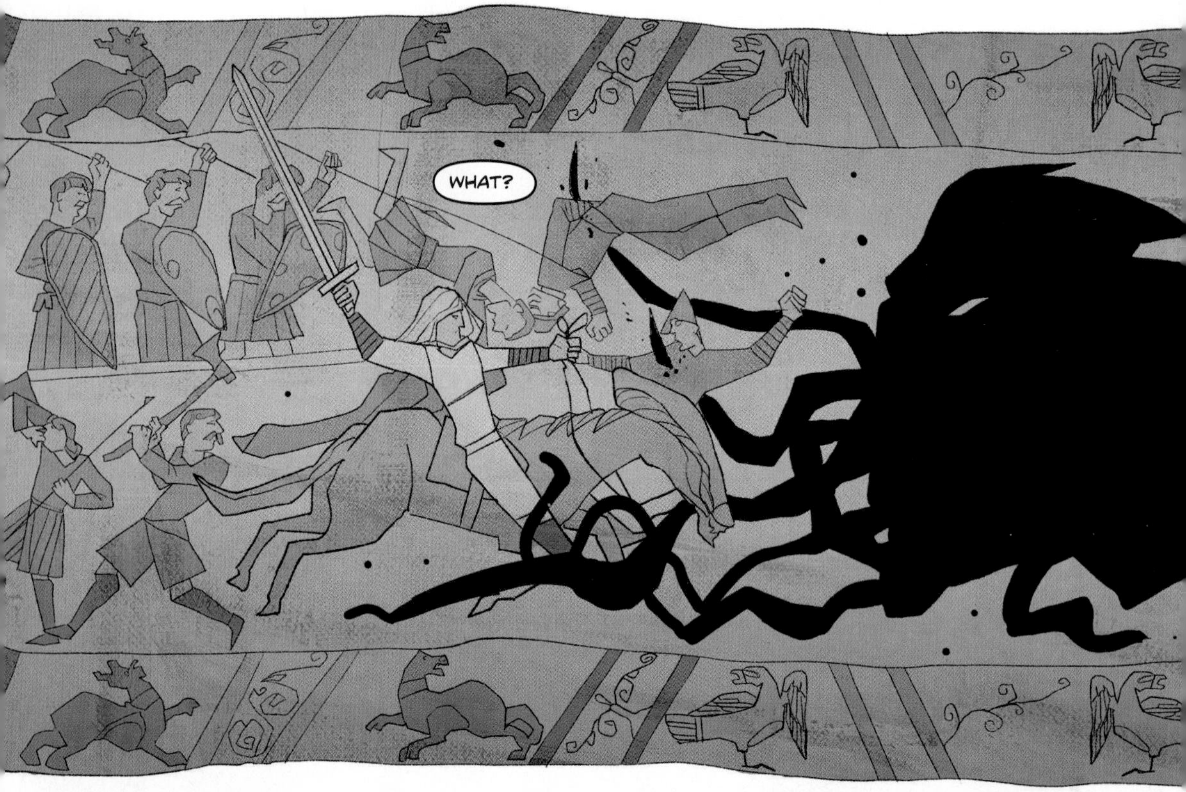
WHAT?

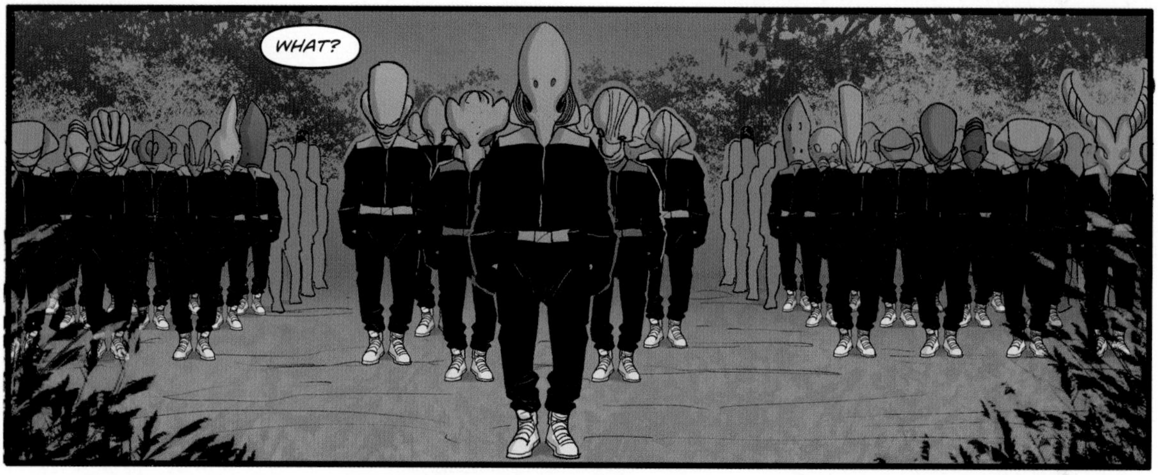
WHAT?

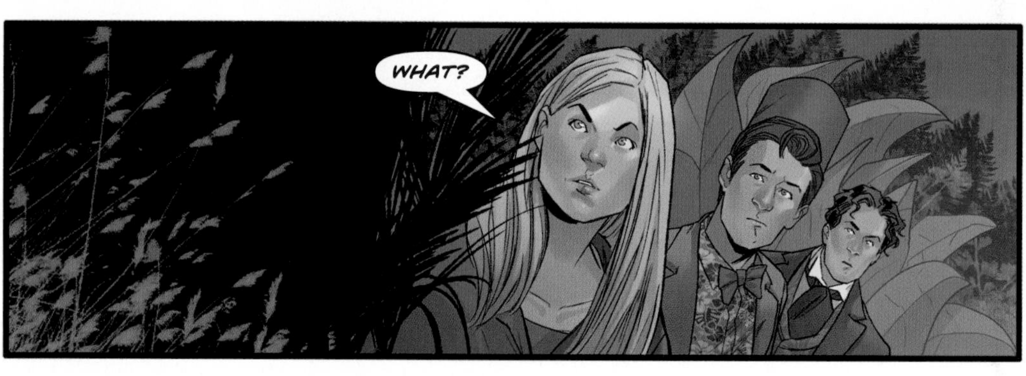
WHAT?

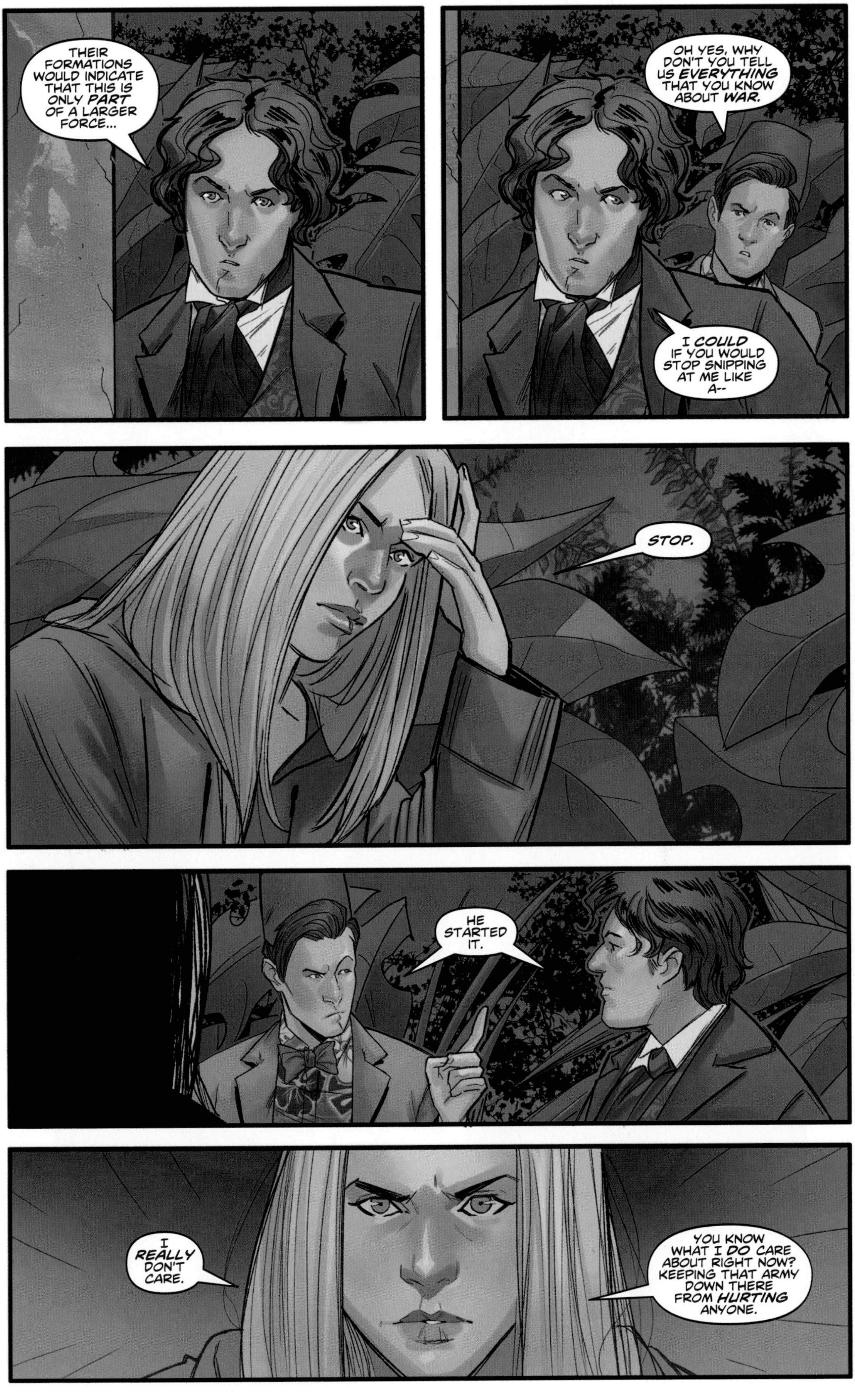
THEIR FORMATIONS WOULD INDICATE THAT THIS IS ONLY *PART* OF A LARGER FORCE...
OH YES, WHY DON'T YOU TELL US *EVERYTHING* THAT YOU KNOW ABOUT *WAR*.
I *COULD* IF YOU WOULD STOP SNIPPING AT ME LIKE A--
STOP.
HE STARTED IT.
I *REALLY* DON'T CARE.
YOU KNOW WHAT I *DO* CARE ABOUT RIGHT NOW? KEEPING THAT ARMY DOWN THERE FROM *HURTING* ANYONE.

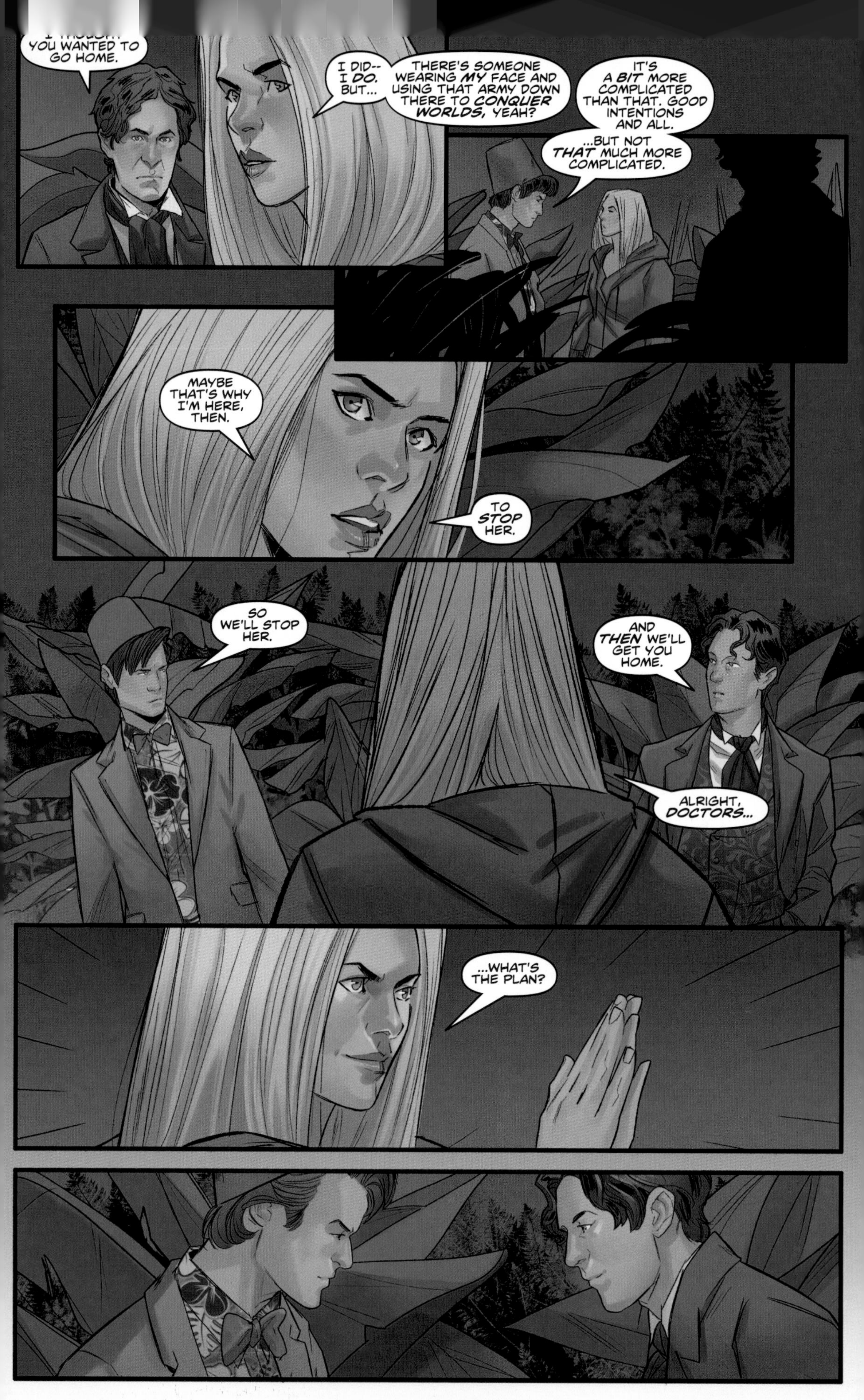
YOU WANTED TO GO HOME.
I DID-- I DO. BUT...
THERE'S SOMEONE WEARING MY FACE AND USING THAT ARMY DOWN THERE TO CONQUER WORLDS, YEAH?
IT'S A BIT MORE COMPLICATED THAN THAT. GOOD INTENTIONS AND ALL.
...BUT NOT THAT MUCH MORE COMPLICATED.
MAYBE THAT'S WHY I'M HERE, THEN.
TO STOP HER.
SO WE'LL STOP HER.
AND THEN WE'LL GET YOU HOME.
ALRIGHT, DOCTORS...
...WHAT'S THE PLAN?

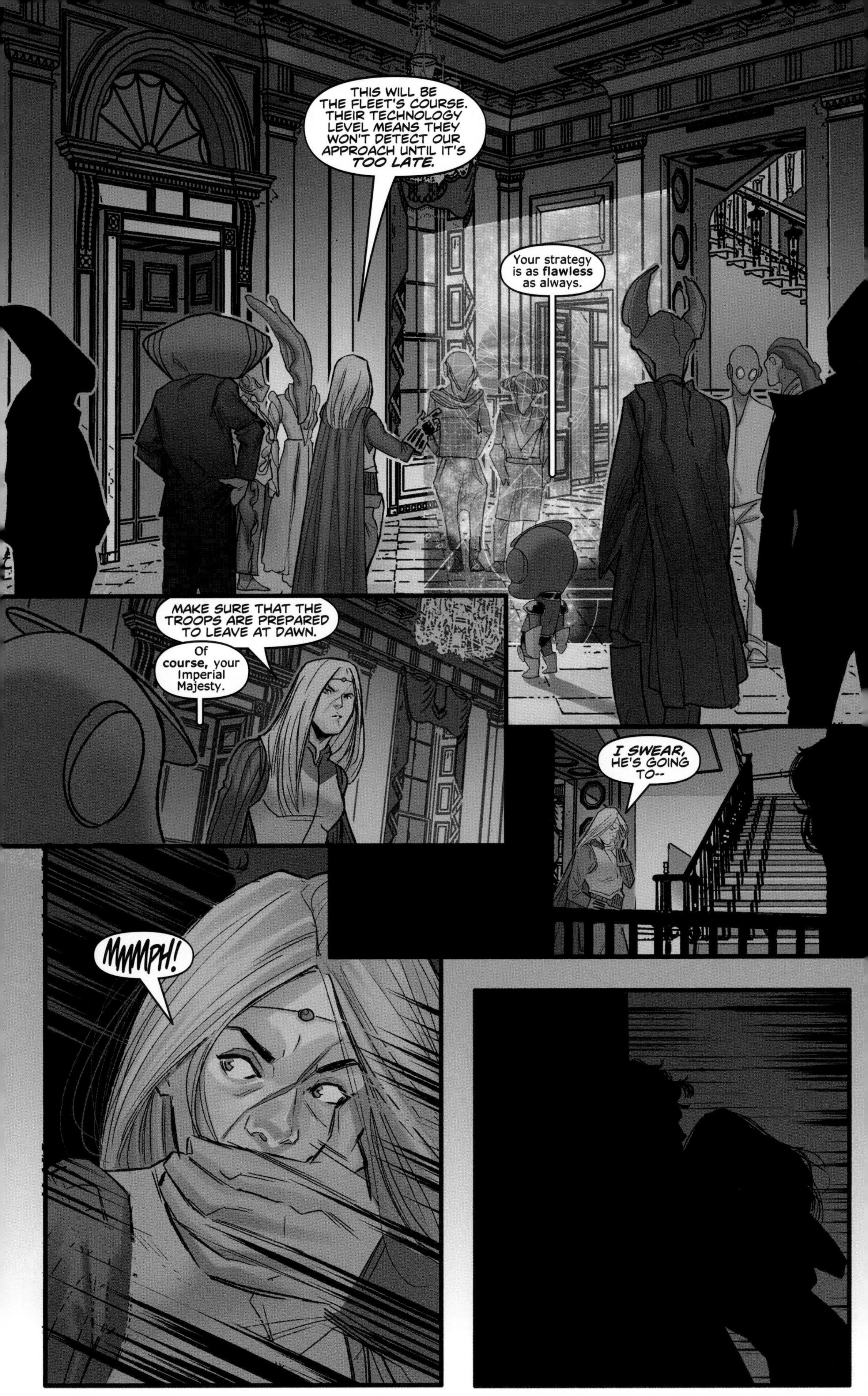
THIS WILL BE THE FLEET'S COURSE. THEIR TECHNOLOGY LEVEL MEANS THEY WON'T DETECT OUR APPROACH UNTIL IT'S *TOO LATE.*
Your strategy is as **flawless** as always.
MAKE SURE THAT THE TROOPS ARE PREPARED TO LEAVE AT DAWN.
Of **course,** your Imperial Majesty.
I SWEAR, HE'S GOING TO--
MMMPH!

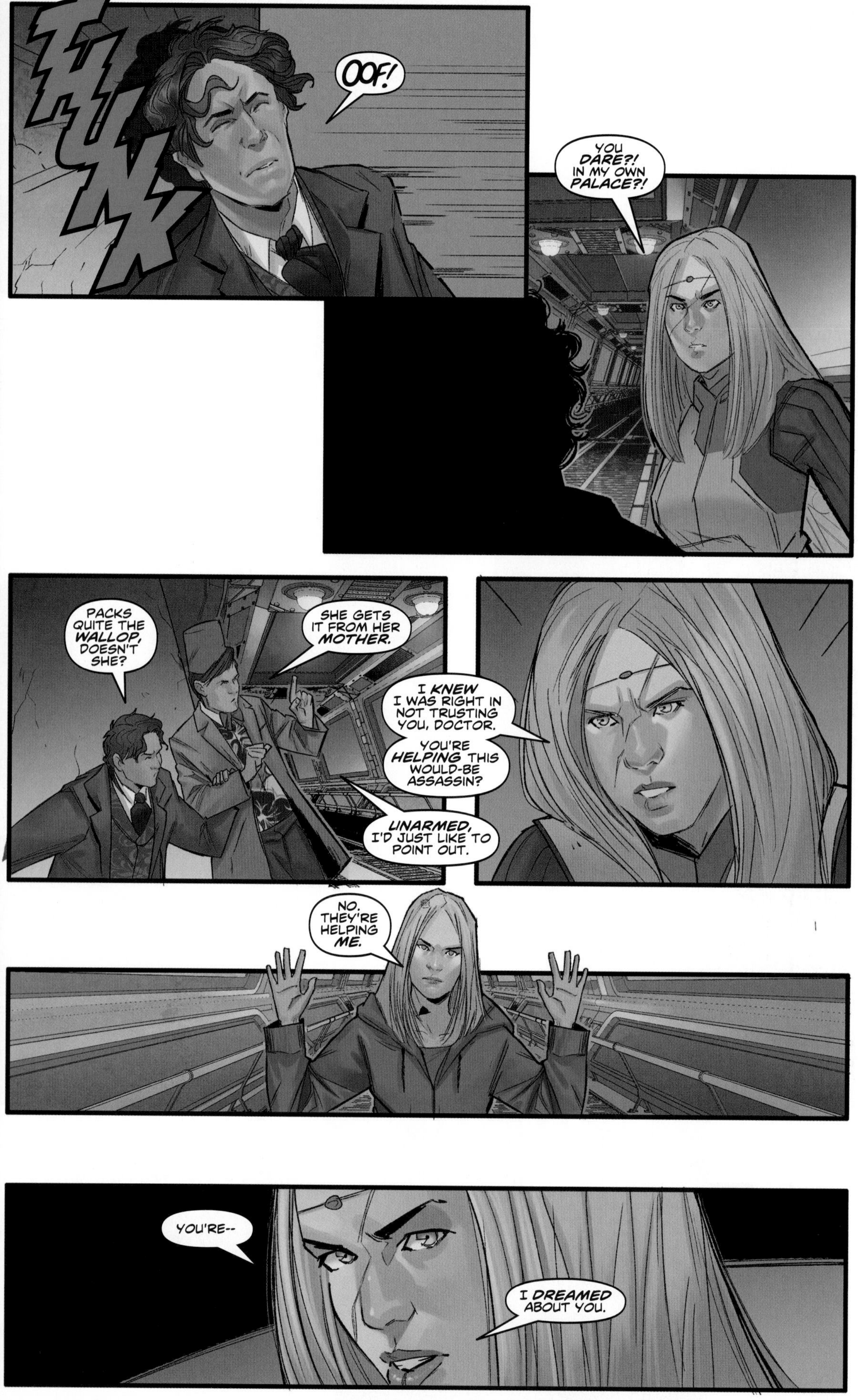
THUNK
OOF!
YOU DARE?! IN MY OWN PALACE?!
PACKS QUITE THE WALLOP, DOESN'T SHE?
SHE GETS IT FROM HER MOTHER.
I KNEW I WAS RIGHT IN NOT TRUSTING YOU, DOCTOR.
YOU'RE HELPING THIS WOULD-BE ASSASSIN?
UNARMED, I'D JUST LIKE TO POINT OUT.
NO. THEY'RE HELPING ME.
YOU'RE--
I DREAMED ABOUT YOU.

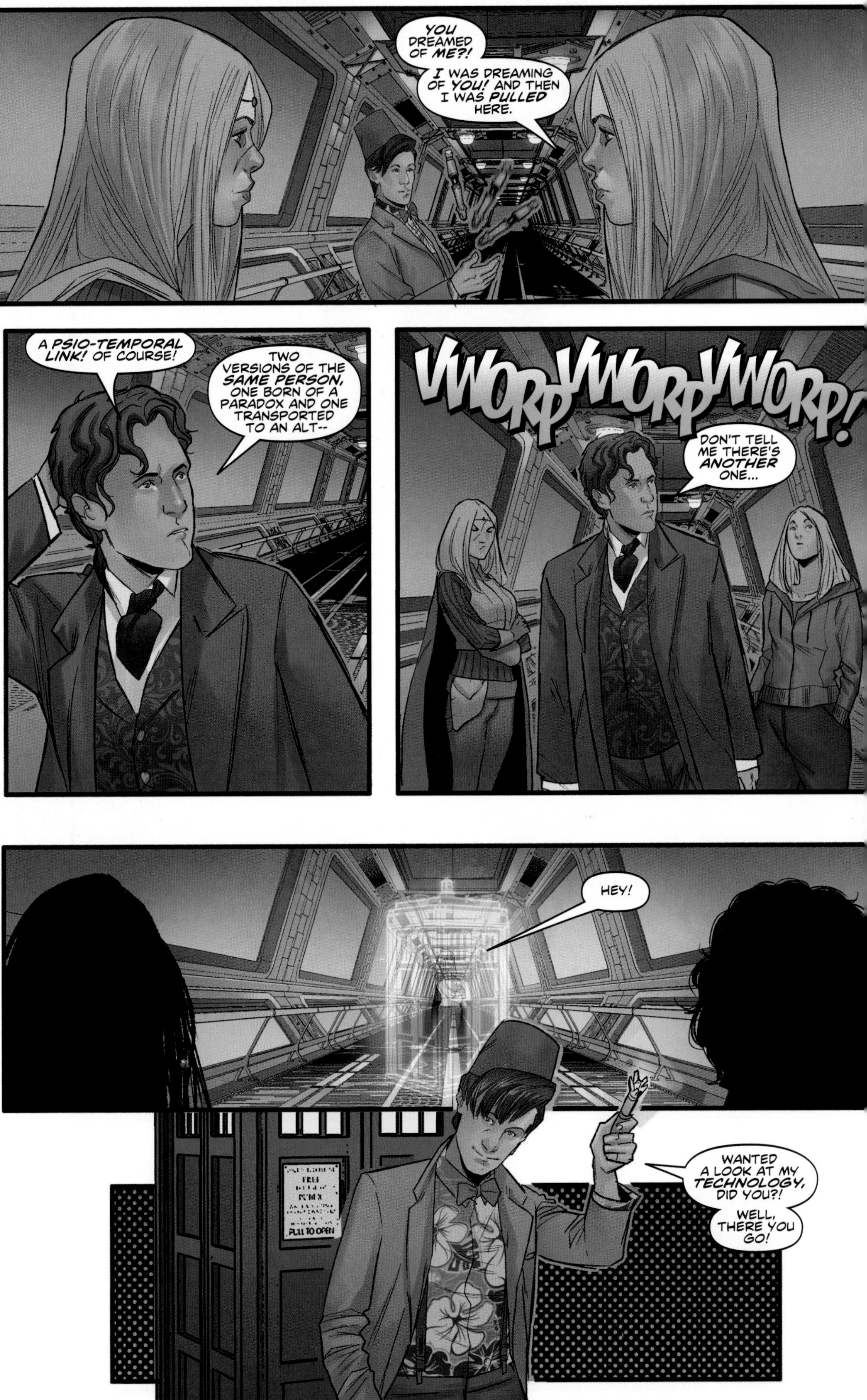
YOU DREAMED OF ME?!
I WAS DREAMING OF YOU! AND THEN I WAS PULLED HERE.
A PSIO-TEMPORAL LINK! OF COURSE!
TWO VERSIONS OF THE SAME PERSON, ONE BORN OF A PARADOX AND ONE TRANSPORTED TO AN ALT--
VWORP VWORP VWORP!
DON'T TELL ME THERE'S ANOTHER ONE...
HEY!
PULL TO OPEN
WANTED A LOOK AT MY TECHNOLOGY, DID YOU?!
WELL, THERE YOU GO!

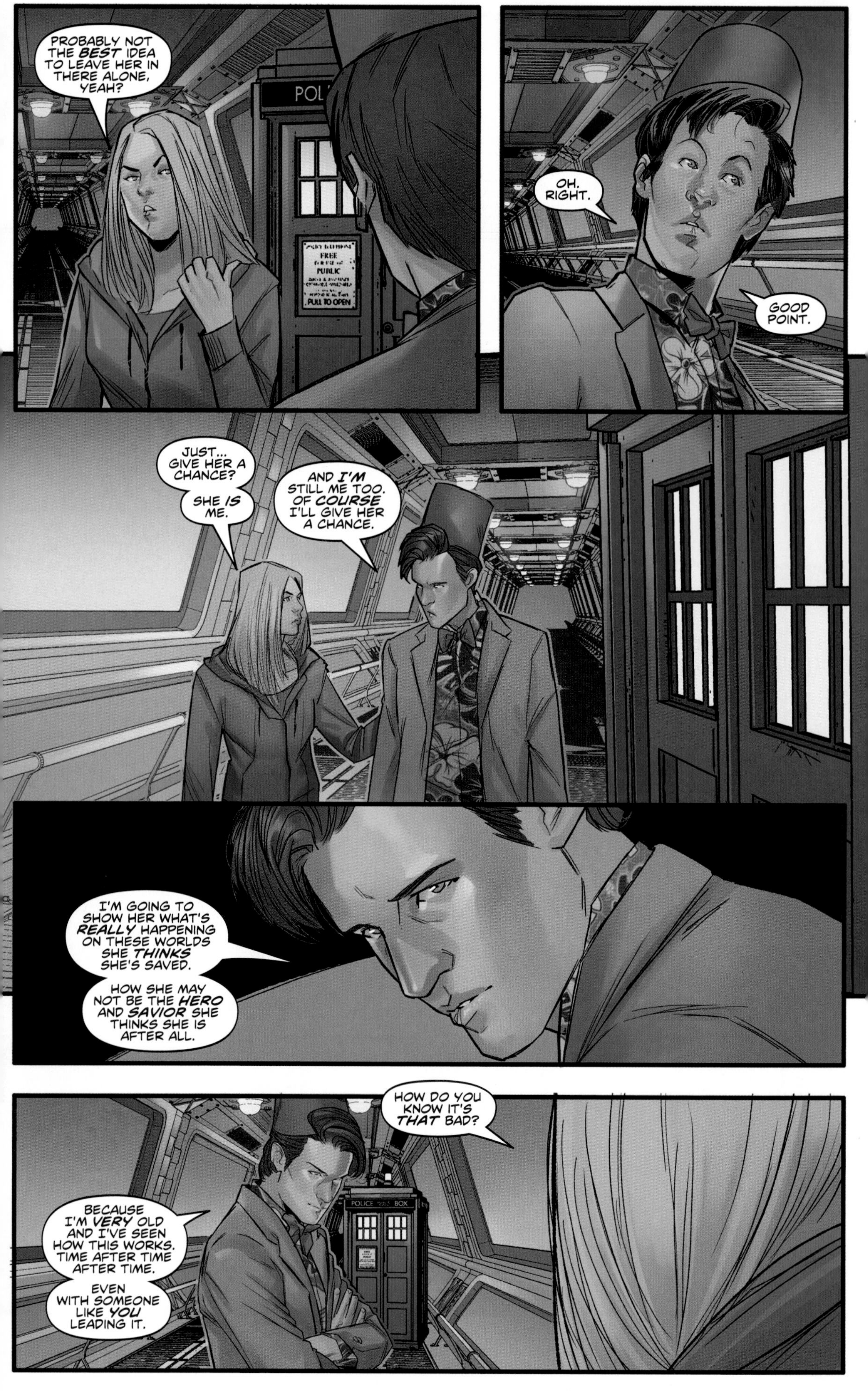
PROBABLY NOT THE BEST IDEA TO LEAVE HER IN THERE ALONE, YEAH?
FREE
PUBLIC
PULL TO OPEN
OH. RIGHT.
GOOD POINT.
JUST... GIVE HER A CHANCE?
SHE IS ME.
AND I'M STILL ME TOO. OF COURSE I'LL GIVE HER A CHANCE.
I'M GOING TO SHOW HER WHAT'S REALLY HAPPENING ON THESE WORLDS SHE THINKS SHE'S SAVED.
HOW SHE MAY NOT BE THE HERO AND SAVIOR SHE THINKS SHE IS AFTER ALL.
HOW DO YOU KNOW IT'S THAT BAD?
POLICE BOX
BECAUSE I'M VERY OLD AND I'VE SEEN HOW THIS WORKS. TIME AFTER TIME AFTER TIME.
EVEN WITH SOMEONE LIKE YOU LEADING IT.

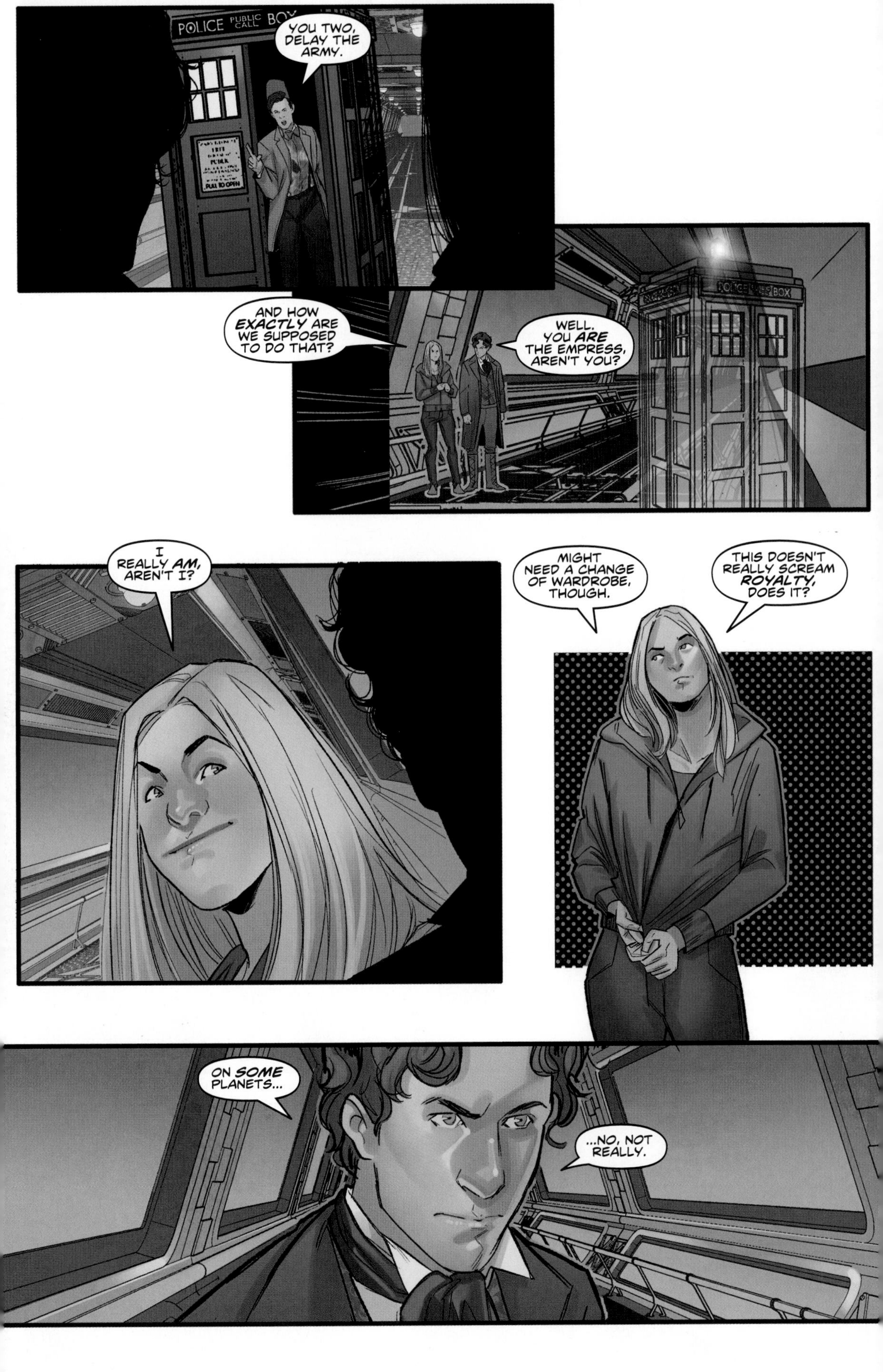
POLICE PUBLIC CALL BOX
YOU TWO, DELAY THE ARMY.
PULL TO OPEN
AND HOW EXACTLY ARE WE SUPPOSED TO DO THAT?
WELL. YOU ARE THE EMPRESS, AREN'T YOU?
I REALLY AM, AREN'T I?
MIGHT NEED A CHANGE OF WARDROBE, THOUGH.
THIS DOESN'T REALLY SCREAM ROYALTY, DOES IT?
ON SOME PLANETS...
...NO, NOT REALLY.

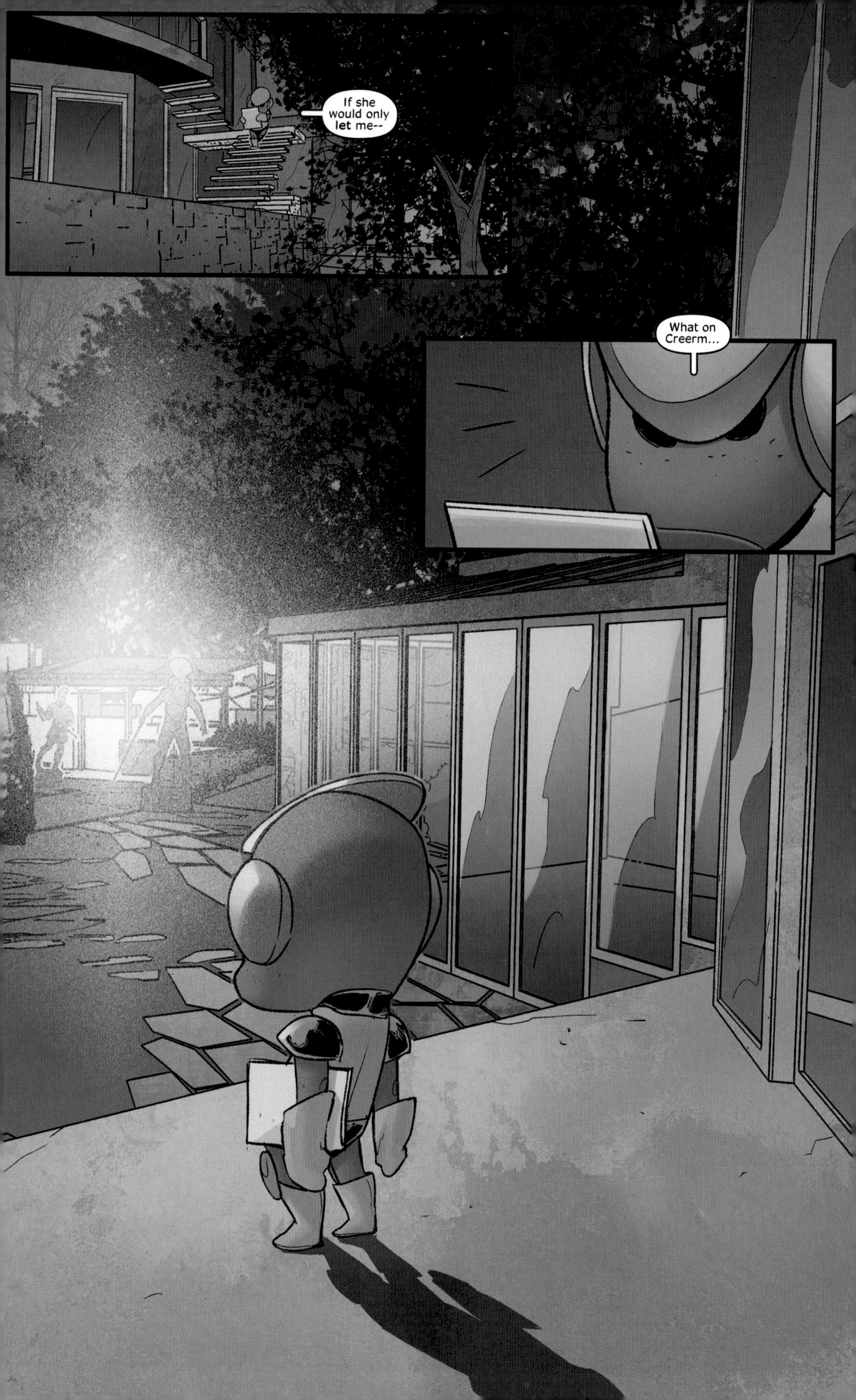
If she would only let me--
What on Creerm...

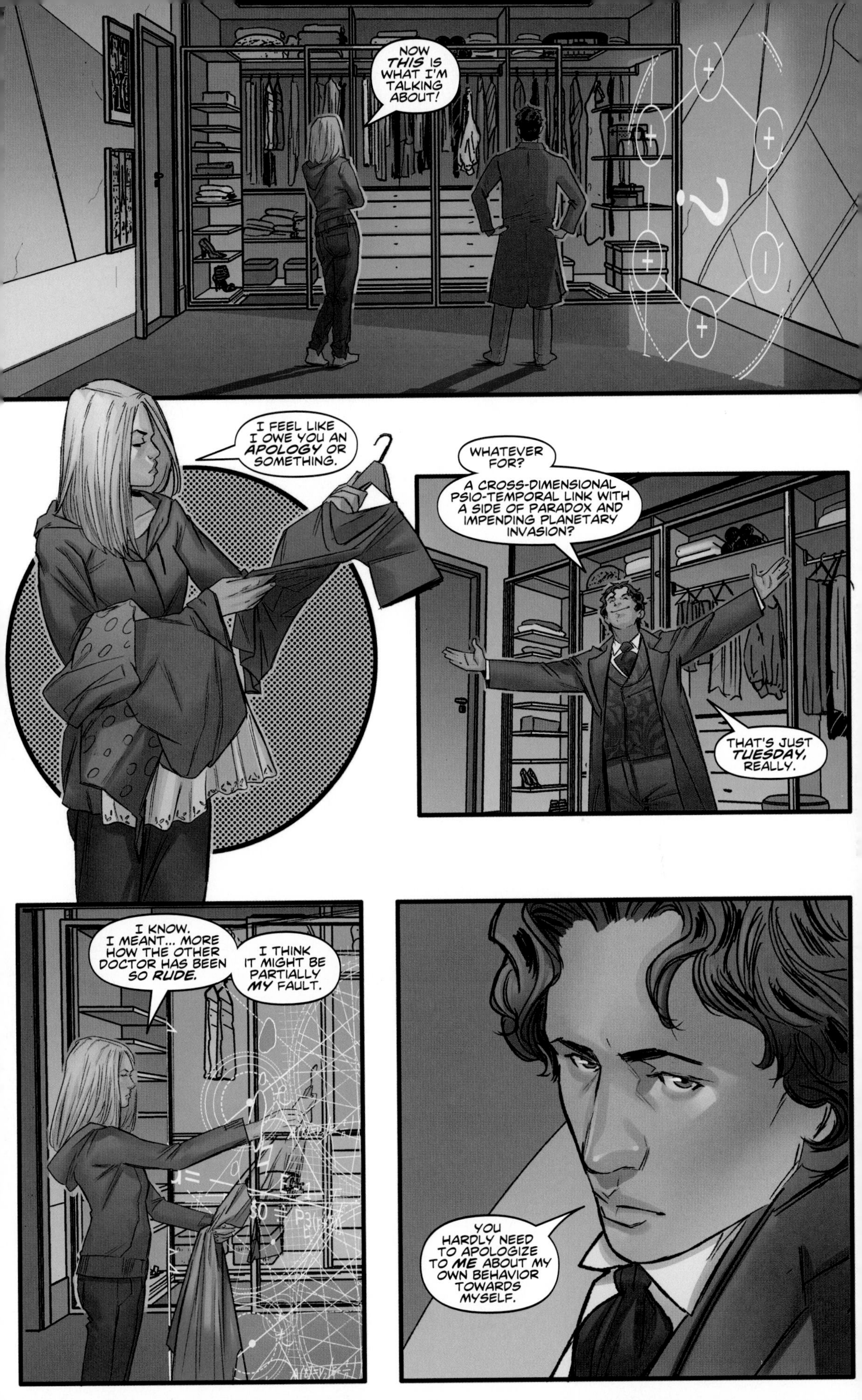
NOW THIS IS WHAT I'M TALKING ABOUT!
I FEEL LIKE I OWE YOU AN APOLOGY OR SOMETHING.
WHATEVER FOR?
A CROSS-DIMENSIONAL PSIO-TEMPORAL LINK WITH A SIDE OF PARADOX AND IMPENDING PLANETARY INVASION?
THAT'S JUST TUESDAY, REALLY.
I KNOW. I MEANT... MORE HOW THE OTHER DOCTOR HAS BEEN SO RUDE.
I THINK IT MIGHT BE PARTIALLY MY FAULT.
YOU HARDLY NEED TO APOLOGIZE TO ME ABOUT MY OWN BEHAVIOR TOWARDS MYSELF.

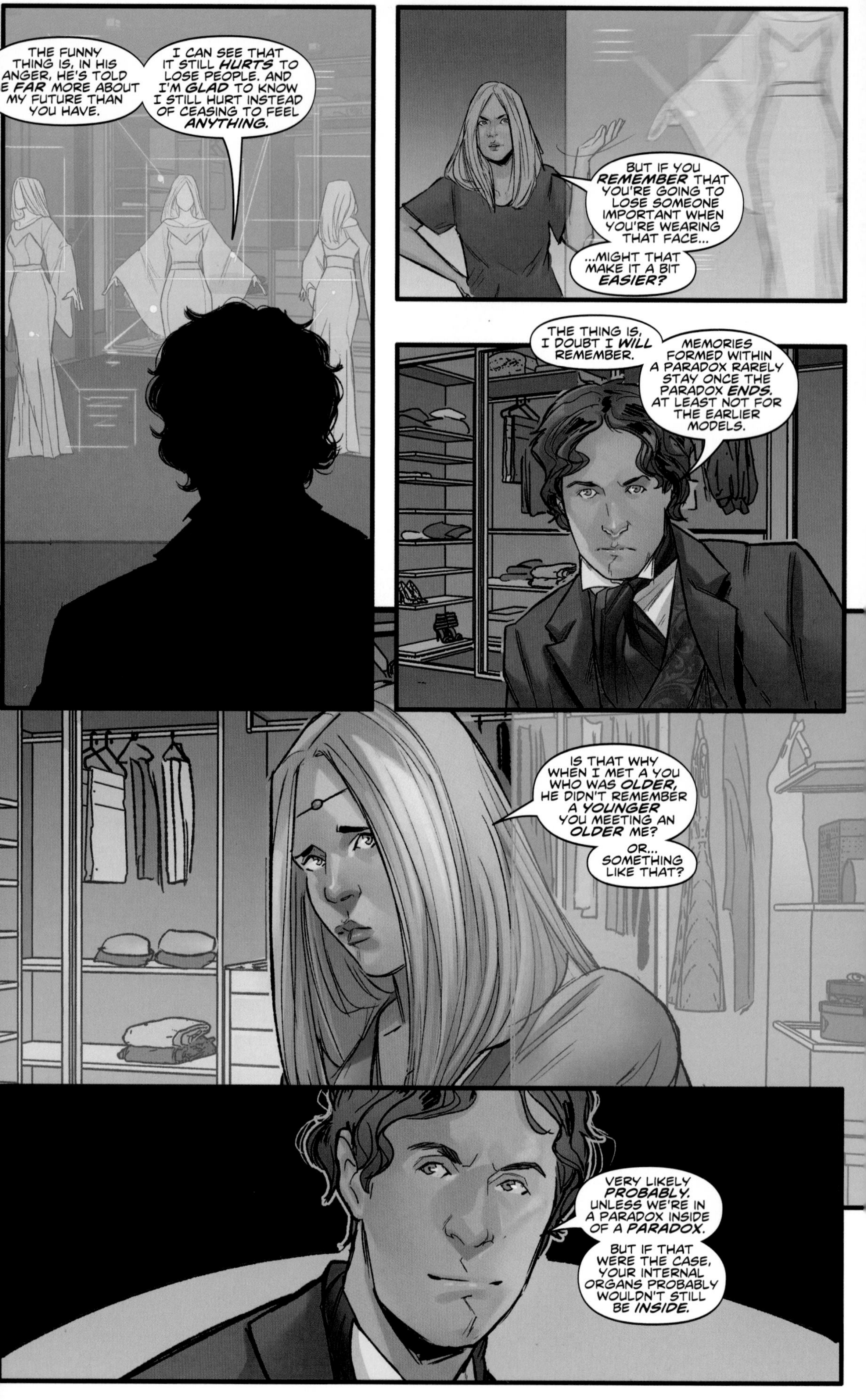
THE FUNNY THING IS, IN HIS ANGER, HE'S TOLD E FAR MORE ABOUT MY FUTURE THAN YOU HAVE.
I CAN SEE THAT IT STILL HURTS TO LOSE PEOPLE. AND I'M GLAD TO KNOW I STILL HURT INSTEAD OF CEASING TO FEEL ANYTHING.
BUT IF YOU REMEMBER THAT YOU'RE GOING TO LOSE SOMEONE IMPORTANT WHEN YOU'RE WEARING THAT FACE...
...MIGHT THAT MAKE IT A BIT EASIER?
THE THING IS, I DOUBT I WILL REMEMBER.
MEMORIES FORMED WITHIN A PARADOX RARELY STAY ONCE THE PARADOX ENDS. AT LEAST NOT FOR THE EARLIER MODELS.
IS THAT WHY WHEN I MET A YOU WHO WAS OLDER, HE DIDN'T REMEMBER A YOUNGER YOU MEETING AN OLDER ME?
OR... SOMETHING LIKE THAT?
VERY LIKELY PROBABLY. UNLESS WE'RE IN A PARADOX INSIDE OF A PARADOX.
BUT IF THAT WERE THE CASE, YOUR INTERNAL ORGANS PROBABLY WOULDN'T STILL BE INSIDE.

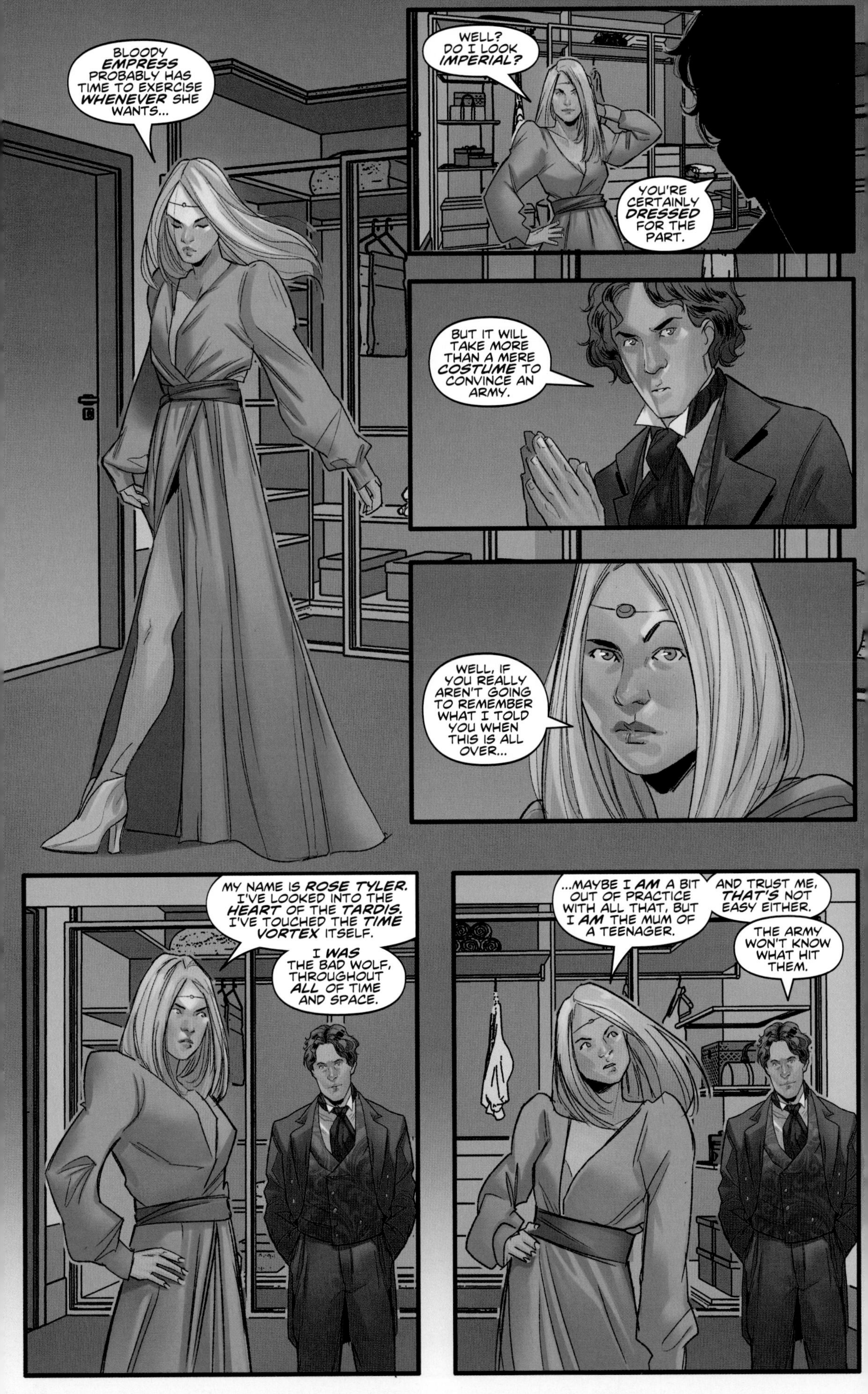
BLOODY EMPRESS PROBABLY HAS TIME TO EXERCISE WHENEVER SHE WANTS...
WELL? DO I LOOK IMPERIAL?
YOU'RE CERTAINLY DRESSED FOR THE PART.
BUT IT WILL TAKE MORE THAN A MERE COSTUME TO CONVINCE AN ARMY.
WELL, IF YOU REALLY AREN'T GOING TO REMEMBER WHAT I TOLD YOU WHEN THIS IS ALL OVER...
MY NAME IS ROSE TYLER. I'VE LOOKED INTO THE HEART OF THE TARDIS. I'VE TOUCHED THE TIME VORTEX ITSELF.
I WAS THE BAD WOLF, THROUGHOUT ALL OF TIME AND SPACE.
...MAYBE I AM A BIT OUT OF PRACTICE WITH ALL THAT, BUT I AM THE MUM OF A TEENAGER.
AND TRUST ME, THAT'S NOT EASY EITHER.
THE ARMY WON'T KNOW WHAT HIT THEM.

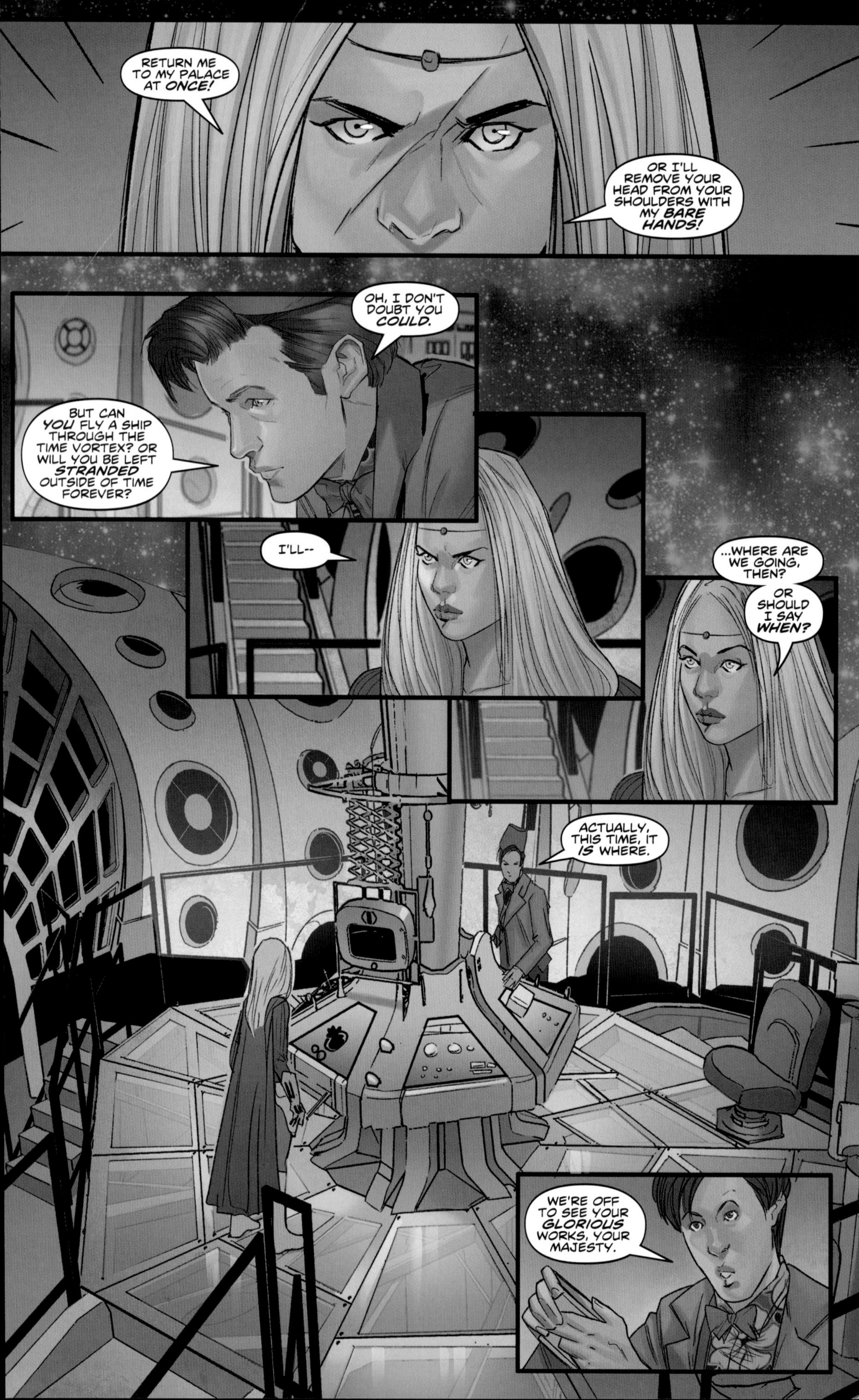
RETURN ME TO MY PALACE AT ONCE!
OR I'LL REMOVE YOUR HEAD FROM YOUR SHOULDERS WITH MY BARE HANDS!
OH, I DON'T DOUBT YOU COULD.
BUT CAN YOU FLY A SHIP THROUGH THE TIME VORTEX? OR WILL YOU BE LEFT STRANDED OUTSIDE OF TIME FOREVER?
I'LL--
...WHERE ARE WE GOING, THEN?
OR SHOULD I SAY WHEN?
ACTUALLY, THIS TIME, IT IS WHERE.
WE'RE OFF TO SEE YOUR GLORIOUS WORKS, YOUR MAJESTY.

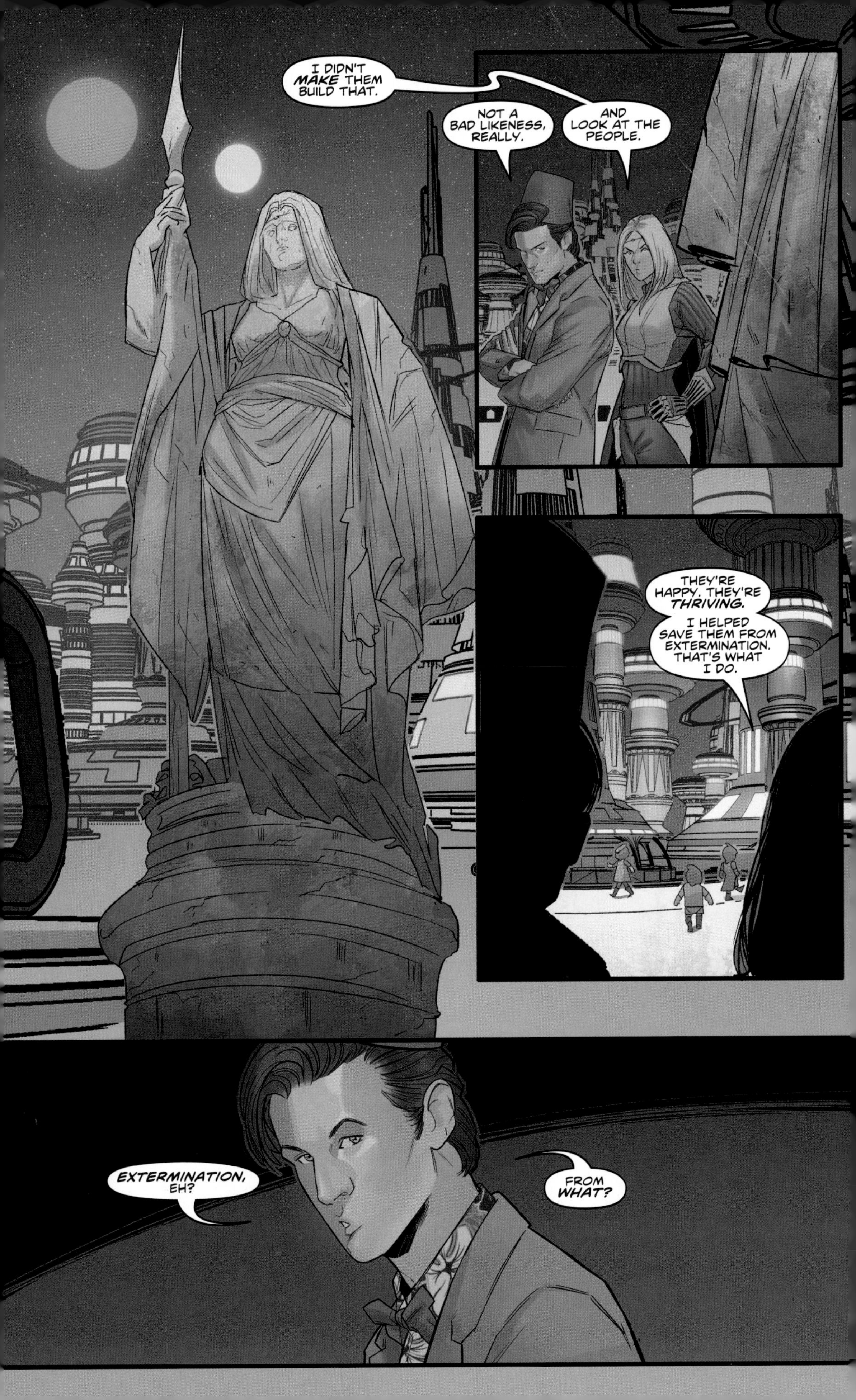
I DIDN'T *MAKE* THEM BUILD THAT.
NOT A BAD LIKENESS, REALLY.
AND LOOK AT THE PEOPLE.
THEY'RE HAPPY. THEY'RE *THRIVING.*
I HELPED SAVE THEM FROM EXTERMINATION. THAT'S WHAT I DO.
EXTERMINATION, EH?
FROM *WHAT?*

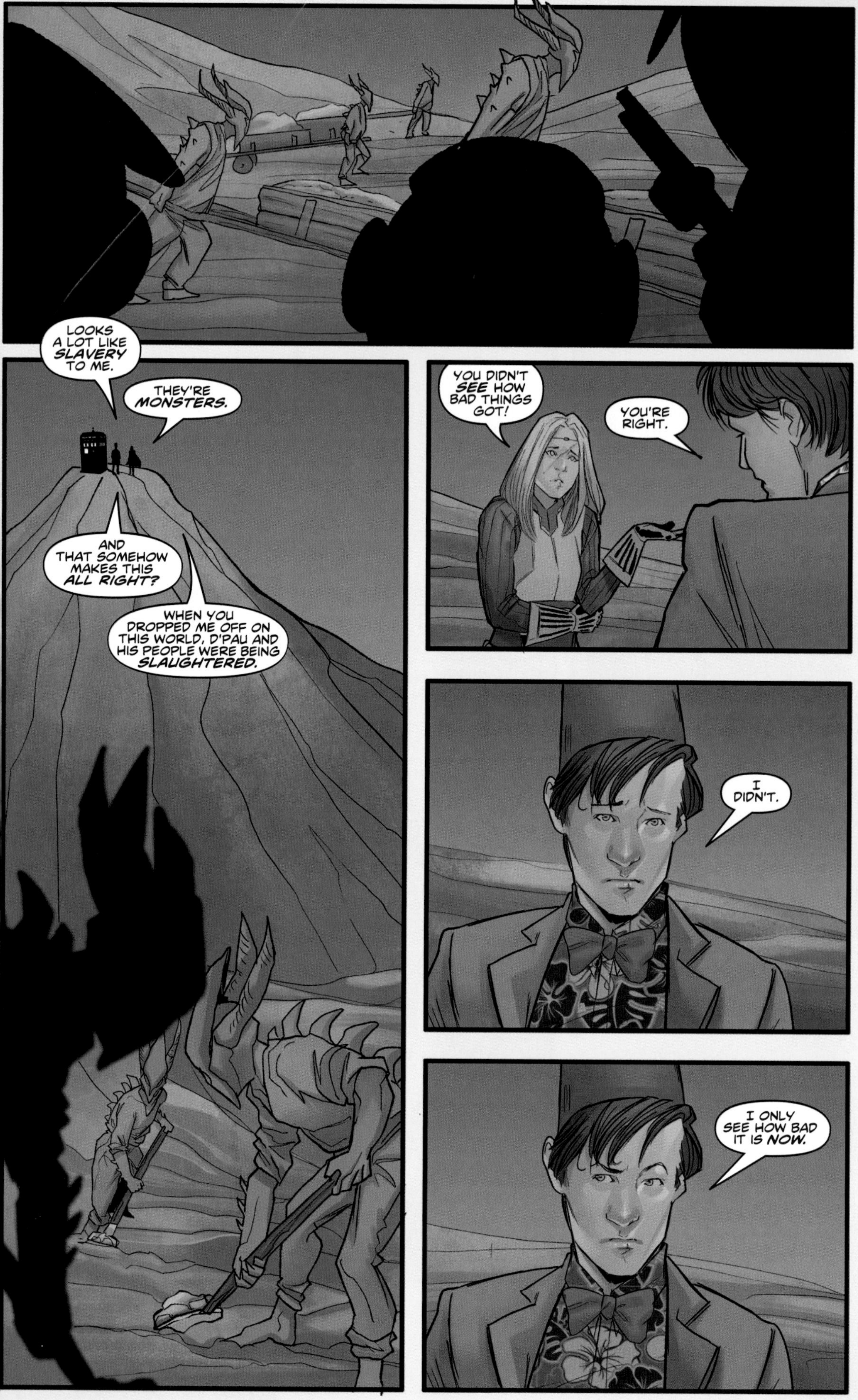
LOOKS A LOT LIKE SLAVERY TO ME.
THEY'RE MONSTERS.
AND THAT SOMEHOW MAKES THIS ALL RIGHT?
WHEN YOU DROPPED ME OFF ON THIS WORLD, D'PAU AND HIS PEOPLE WERE BEING SLAUGHTERED.
YOU DIDN'T SEE HOW BAD THINGS GOT!
YOU'RE RIGHT.
I DIDN'T.
I ONLY SEE HOW BAD IT IS NOW.

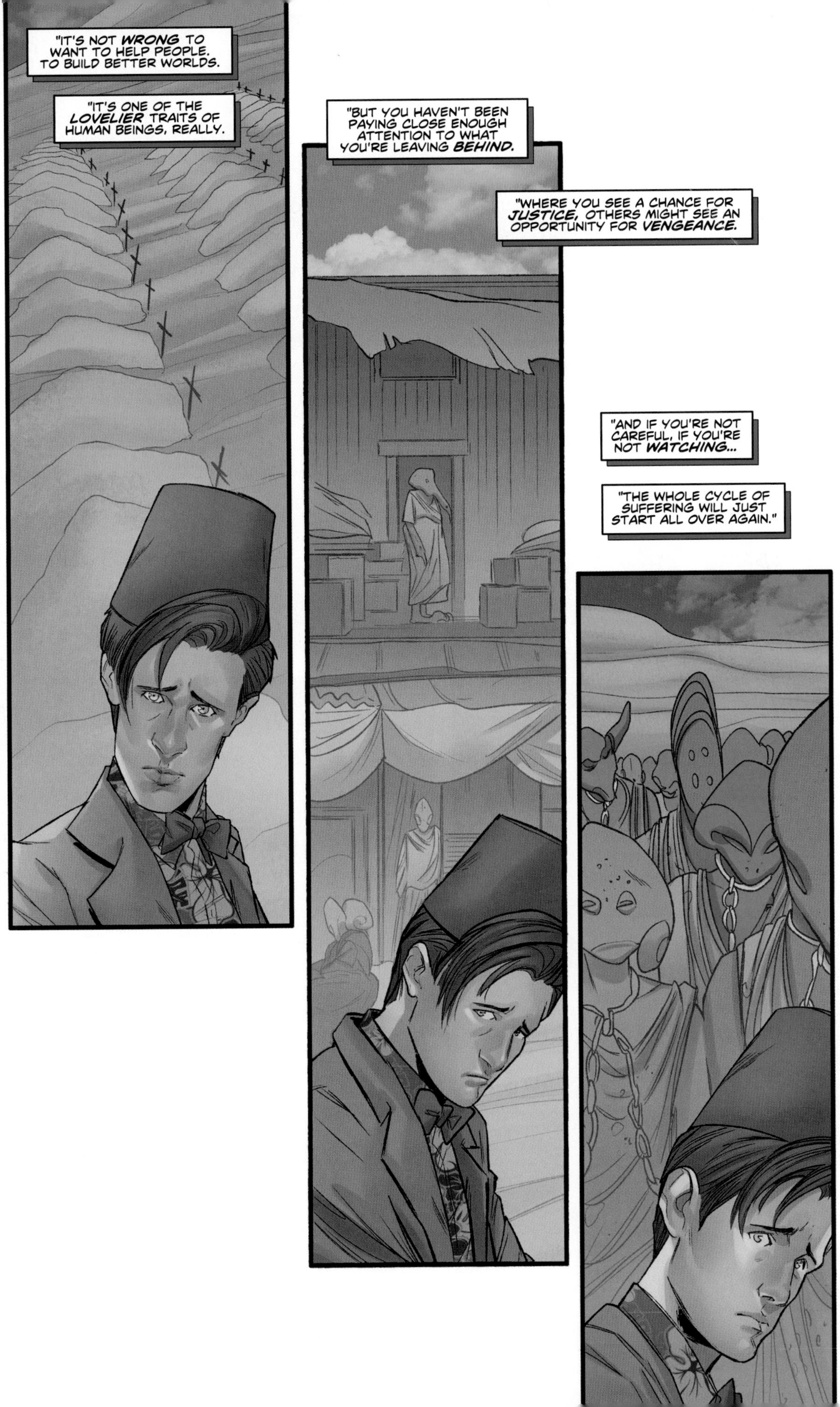
"IT'S NOT WRONG TO WANT TO HELP PEOPLE. TO BUILD BETTER WORLDS.
"IT'S ONE OF THE LOVELIER TRAITS OF HUMAN BEINGS, REALLY.
"BUT YOU HAVEN'T BEEN PAYING CLOSE ENOUGH ATTENTION TO WHAT YOU'RE LEAVING BEHIND.
"WHERE YOU SEE A CHANCE FOR JUSTICE, OTHERS MIGHT SEE AN OPPORTUNITY FOR VENGEANCE.
"AND IF YOU'RE NOT CAREFUL, IF YOU'RE NOT WATCHING...
"THE WHOLE CYCLE OF SUFFERING WILL JUST START ALL OVER AGAIN."

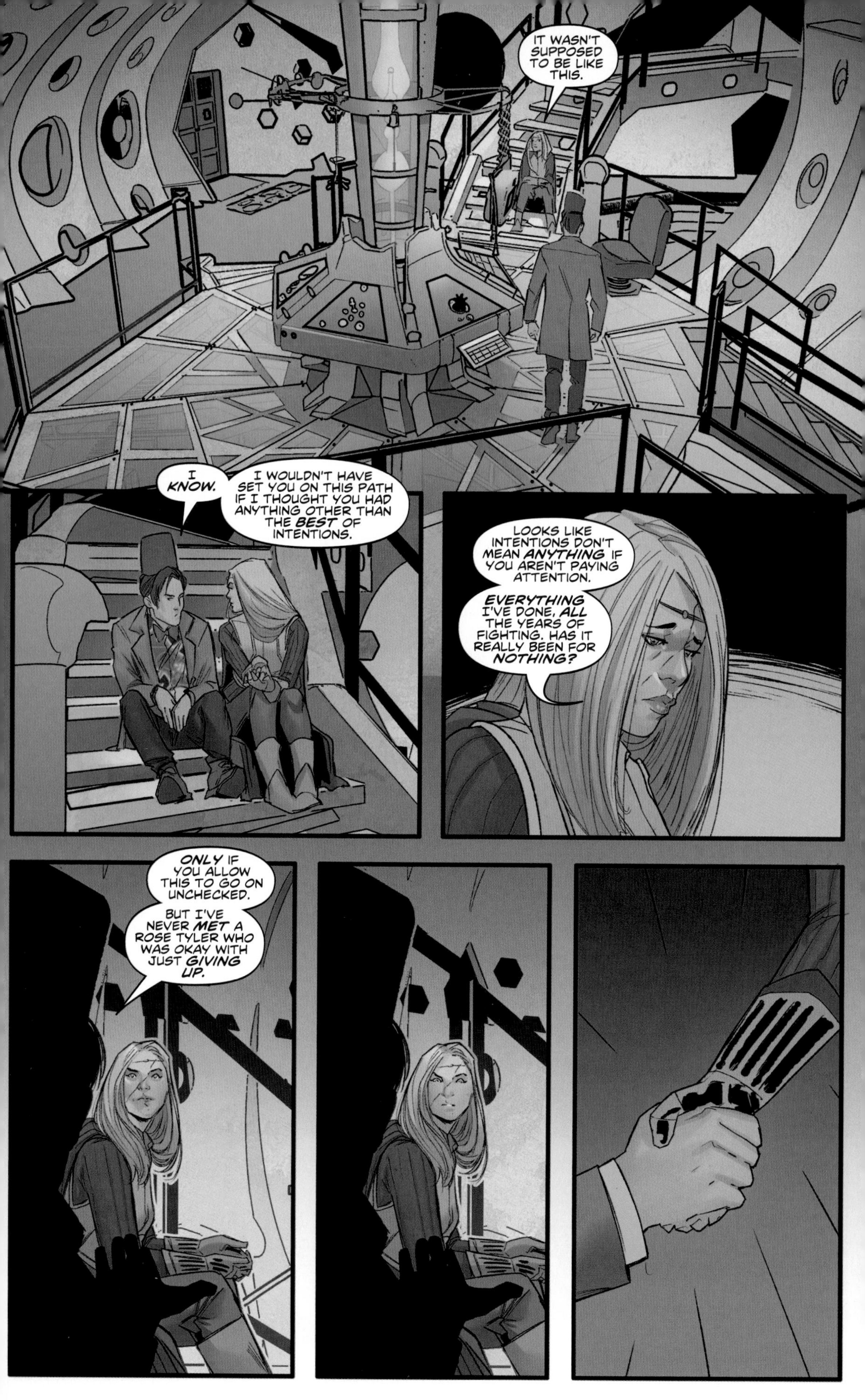

IT WASN'T SUPPOSED TO BE LIKE THIS.
I KNOW.
I WOULDN'T HAVE SET YOU ON THIS PATH IF I THOUGHT YOU HAD ANYTHING OTHER THAN THE BEST OF INTENTIONS.
LOOKS LIKE INTENTIONS DON'T MEAN ANYTHING IF YOU AREN'T PAYING ATTENTION.
EVERYTHING I'VE DONE, ALL THE YEARS OF FIGHTING. HAS IT REALLY BEEN FOR NOTHING?
ONLY IF YOU ALLOW THIS TO GO ON UNCHECKED.
BUT I'VE NEVER MET A ROSE TYLER WHO WAS OKAY WITH JUST GIVING UP.

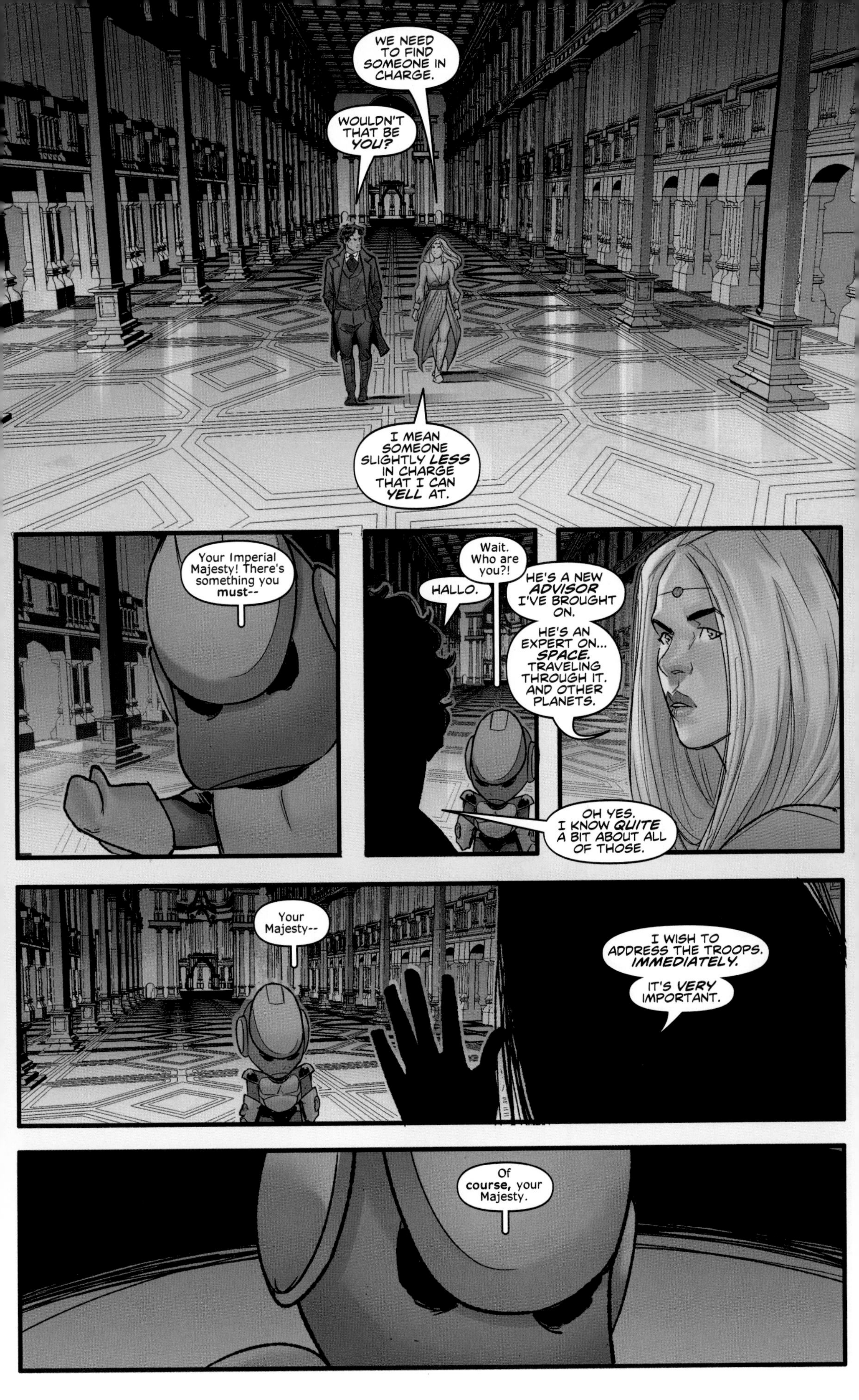
WE NEED TO FIND SOMEONE IN CHARGE.
WOULDN'T THAT BE *YOU?*
I MEAN SOMEONE SLIGHTLY *LESS* IN CHARGE THAT I CAN *YELL* AT.
Your Imperial Majesty! There's something you **must**--
HALLO.
Wait. Who are you?!
HE'S A NEW *ADVISOR* I'VE BROUGHT ON.
HE'S AN EXPERT ON... *SPACE.* TRAVELING THROUGH IT. AND OTHER PLANETS.
OH YES. I KNOW *QUITE* A BIT ABOUT ALL OF THOSE.
Your Majesty--
I WISH TO ADDRESS THE TROOPS. *IMMEDIATELY.*
IT'S *VERY* IMPORTANT.
Of **course,** your Majesty.

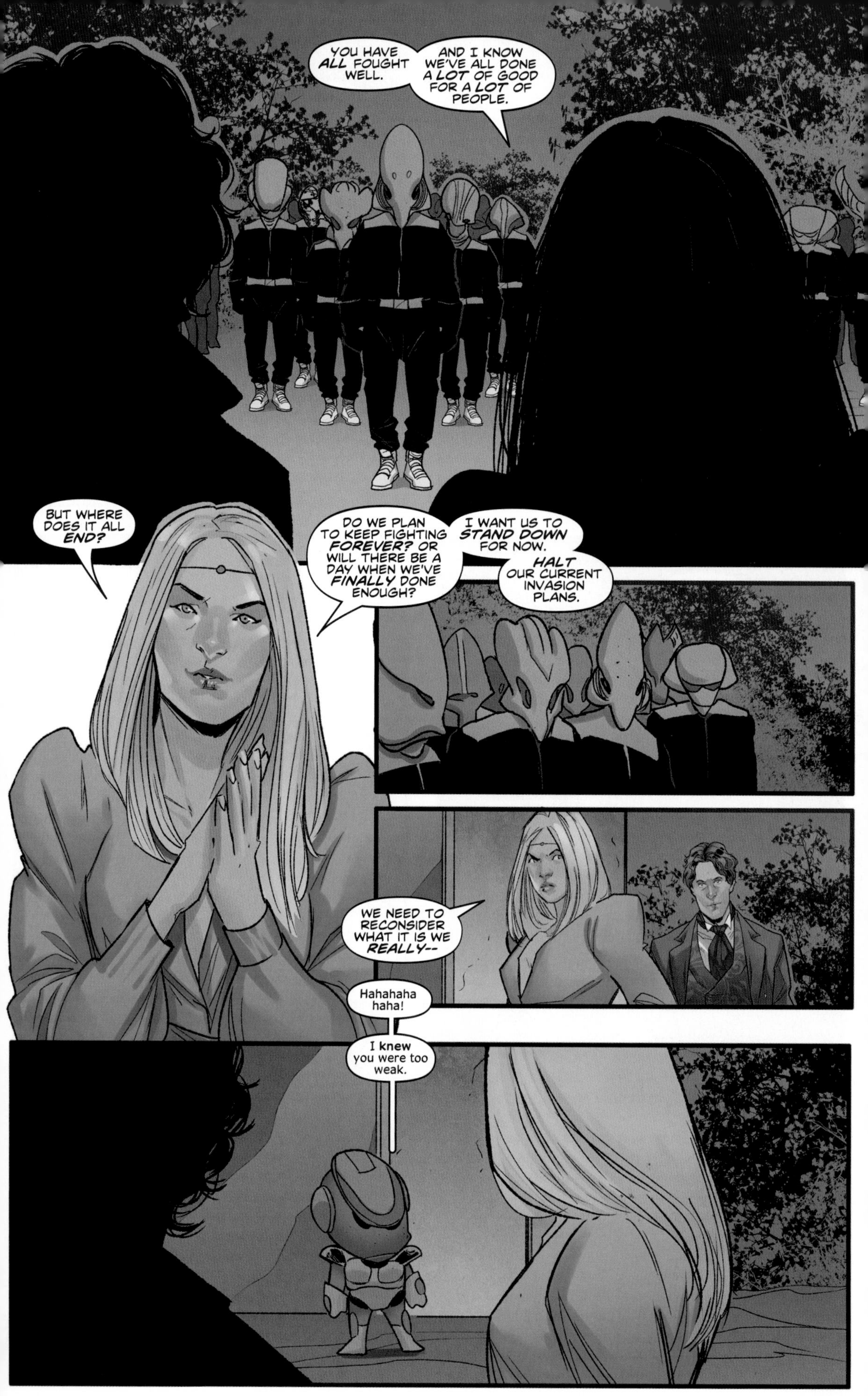
YOU HAVE ALL FOUGHT WELL.
AND I KNOW WE'VE ALL DONE A LOT OF GOOD FOR A LOT OF PEOPLE.
BUT WHERE DOES IT ALL END?
DO WE PLAN TO KEEP FIGHTING FOREVER? OR WILL THERE BE A DAY WHEN WE'VE FINALLY DONE ENOUGH?
I WANT US TO STAND DOWN FOR NOW.
HALT OUR CURRENT INVASION PLANS.
WE NEED TO RECONSIDER WHAT IT IS WE REALLY--
Hahahaha haha!
I knew you were too weak.

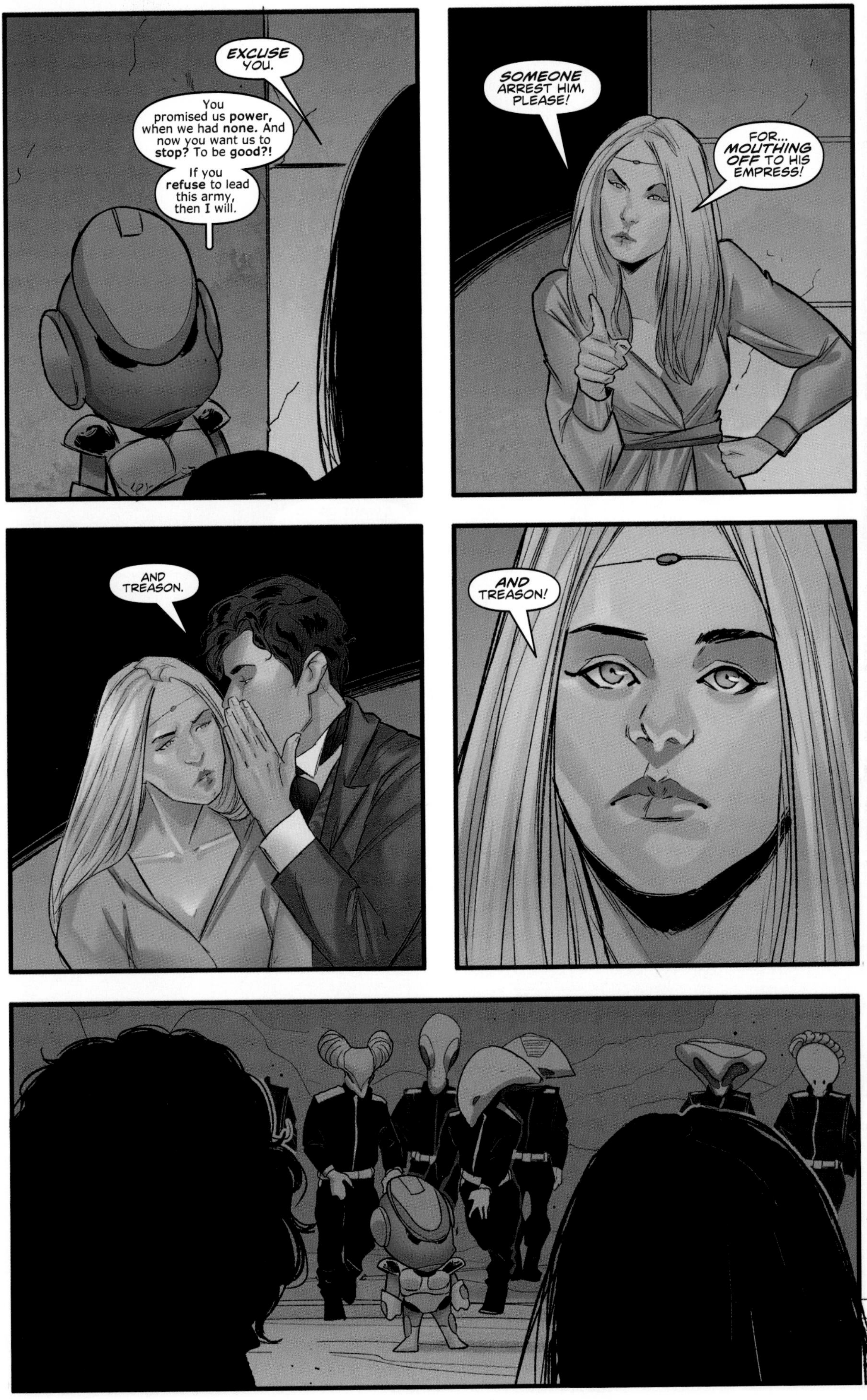
EXCUSE YOU.
You promised us power, when we had none. And now you want us to stop? To be good?!
If you refuse to lead this army, then I will.
SOMEONE ARREST HIM, PLEASE!
FOR... MOUTHING OFF TO HIS EMPRESS!
AND TREASON.
AND TREASON!

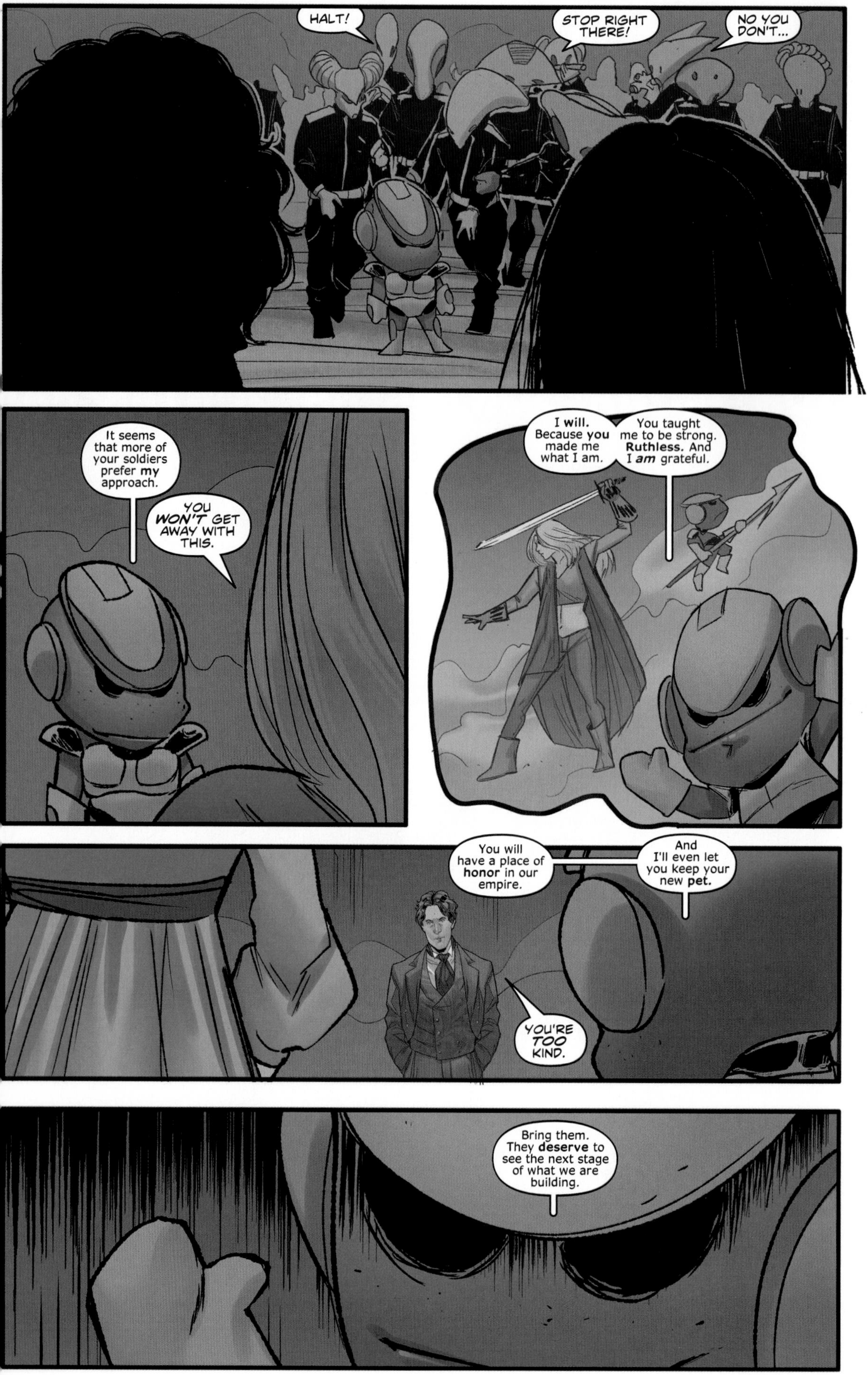
HALT!
STOP RIGHT THERE!
NO YOU DON'T...
It seems that more of your soldiers prefer **my** approach.
YOU ***WON'T*** GET AWAY WITH THIS.
I will. Because **you** made me what I am.
You taught me to be strong. **Ruthless.** And I ***am*** grateful.
You will have a place of **honor** in our empire.
And I'll even let you keep your new **pet.**
YOU'RE *TOO* KIND.
Bring them. They **deserve** to see the next stage of what we are building.

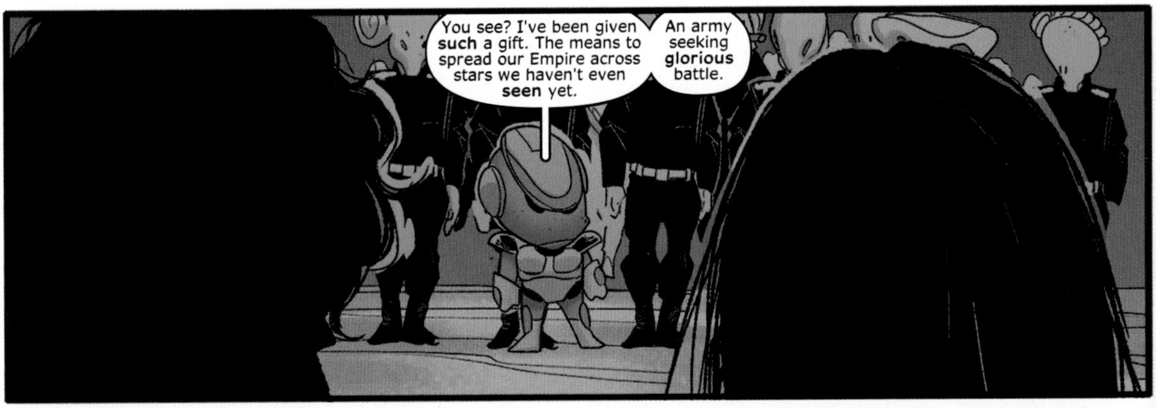
You see? I've been given **such** a gift. The means to spread our Empire across stars we haven't even **seen** yet.
An army seeking **glorious** battle.

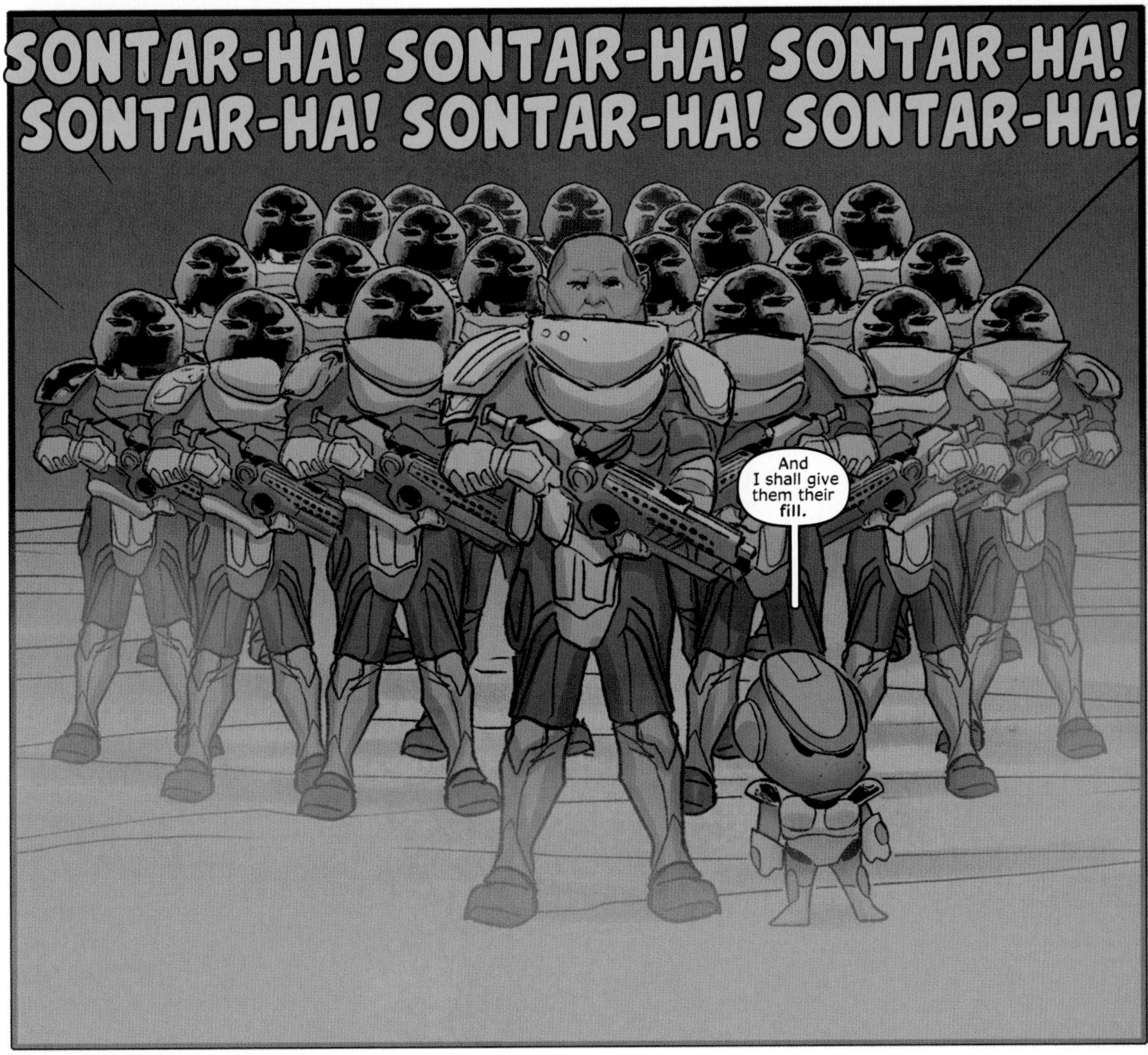
SONTAR-HA! SONTAR-HA! SONTAR-HA! SONTAR-HA! SONTAR-HA! SONTAR-HA!
And I shall give them their **fill.**

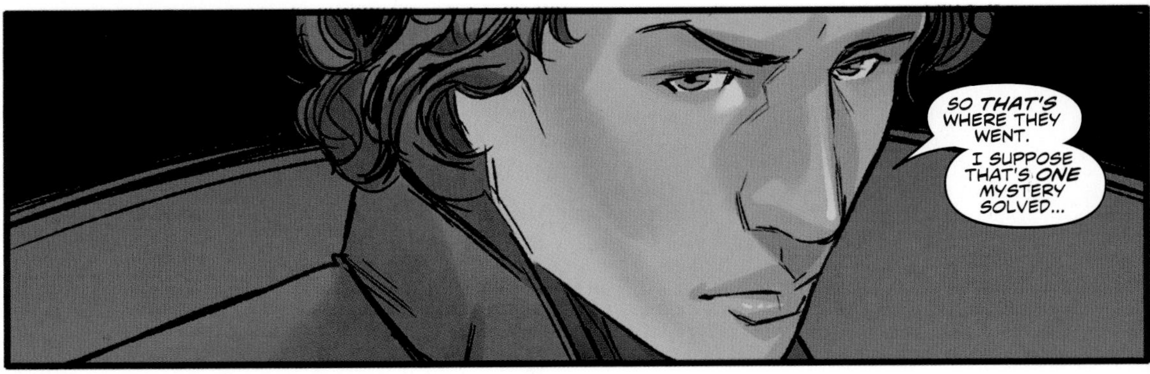
SO *THAT'S* WHERE THEY WENT.
I SUPPOSE THAT'S *ONE* MYSTERY SOLVED...

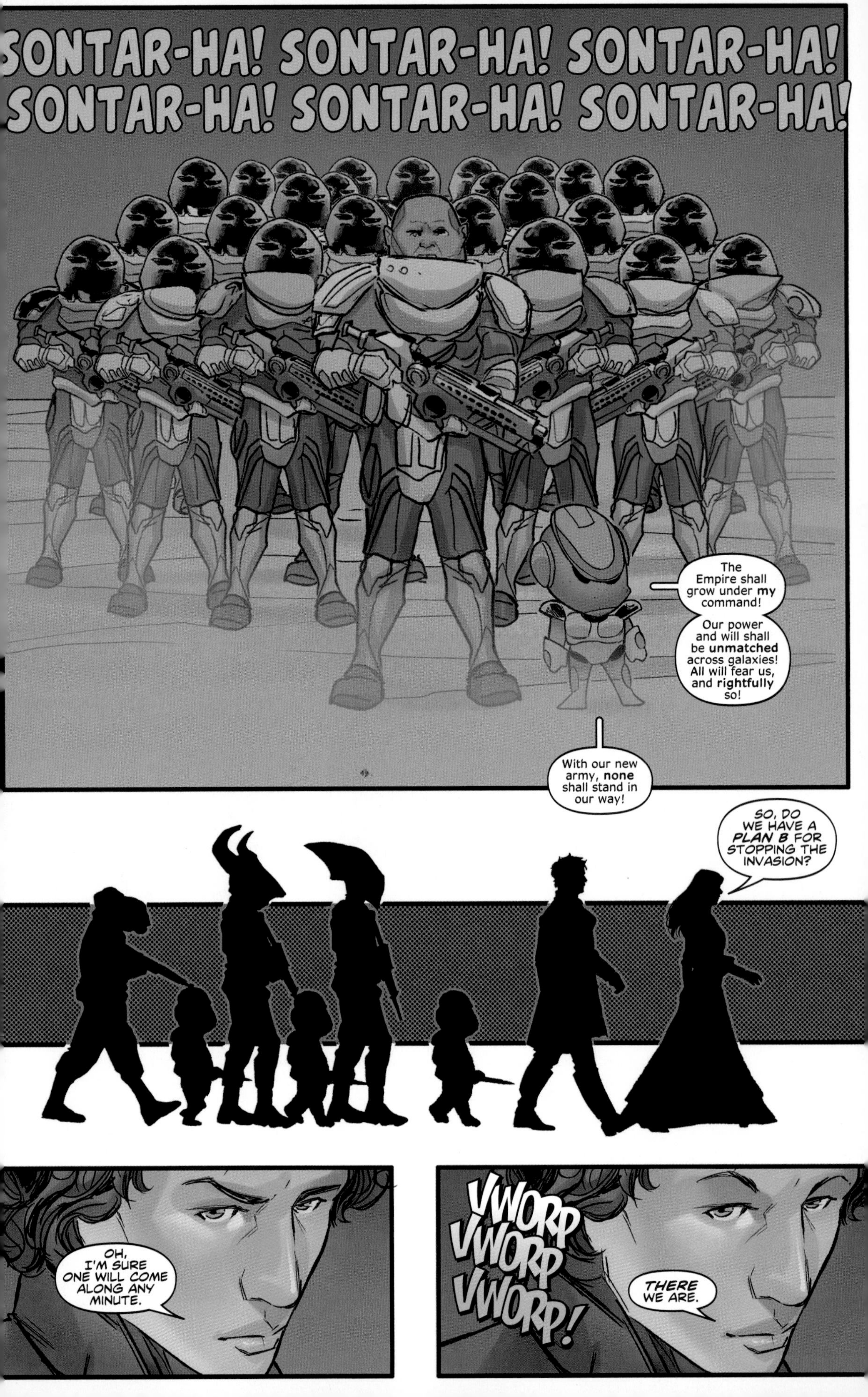
SONTAR-HA! SONTAR-HA! SONTAR-HA! SONTAR-HA! SONTAR-HA! SONTAR-HA!
The Empire shall grow under **my** command!
Our power and will shall be **unmatched** across galaxies! All will fear us, and **rightfully** so!
With our new army, **none** shall stand in our way!
SO, DO WE HAVE A ***PLAN B*** FOR STOPPING THE INVASION?
OH, I'M SURE ONE WILL COME ALONG ANY MINUTE.
VWORP VWORP VWORP!
THERE WE ARE.

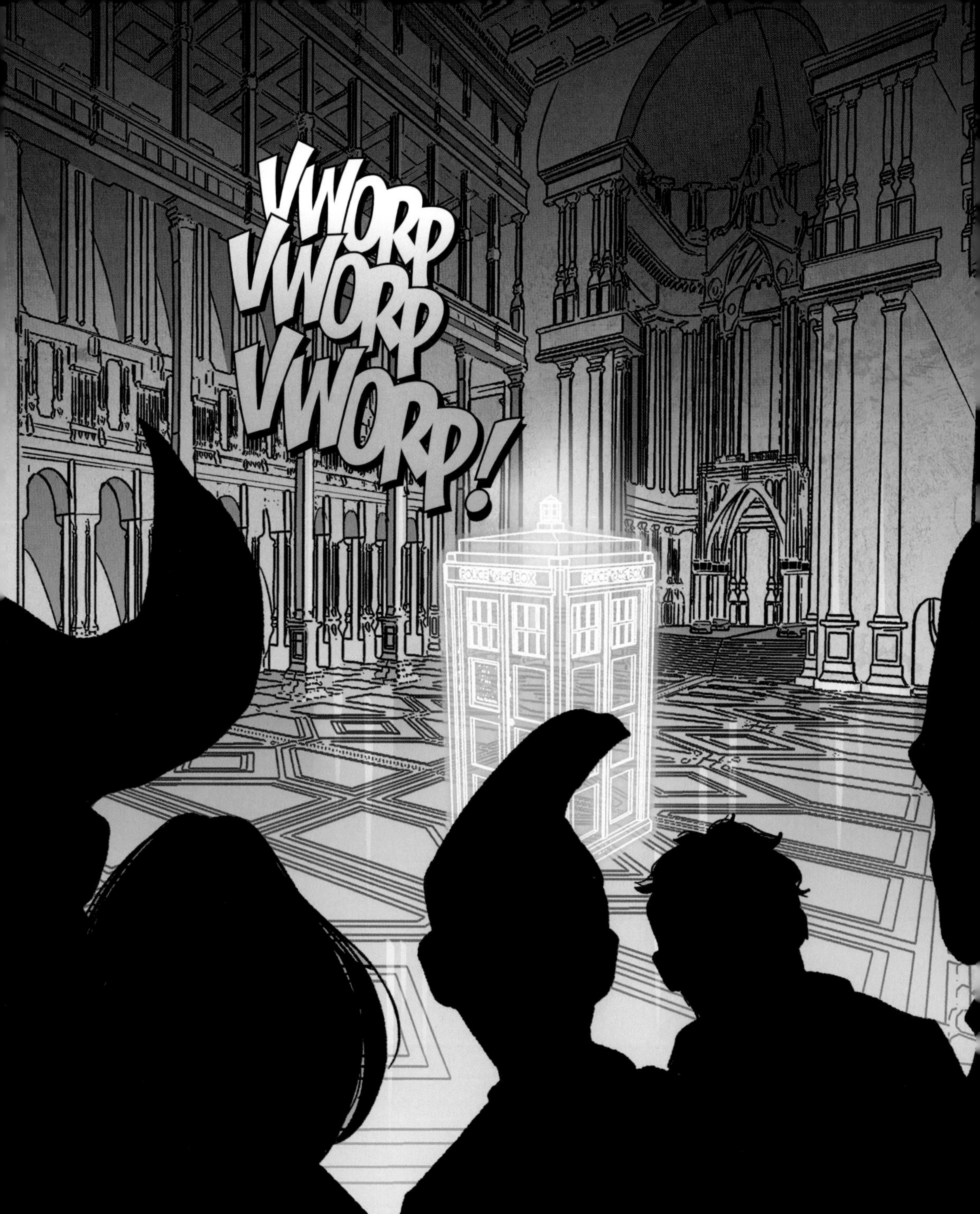
VWORP
VWORP
VWORP!
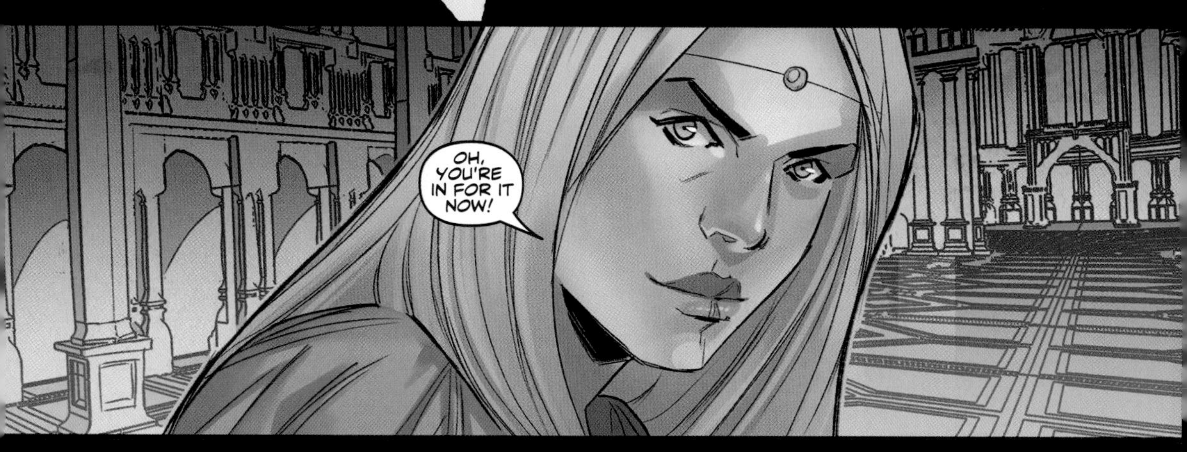
OH, YOU'RE IN FOR IT NOW!

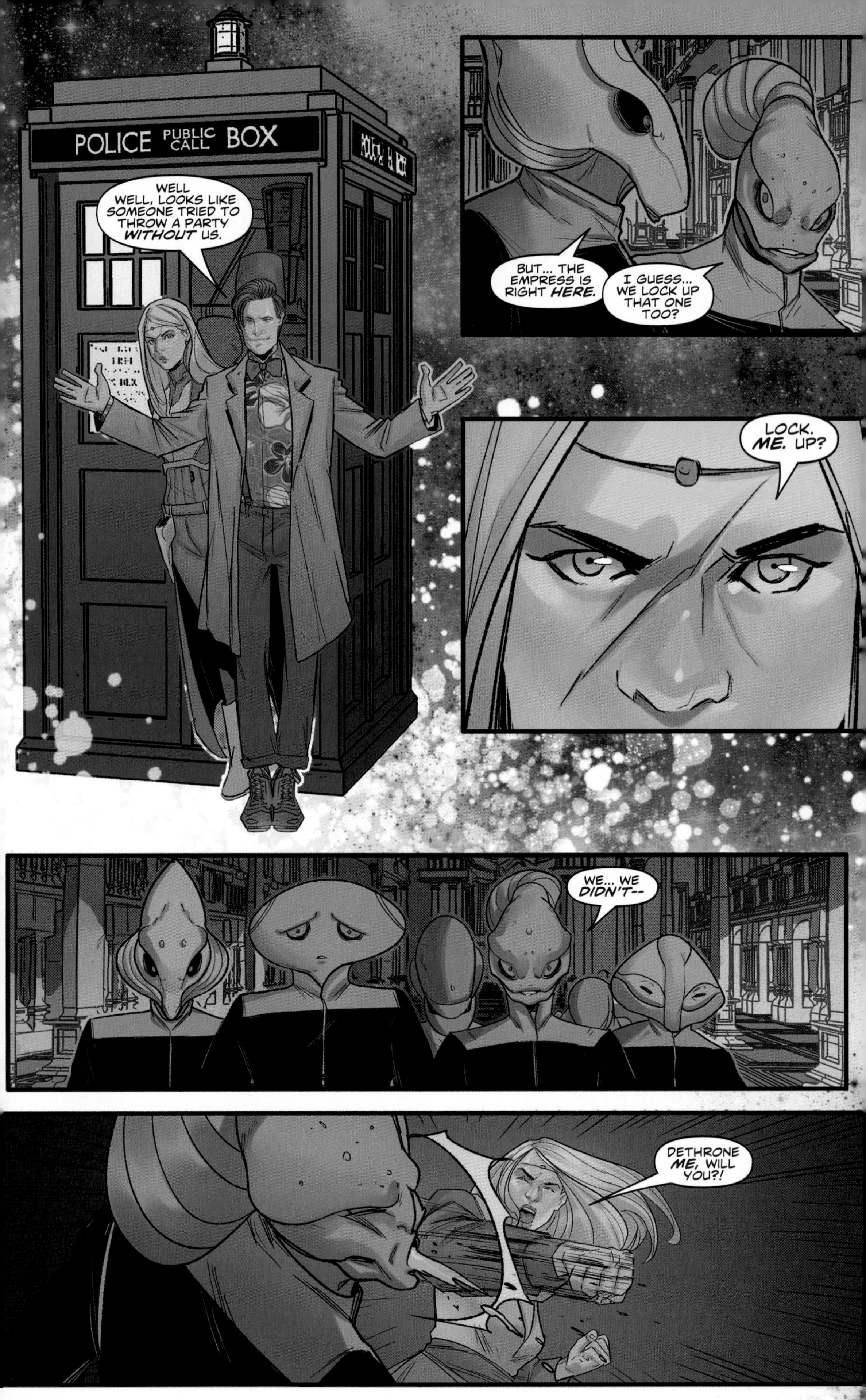
POLICE PUBLIC CALL BOX
WELL WELL, LOOKS LIKE SOMEONE TRIED TO THROW A PARTY *WITHOUT* US.
BUT... THE EMPRESS IS RIGHT *HERE*.
I GUESS... WE LOCK UP THAT ONE TOO?
LOCK. *ME.* UP?
WE... WE *DIDN'T*--
DETHRONE *ME,* WILL YOU?!

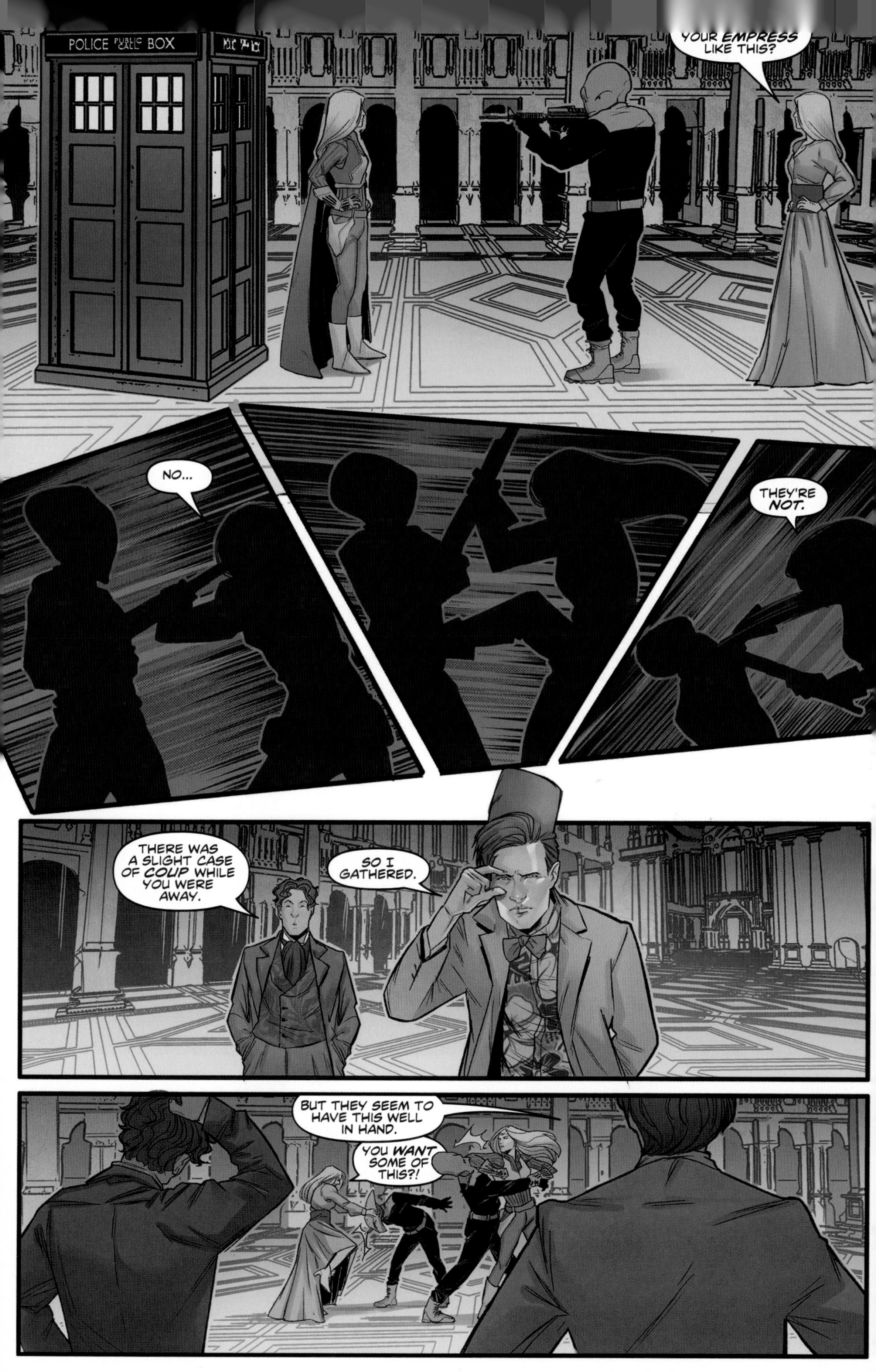
POLICE PUBLIC CALL BOX
YOUR EMPRESS LIKE THIS?
NO...
THEY'RE NOT.
THERE WAS A SLIGHT CASE OF COUP WHILE YOU WERE AWAY.
SO I GATHERED.
BUT THEY SEEM TO HAVE THIS WELL IN HAND.
YOU WANT SOME OF THIS?!

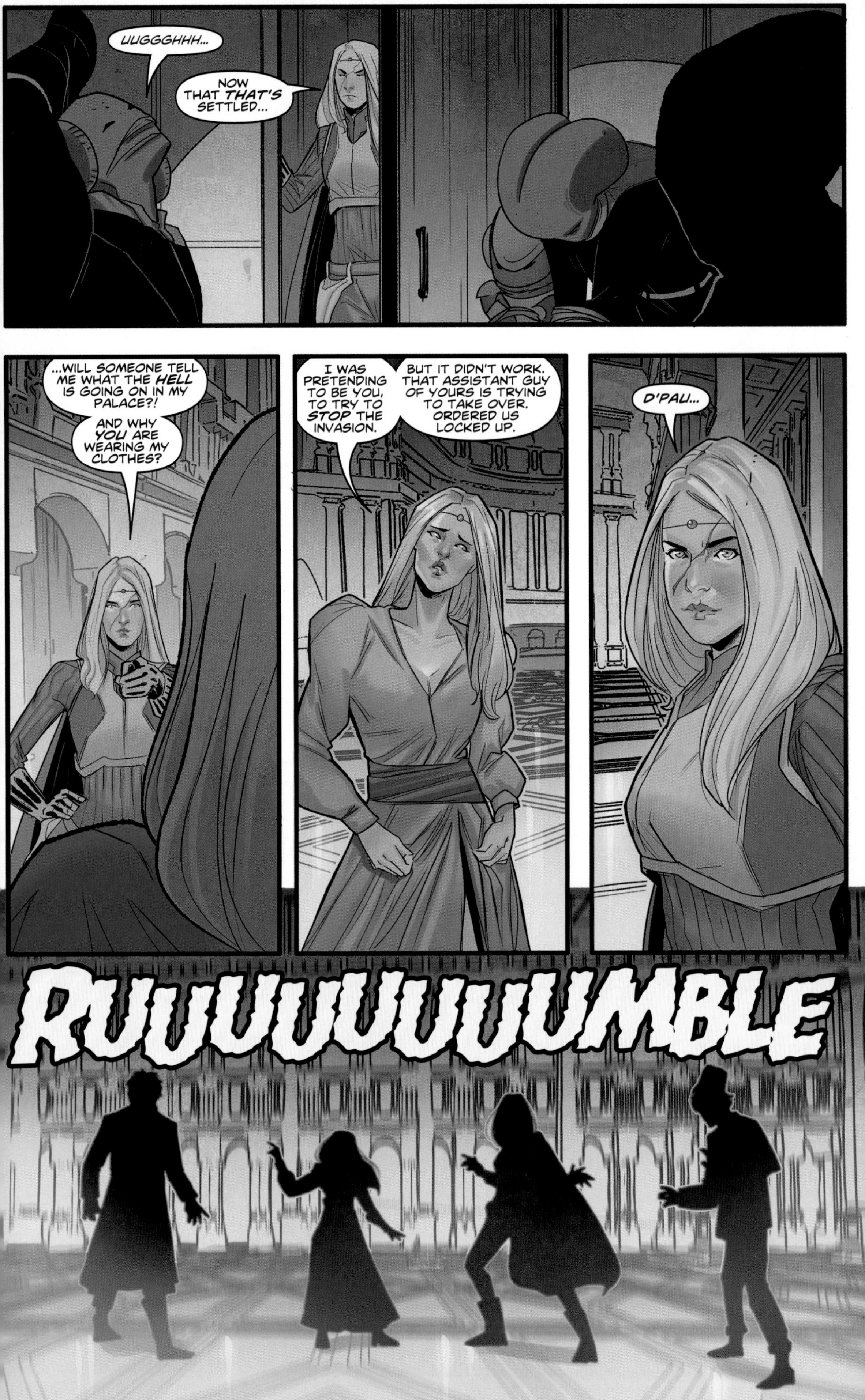
UUGGGHHH...
NOW THAT THAT'S SETTLED...
...WILL SOMEONE TELL ME WHAT THE HELL IS GOING ON IN MY PALACE?!
AND WHY YOU ARE WEARING MY CLOTHES?
I WAS PRETENDING TO BE YOU, TO TRY TO STOP THE INVASION.
BUT IT DIDN'T WORK. THAT ASSISTANT GUY OF YOURS IS TRYING TO TAKE OVER. ORDERED US LOCKED UP.
D'PAU...
RUUUUUUUUMBLE

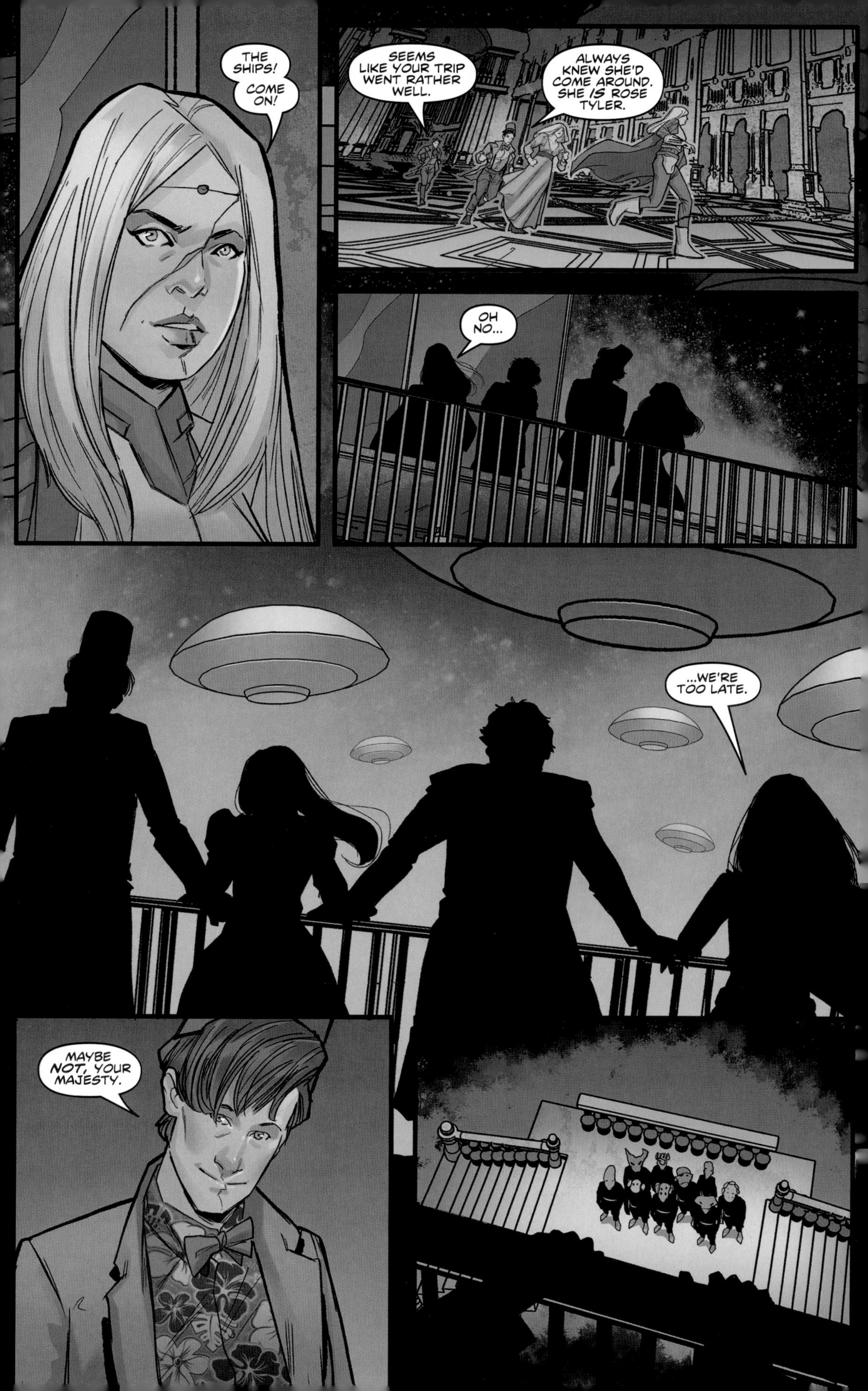
THE SHIPS! COME ON!
SEEMS LIKE YOUR TRIP WENT RATHER WELL.
ALWAYS KNEW SHE'D COME AROUND. SHE *IS* ROSE TYLER.
OH NO...
...WE'RE TOO LATE.
MAYBE *NOT*, YOUR MAJESTY.

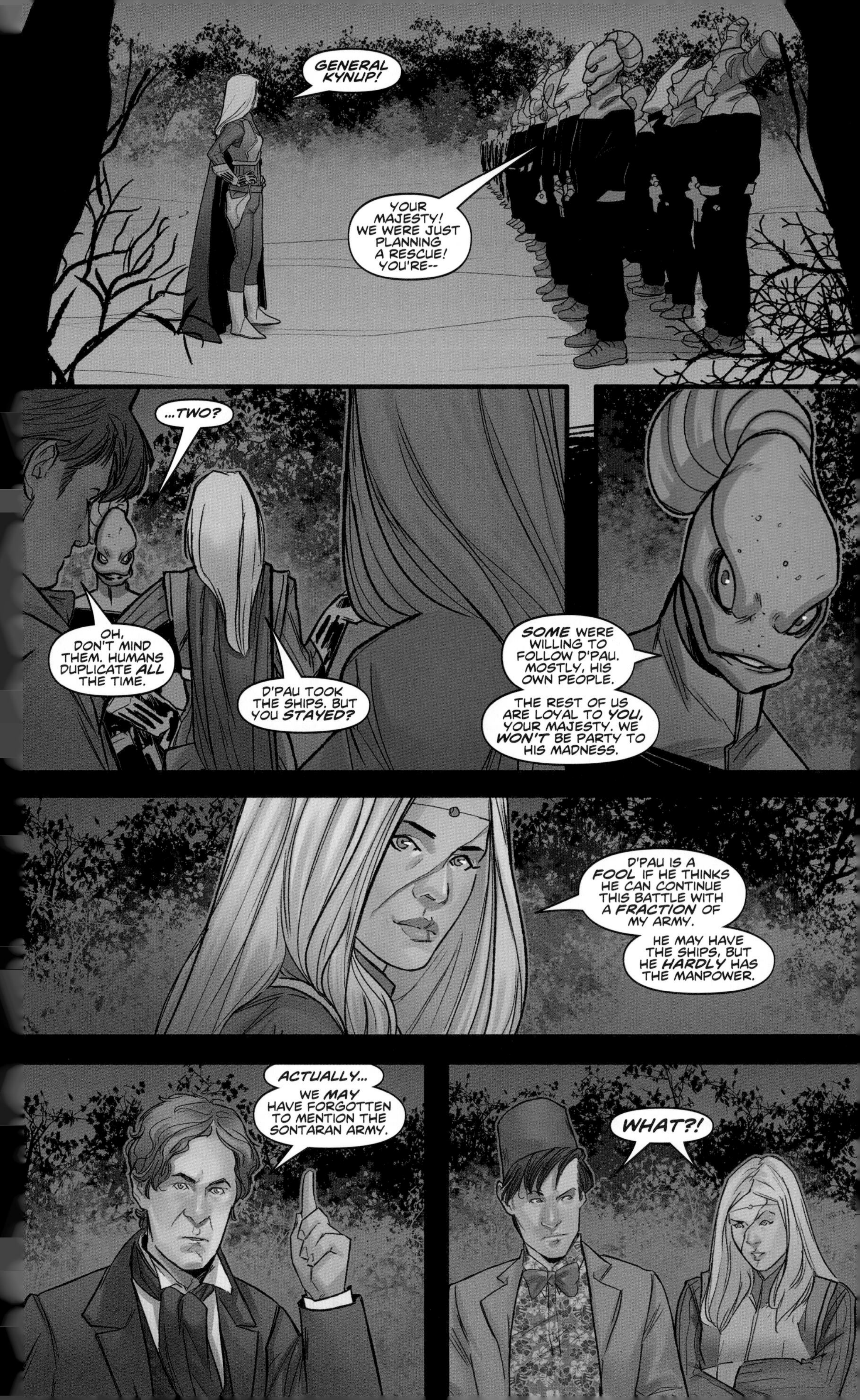
GENERAL KYNUP!
YOUR MAJESTY! WE WERE JUST PLANNING A RESCUE! YOU'RE--
...TWO?
OH, DON'T MIND THEM. HUMANS DUPLICATE ALL THE TIME.
D'PAU TOOK THE SHIPS. BUT YOU STAYED?
SOME WERE WILLING TO FOLLOW D'PAU. MOSTLY, HIS OWN PEOPLE.
THE REST OF US ARE LOYAL TO YOU, YOUR MAJESTY. WE WON'T BE PARTY TO HIS MADNESS.
D'PAU IS A FOOL IF HE THINKS HE CAN CONTINUE THIS BATTLE WITH A FRACTION OF MY ARMY.
HE MAY HAVE THE SHIPS, BUT HE HARDLY HAS THE MANPOWER.
ACTUALLY...
WE MAY HAVE FORGOTTEN TO MENTION THE SONTARAN ARMY.
WHAT?!

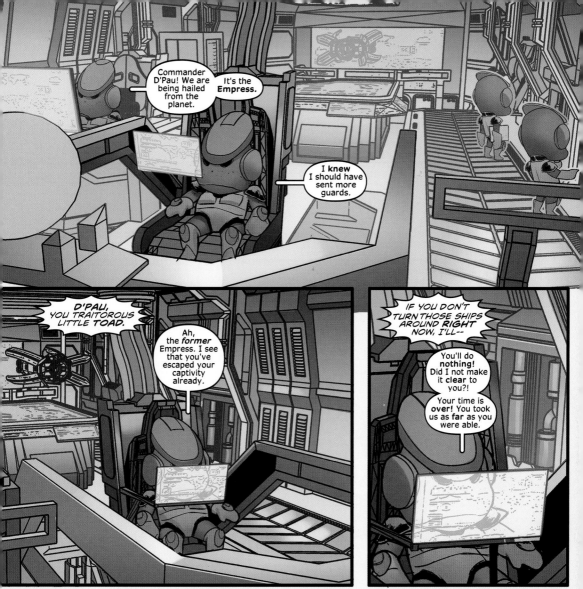

Commander D'Pau! We are being hailed from the planet.

It's the **Empress**.

I **knew** I should have sent more guards.

D'PAU, YOU TRAITOROUS LITTLE **TOAD**.

Ah, the *former* Empress. I see that you've escaped your captivity already.

IF YOU DON'T TURN THOSE SHIPS AROUND **RIGHT** NOW, I'LL--

You'll do **nothing**! Did I not make it **clear** to you?!

Your time is **over**! You took us as far as you were able.

SONTAR-HA! SONTAR-HA! SONTAR-HA!

"Me and my new army...

"...**We'll** take things from here."

HE... HE IS...

...HE IS WHAT I **MADE** HIM.

ISN'T HE, DOCTOR?

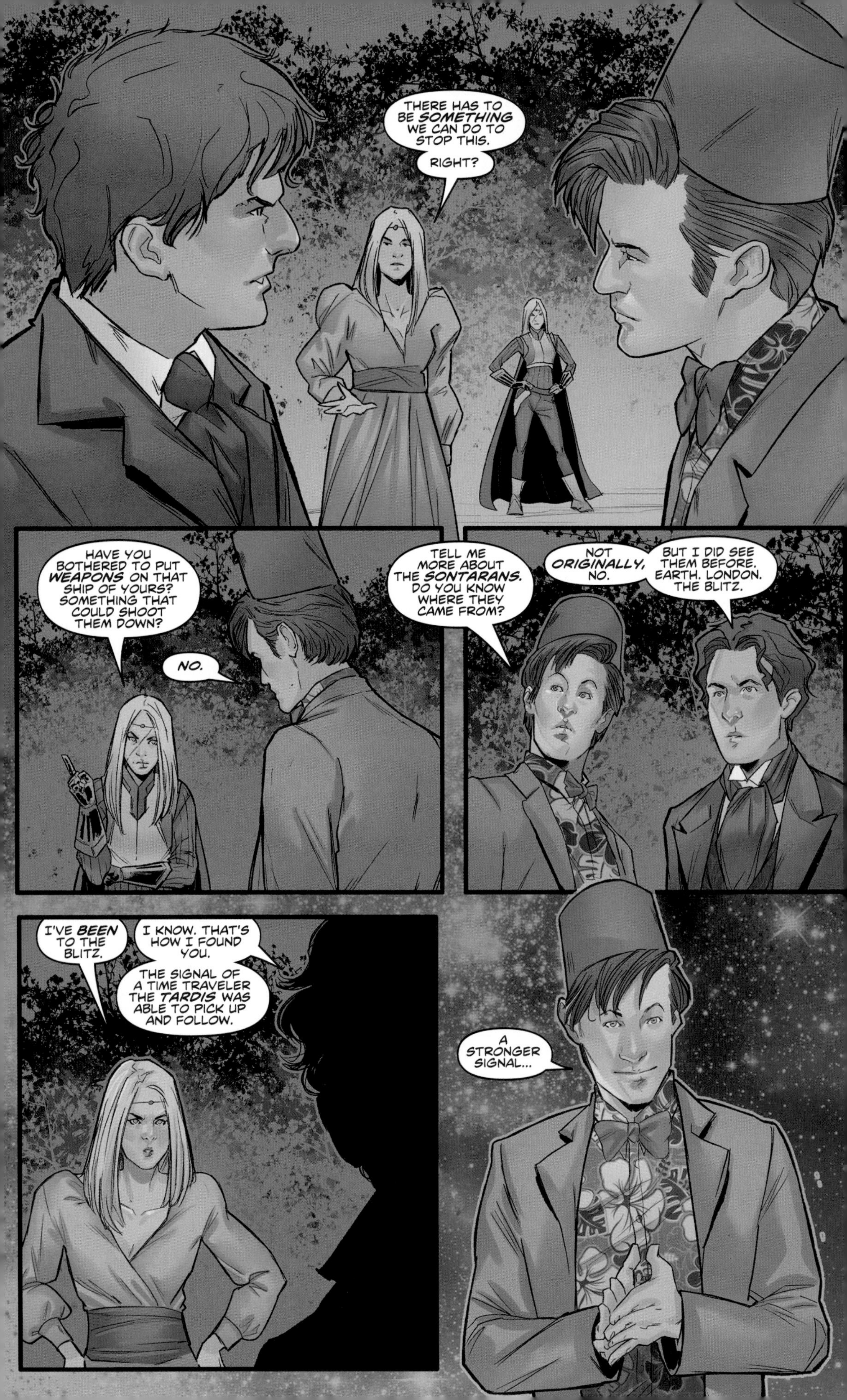
THERE HAS TO BE *SOMETHING* WE CAN DO TO STOP THIS.
RIGHT?
HAVE YOU BOTHERED TO PUT *WEAPONS* ON THAT SHIP OF YOURS? SOMETHING THAT COULD SHOOT THEM DOWN?
NO.
TELL ME MORE ABOUT THE *SONTARANS.* DO YOU KNOW WHERE THEY CAME FROM?
NOT *ORIGINALLY,* NO.
BUT I DID SEE THEM BEFORE. EARTH. LONDON. THE BLITZ.
I'VE *BEEN* TO THE BLITZ.
I KNOW. THAT'S HOW I FOUND YOU.
THE SIGNAL OF A TIME TRAVELER THE *TARDIS* WAS ABLE TO PICK UP AND FOLLOW.
A STRONGER SIGNAL...

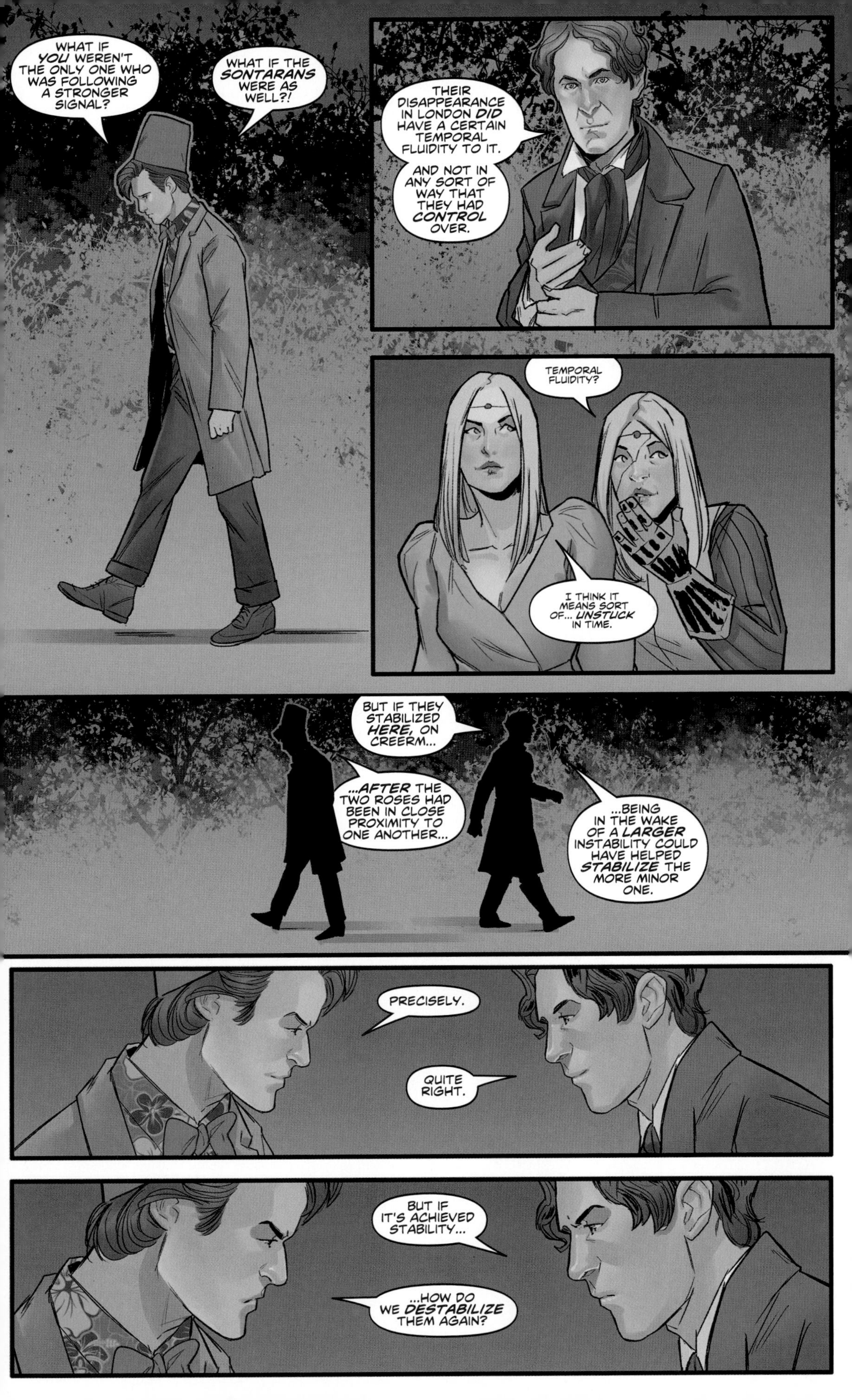
WHAT IF YOU WEREN'T THE ONLY ONE WHO WAS FOLLOWING A STRONGER SIGNAL?
WHAT IF THE SONTARANS WERE AS WELL?!
THEIR DISAPPEARANCE IN LONDON DID HAVE A CERTAIN TEMPORAL FLUIDITY TO IT.
AND NOT IN ANY SORT OF WAY THAT THEY HAD CONTROL OVER.
TEMPORAL FLUIDITY?
I THINK IT MEANS SORT OF... UNSTUCK IN TIME.
BUT IF THEY STABILIZED HERE, ON CREERM...
...AFTER THE TWO ROSES HAD BEEN IN CLOSE PROXIMITY TO ONE ANOTHER...
...BEING IN THE WAKE OF A LARGER INSTABILITY COULD HAVE HELPED STABILIZE THE MORE MINOR ONE.
PRECISELY.
QUITE RIGHT.
BUT IF IT'S ACHIEVED STABILITY...
...HOW DO WE DESTABILIZE THEM AGAIN?

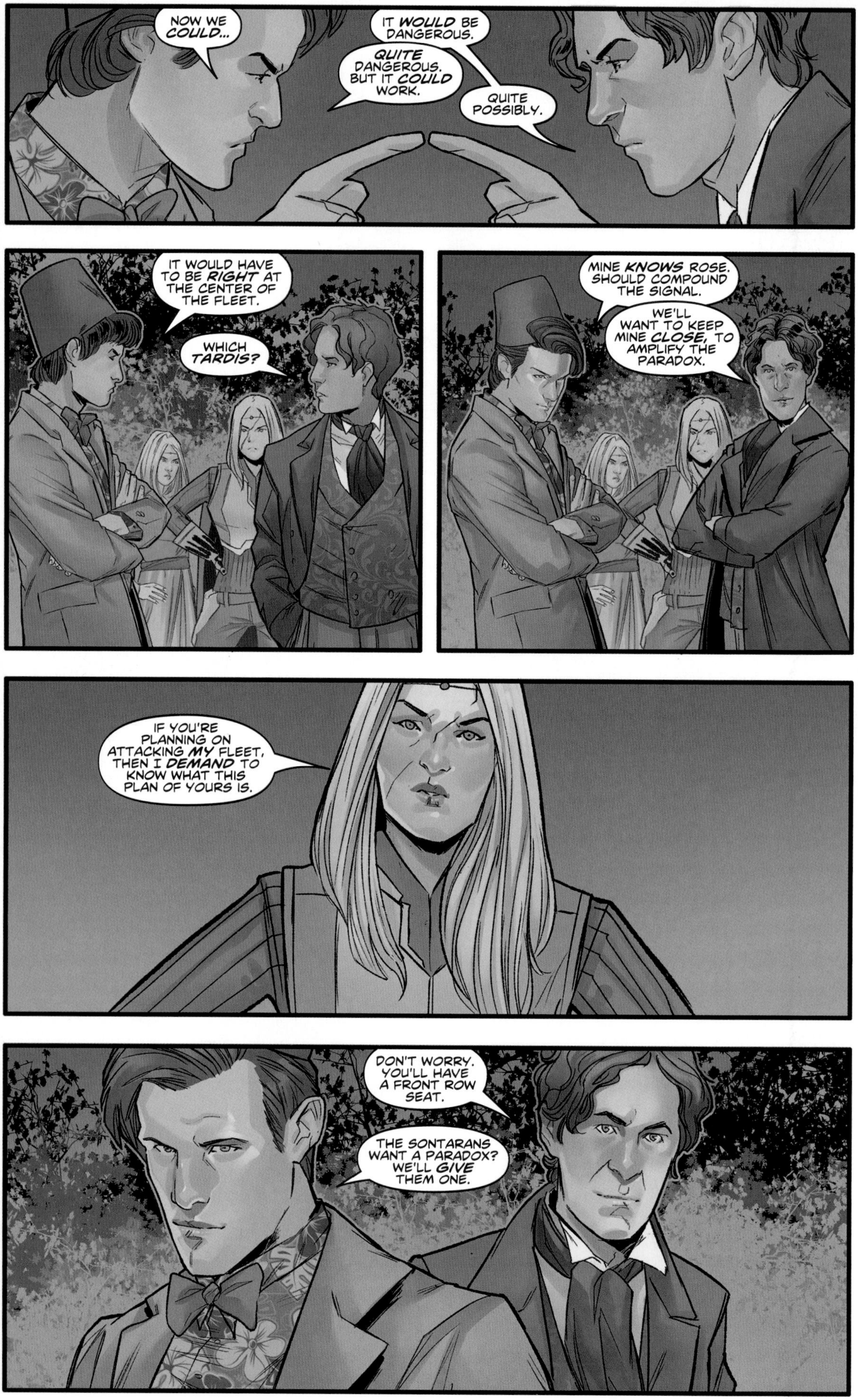
NOW WE COULD...
IT WOULD BE DANGEROUS.
QUITE DANGEROUS. BUT IT COULD WORK.
QUITE POSSIBLY.
IT WOULD HAVE TO BE RIGHT AT THE CENTER OF THE FLEET.
WHICH TARDIS?
MINE KNOWS ROSE. SHOULD COMPOUND THE SIGNAL.
WE'LL WANT TO KEEP MINE CLOSE, TO AMPLIFY THE PARADOX.
IF YOU'RE PLANNING ON ATTACKING MY FLEET, THEN I DEMAND TO KNOW WHAT THIS PLAN OF YOURS IS.
DON'T WORRY. YOU'LL HAVE A FRONT ROW SEAT.
THE SONTARANS WANT A PARADOX? WE'LL GIVE THEM ONE.

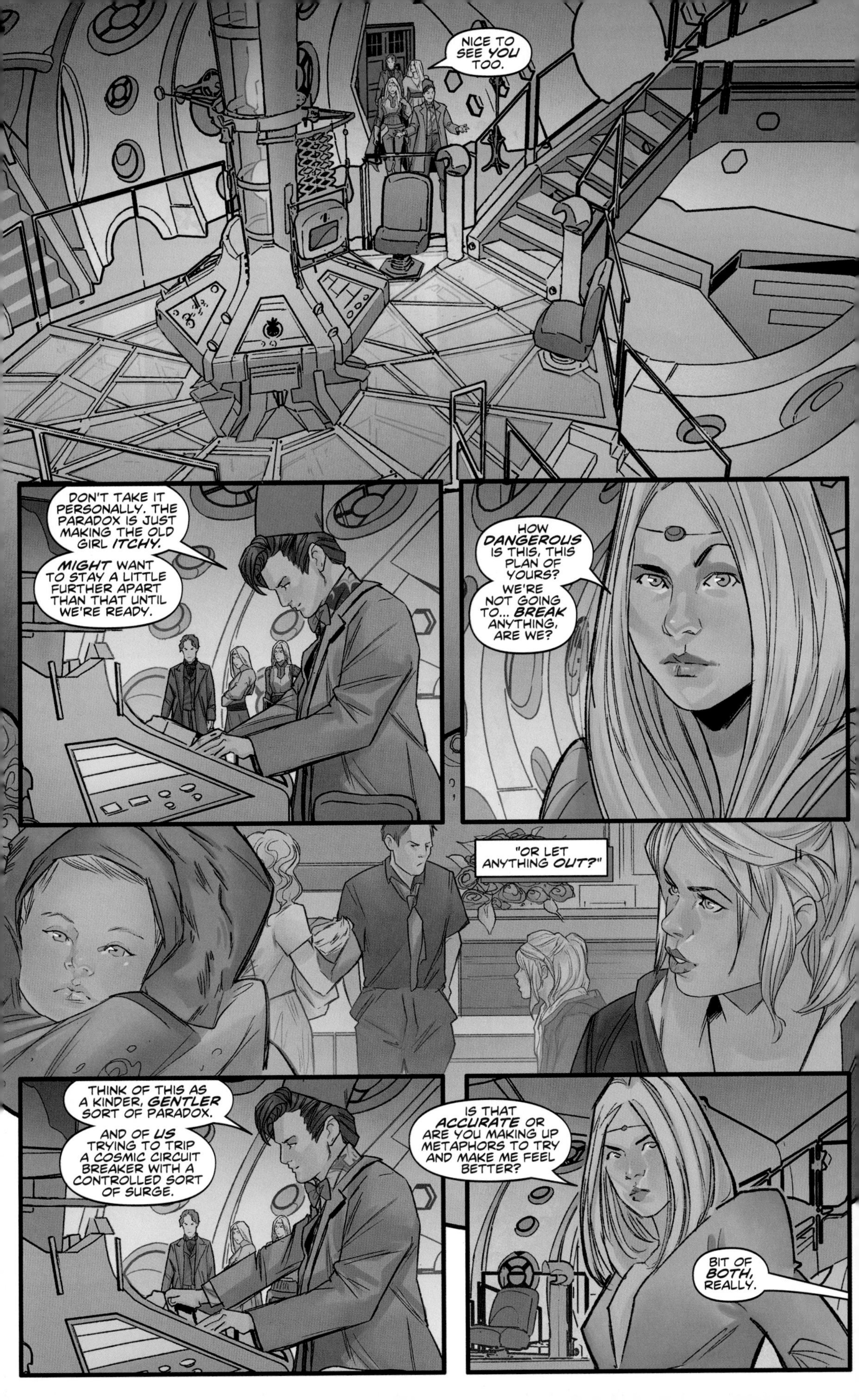
NICE TO SEE *YOU* TOO.
DON'T TAKE IT PERSONALLY. THE PARADOX IS JUST MAKING THE OLD GIRL *ITCHY.*
MIGHT WANT TO STAY A LITTLE FURTHER APART THAN THAT UNTIL WE'RE READY.
HOW *DANGEROUS* IS THIS, THIS PLAN OF YOURS? WE'RE NOT GOING TO... *BREAK* ANYTHING, ARE WE?
"OR LET ANYTHING *OUT?*"
THINK OF THIS AS A KINDER, *GENTLER* SORT OF PARADOX.
AND OF *US* TRYING TO TRIP A COSMIC CIRCUIT BREAKER WITH A CONTROLLED SORT OF SURGE.
IS THAT *ACCURATE* OR ARE YOU MAKING UP METAPHORS TO TRY AND MAKE ME FEEL BETTER?
BIT OF *BOTH,* REALLY.

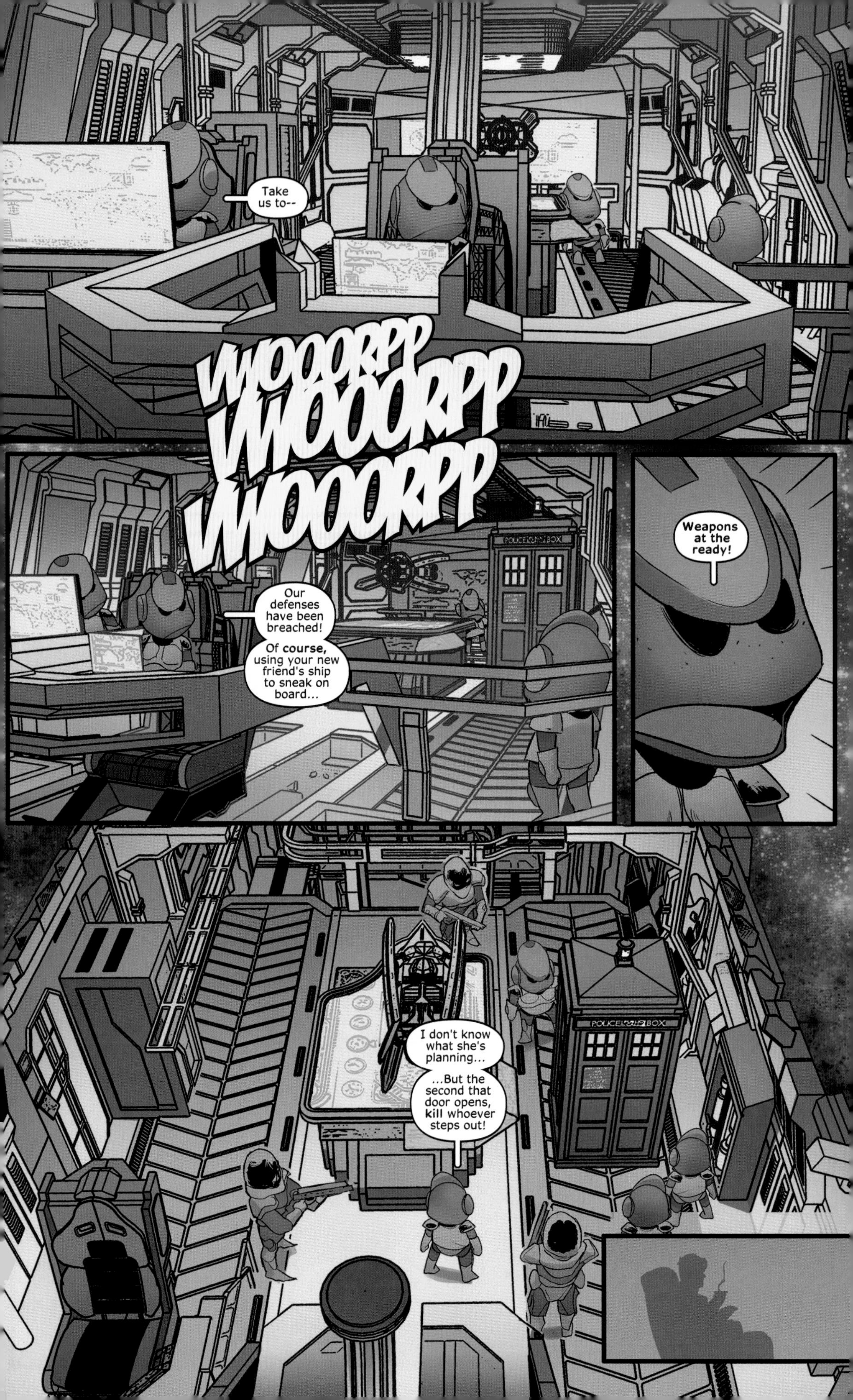
Take us to--
VWOOORPP VWOOORPP VWOOORPP
Our defenses have been breached!
Of **course,** using your new friend's ship to sneak on board...
POLICE PUBLIC CALL BOX
Weapons at the ready!
I don't know what she's planning...
...But the second that door opens, **kill** whoever steps out!
POLICE PUBLIC CALL BOX

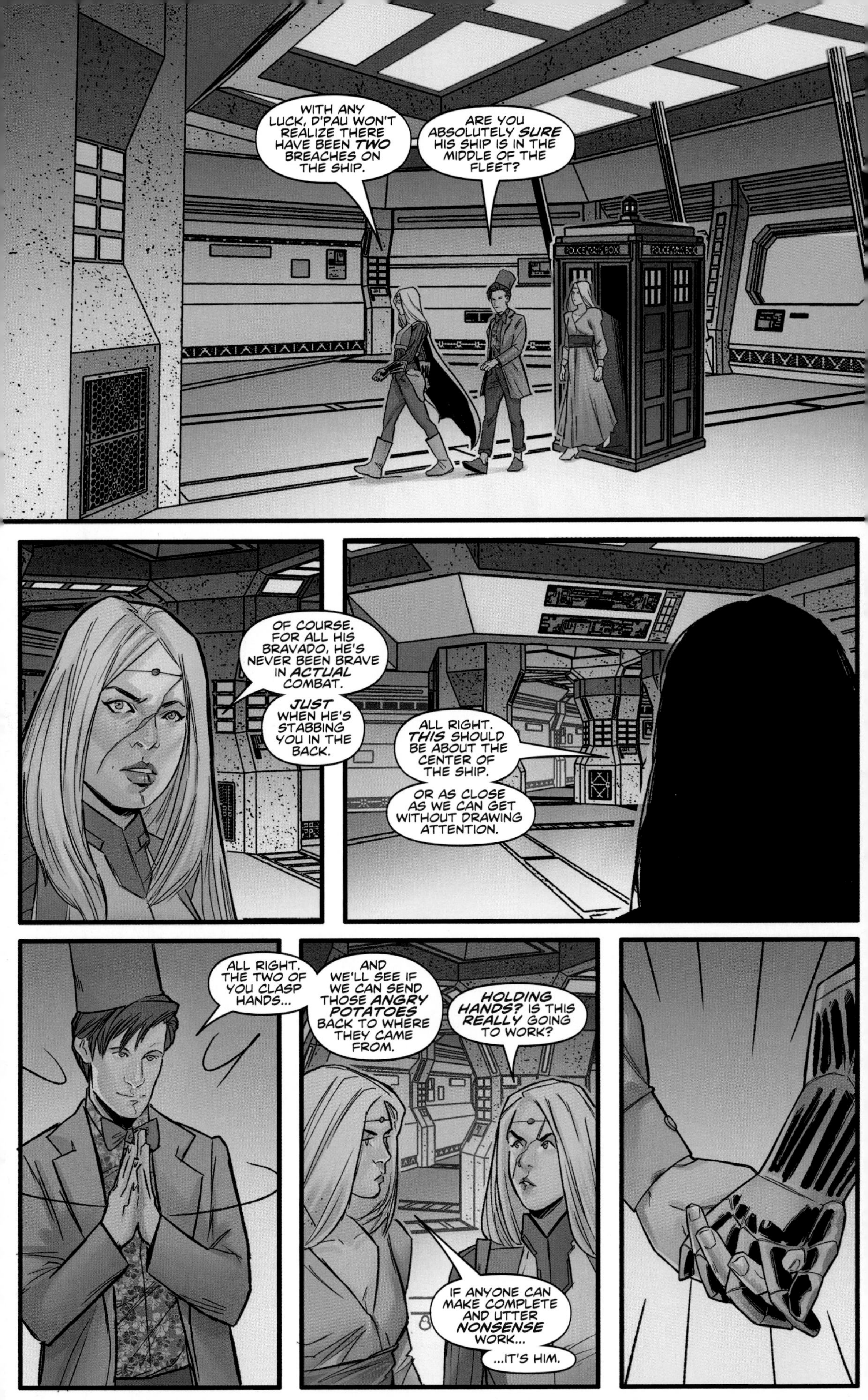
WITH ANY LUCK, D'PAU WON'T REALIZE THERE HAVE BEEN *TWO* BREACHES ON THE SHIP.
ARE YOU ABSOLUTELY *SURE* HIS SHIP IS IN THE MIDDLE OF THE FLEET?
OF COURSE. FOR ALL HIS BRAVADO, HE'S NEVER BEEN BRAVE IN *ACTUAL* COMBAT.
JUST WHEN HE'S STABBING YOU IN THE BACK.
ALL RIGHT. *THIS* SHOULD BE ABOUT THE CENTER OF THE SHIP.
OR AS CLOSE AS WE CAN GET WITHOUT DRAWING ATTENTION.
ALL RIGHT. THE TWO OF YOU CLASP HANDS...
AND WE'LL SEE IF WE CAN SEND THOSE *ANGRY POTATOES* BACK TO WHERE THEY CAME FROM.
HOLDING HANDS? IS THIS *REALLY* GOING TO WORK?
IF ANYONE CAN MAKE COMPLETE AND UTTER *NONSENSE* WORK...
...IT'S HIM.

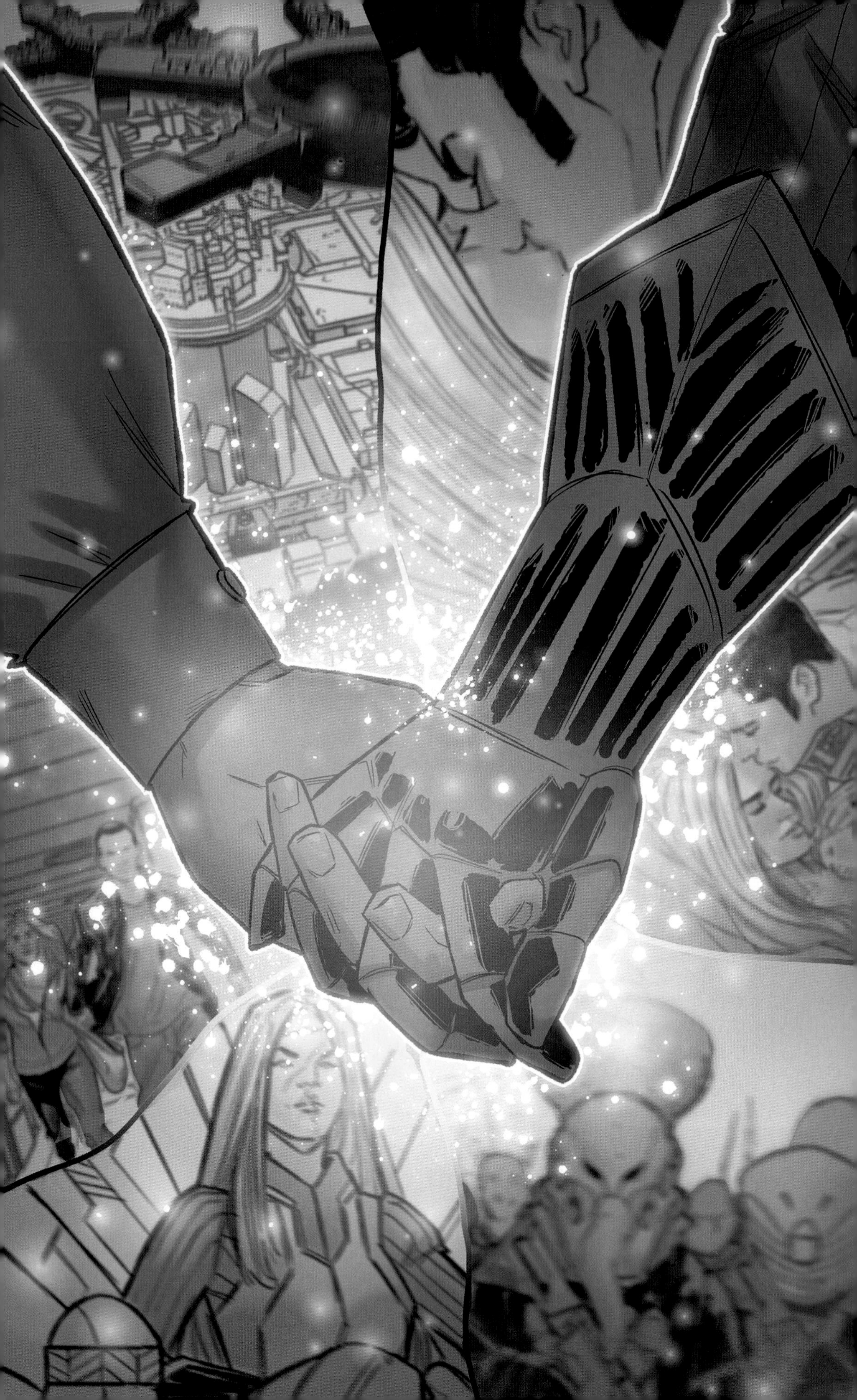

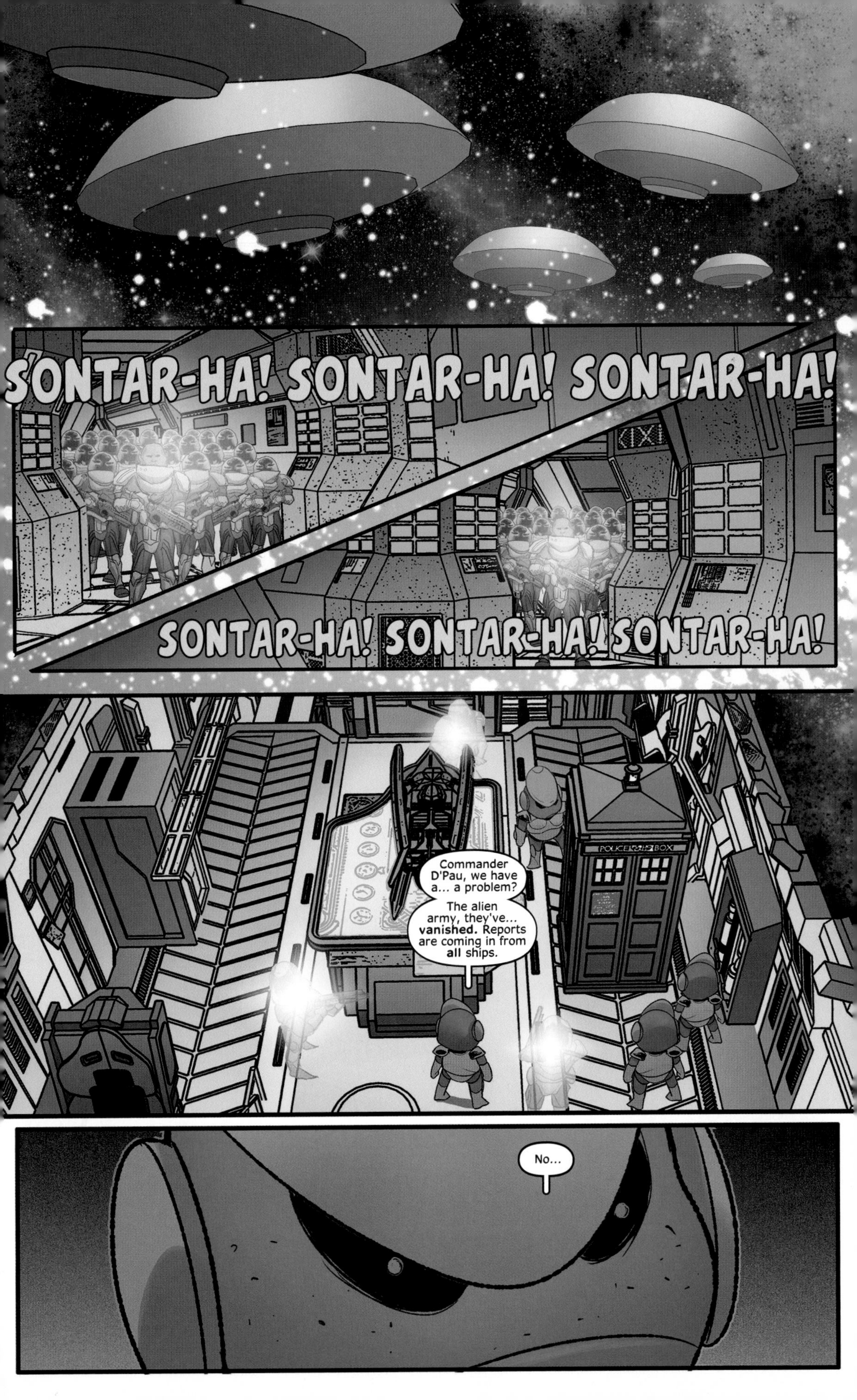
SONTAR-HA! SONTAR-HA! SONTAR-HA!
SONTAR-HA! SONTAR-HA! SONTAR-HA!
POLICE BOX
Commander D'Pau, we have a... a problem?
The alien army, they've... **vanished.** Reports are coming in from **all** ships.
No...

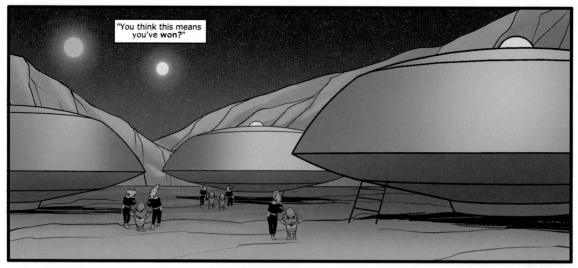

"You think this means you've won?"

I HAVE MY SHIPS BACK AND *YOU'VE* LOST YOUR ARMY.

SO YES, I *DO*.

Perhaps the battle. But the war has only begun.

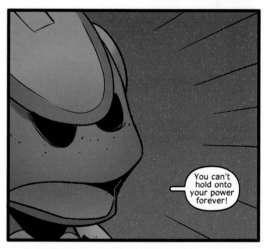

You can't hold onto your power forever!

DO YOU THINK HE'S RIGHT?

IT'S HARD TO SAY, YOUR MAJESTY.

THOSE WHO REMAINED LOYAL TO YOU THROUGH THIS MAY NOT ALWAYS BE SO.

IS THE POWER *REALLY* THE POINT HERE?

OR IS IT ABOUT CONTINUING TO BUILD SOMETHING *BETTER*?

AS ANNOYING AS IT IS, YOU'RE RIGHT. *AGAIN.*

I GENERALLY AM.

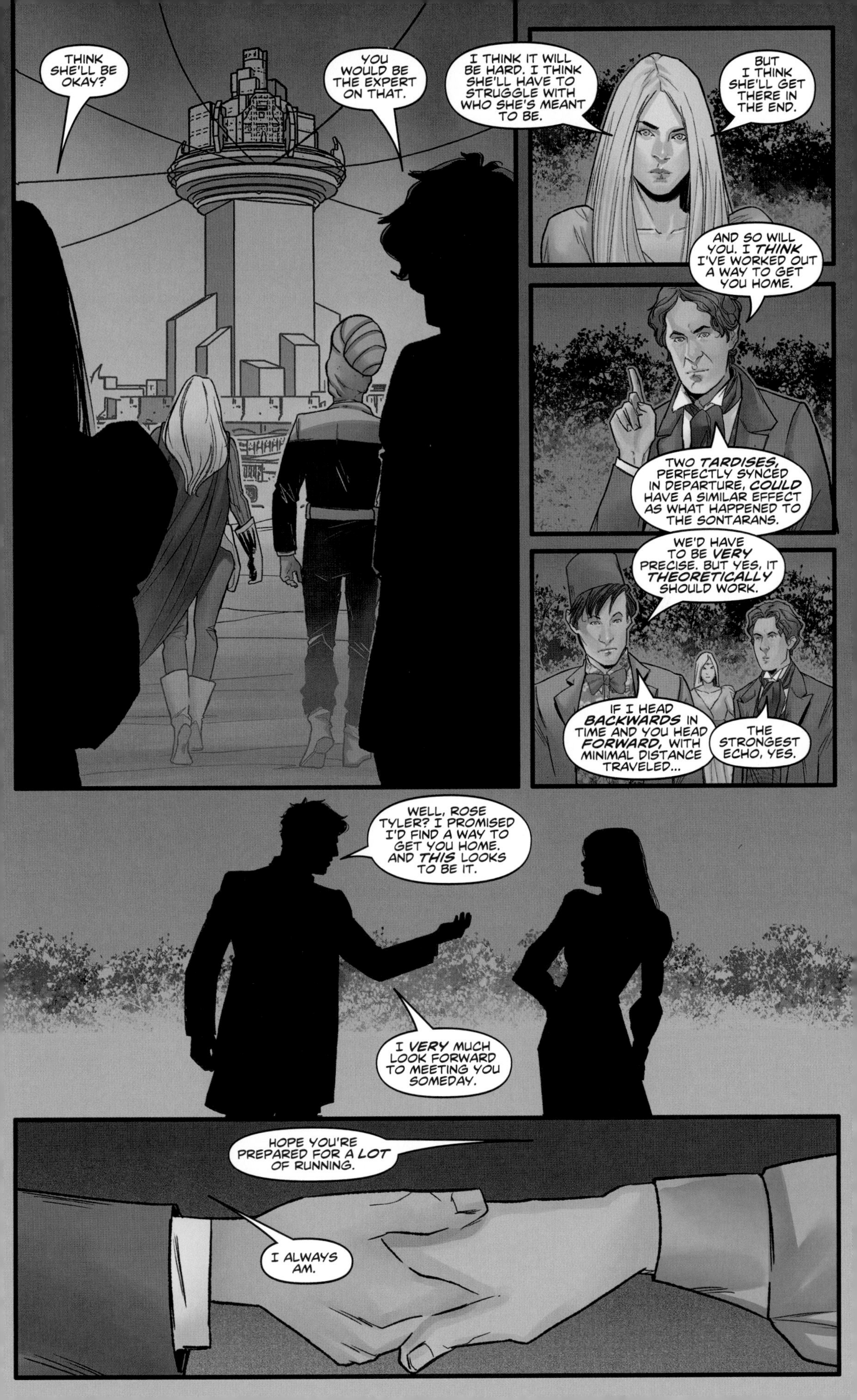
THINK SHE'LL BE OKAY?
YOU WOULD BE THE EXPERT ON THAT.
I THINK IT WILL BE HARD. I THINK SHE'LL HAVE TO STRUGGLE WITH WHO SHE'S MEANT TO BE.
BUT I THINK SHE'LL GET THERE IN THE END.
AND SO WILL YOU. I THINK I'VE WORKED OUT A WAY TO GET YOU HOME.
TWO TARDISES, PERFECTLY SYNCED IN DEPARTURE, COULD HAVE A SIMILAR EFFECT AS WHAT HAPPENED TO THE SONTARANS.
WE'D HAVE TO BE VERY PRECISE. BUT YES, IT THEORETICALLY SHOULD WORK.
IF I HEAD BACKWARDS IN TIME AND YOU HEAD FORWARD, WITH MINIMAL DISTANCE TRAVELED...
THE STRONGEST ECHO, YES.
WELL, ROSE TYLER? I PROMISED I'D FIND A WAY TO GET YOU HOME. AND THIS LOOKS TO BE IT.
I VERY MUCH LOOK FORWARD TO MEETING YOU SOMEDAY.
HOPE YOU'RE PREPARED FOR A LOT OF RUNNING.
I ALWAYS AM.

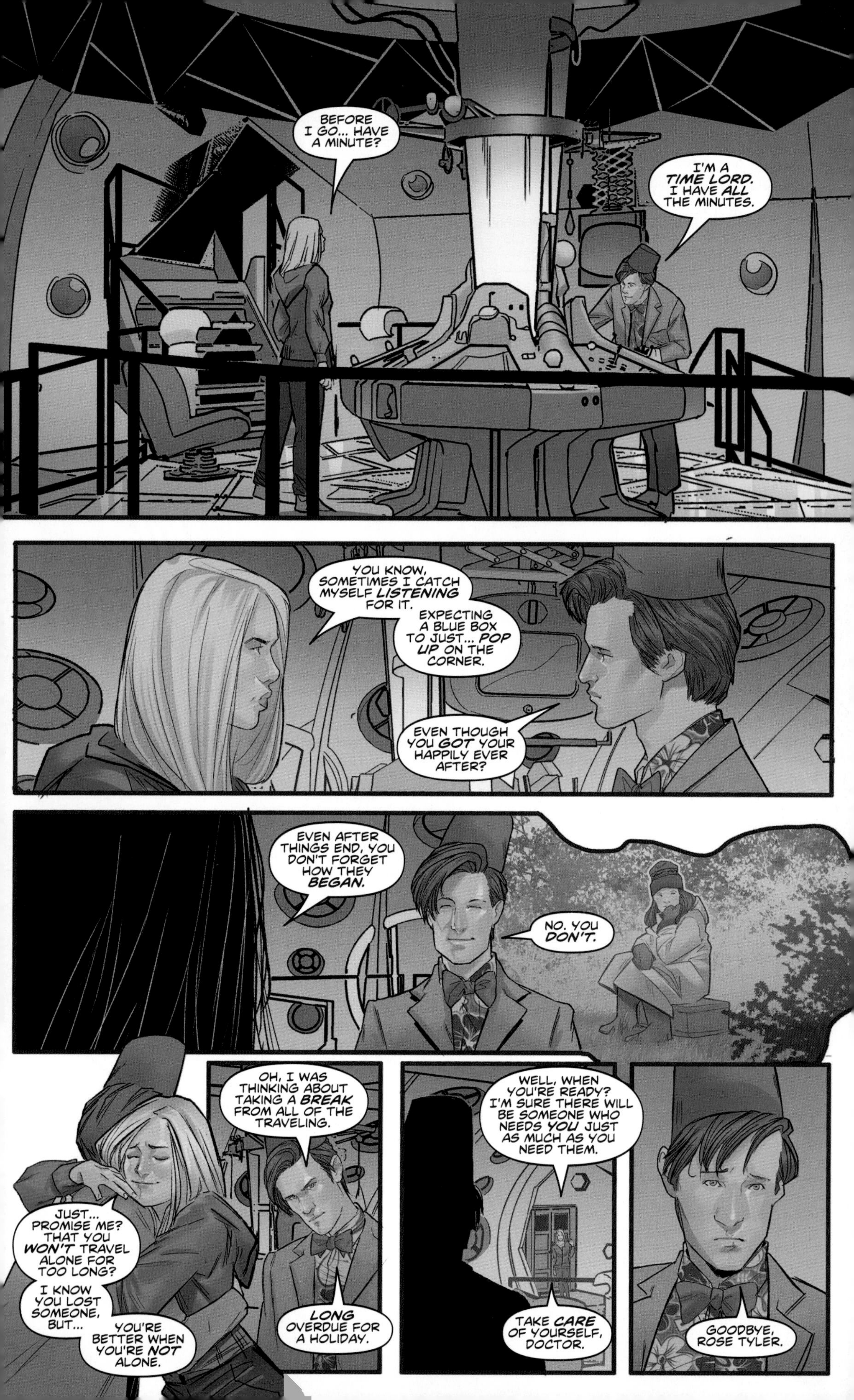
BEFORE I GO... HAVE A MINUTE?
I'M A TIME LORD. I HAVE ALL THE MINUTES.
YOU KNOW, SOMETIMES I CATCH MYSELF LISTENING FOR IT.
EXPECTING A BLUE BOX TO JUST... POP UP ON THE CORNER.
EVEN THOUGH YOU GOT YOUR HAPPILY EVER AFTER?
EVEN AFTER THINGS END, YOU DON'T FORGET HOW THEY BEGAN.
NO. YOU DON'T.
JUST... PROMISE ME? THAT YOU WON'T TRAVEL ALONE FOR TOO LONG?
I KNOW YOU LOST SOMEONE, BUT...
YOU'RE BETTER WHEN YOU'RE NOT ALONE.
OH, I WAS THINKING ABOUT TAKING A BREAK FROM ALL OF THE TRAVELING.
LONG OVERDUE FOR A HOLIDAY.
WELL, WHEN YOU'RE READY? I'M SURE THERE WILL BE SOMEONE WHO NEEDS YOU JUST AS MUCH AS YOU NEED THEM.
TAKE CARE OF YOURSELF, DOCTOR.
GOODBYE, ROSE TYLER.

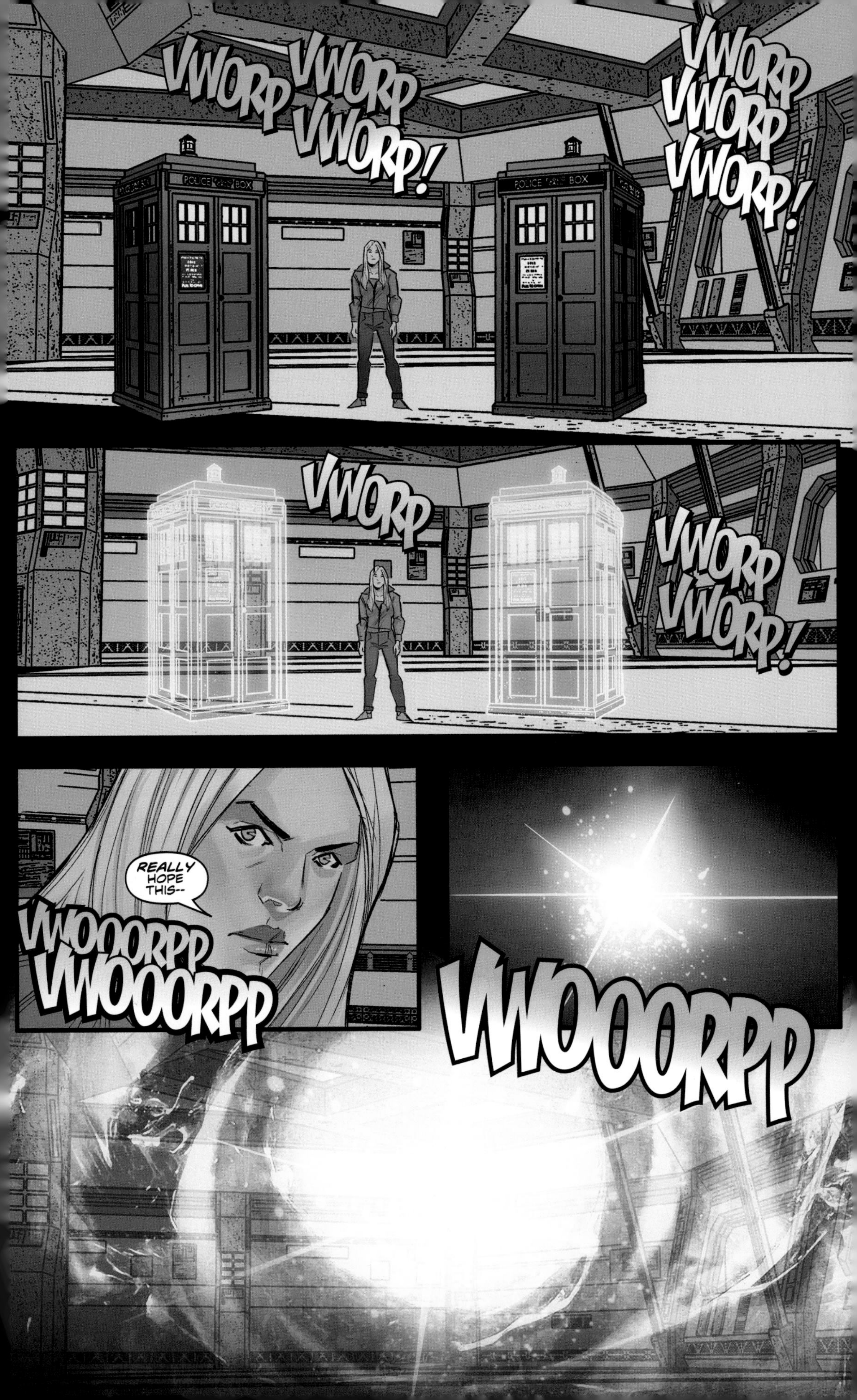
VWORP VWORP VWORP!
VWORP VWORP VWORP!
VWORP
VWORP VWORP!
REALLY HOPE THIS--
VWOOORPP VWOOORPP
VWOOORPP

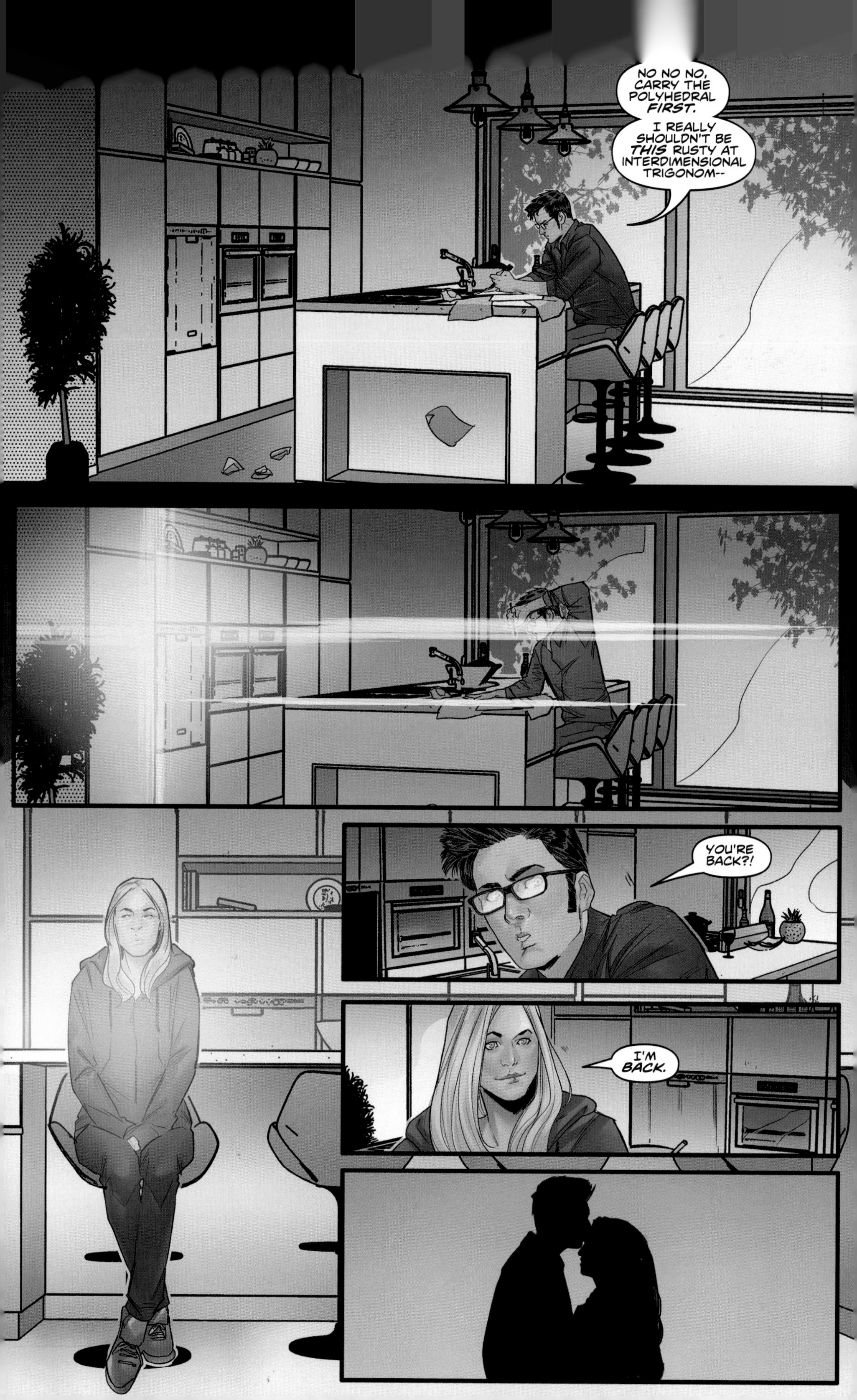
NO NO NO, CARRY THE POLYHEDRAL FIRST.
I REALLY SHOULDN'T BE THIS RUSTY AT INTERDIMENSIONAL TRIGONOM--
YOU'RE BACK?!
I'M BACK.

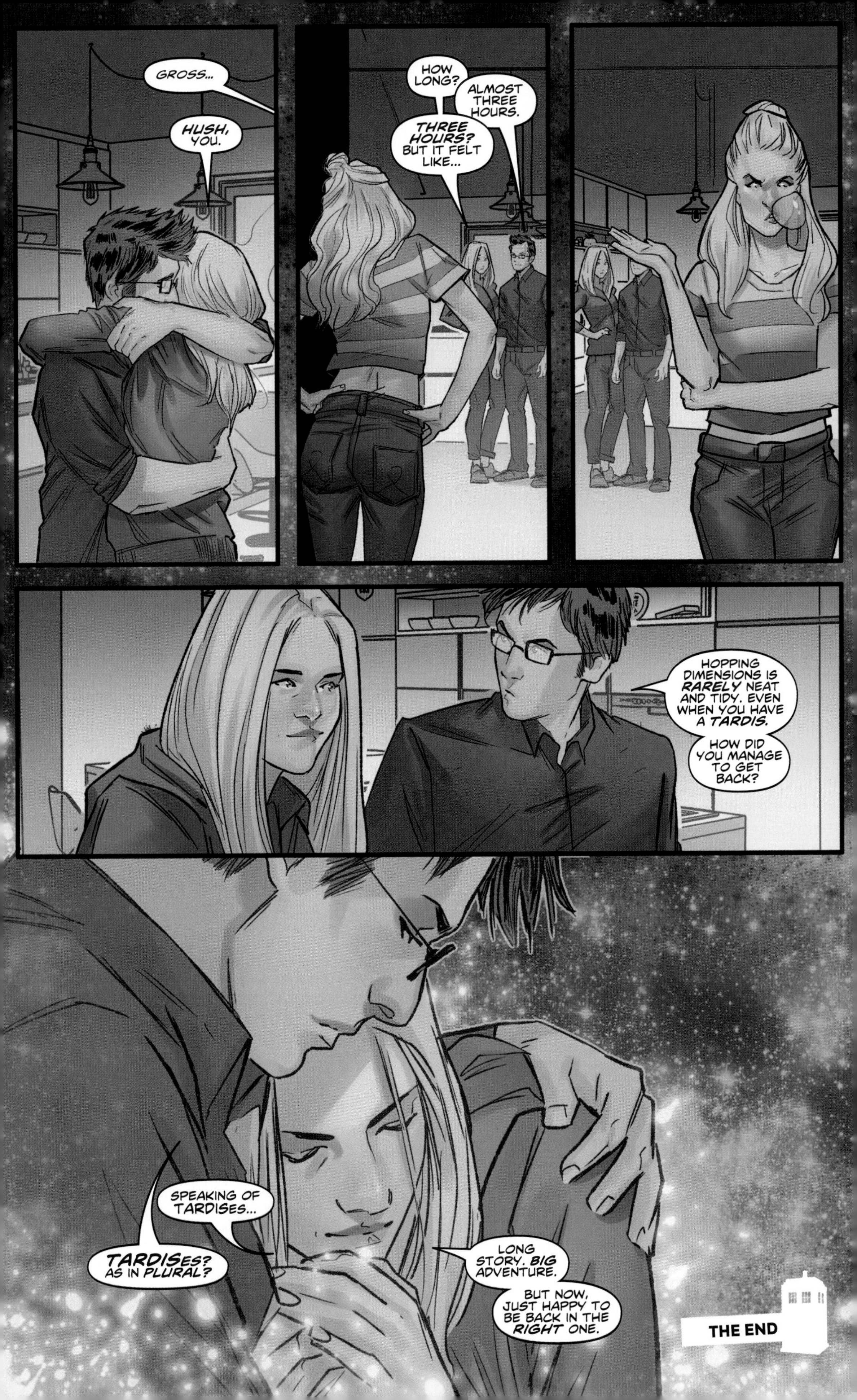
GROSS...
HUSH, YOU.
HOW LONG?
ALMOST THREE HOURS.
THREE HOURS? BUT IT FELT LIKE...
HOPPING DIMENSIONS IS RARELY NEAT AND TIDY. EVEN WHEN YOU HAVE A TARDIS.
HOW DID YOU MANAGE TO GET BACK?
SPEAKING OF TARDISES...
TARDISes? AS IN PLURAL?
LONG STORY. BIG ADVENTURE.
BUT NOW, JUST HAPPY TO BE BACK IN THE RIGHT ONE.
THE END

BBC

DOCTOR WHO

COMIC

Covers Gallery

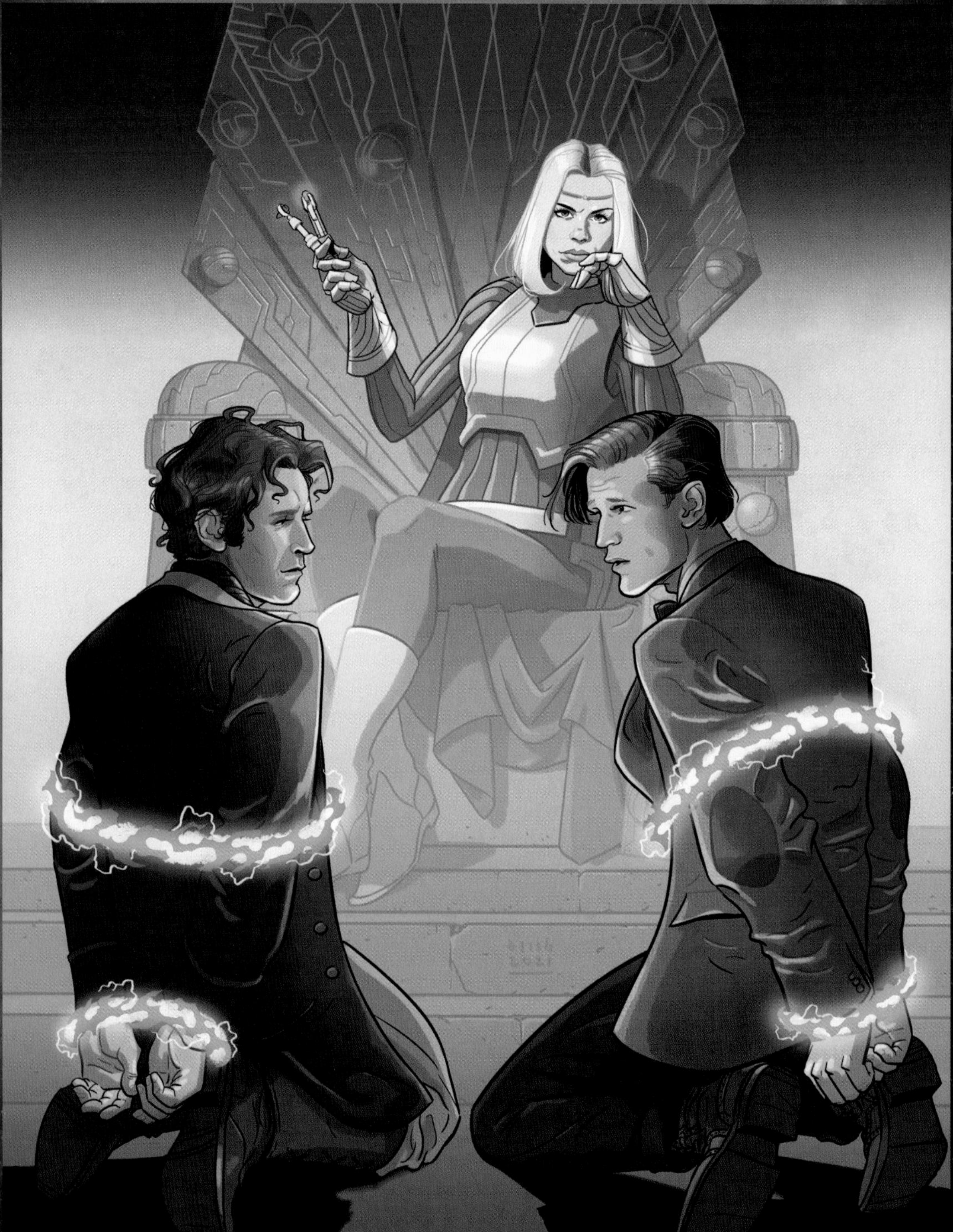

ISSUE #1 COVER A • DAVID BUISÁN

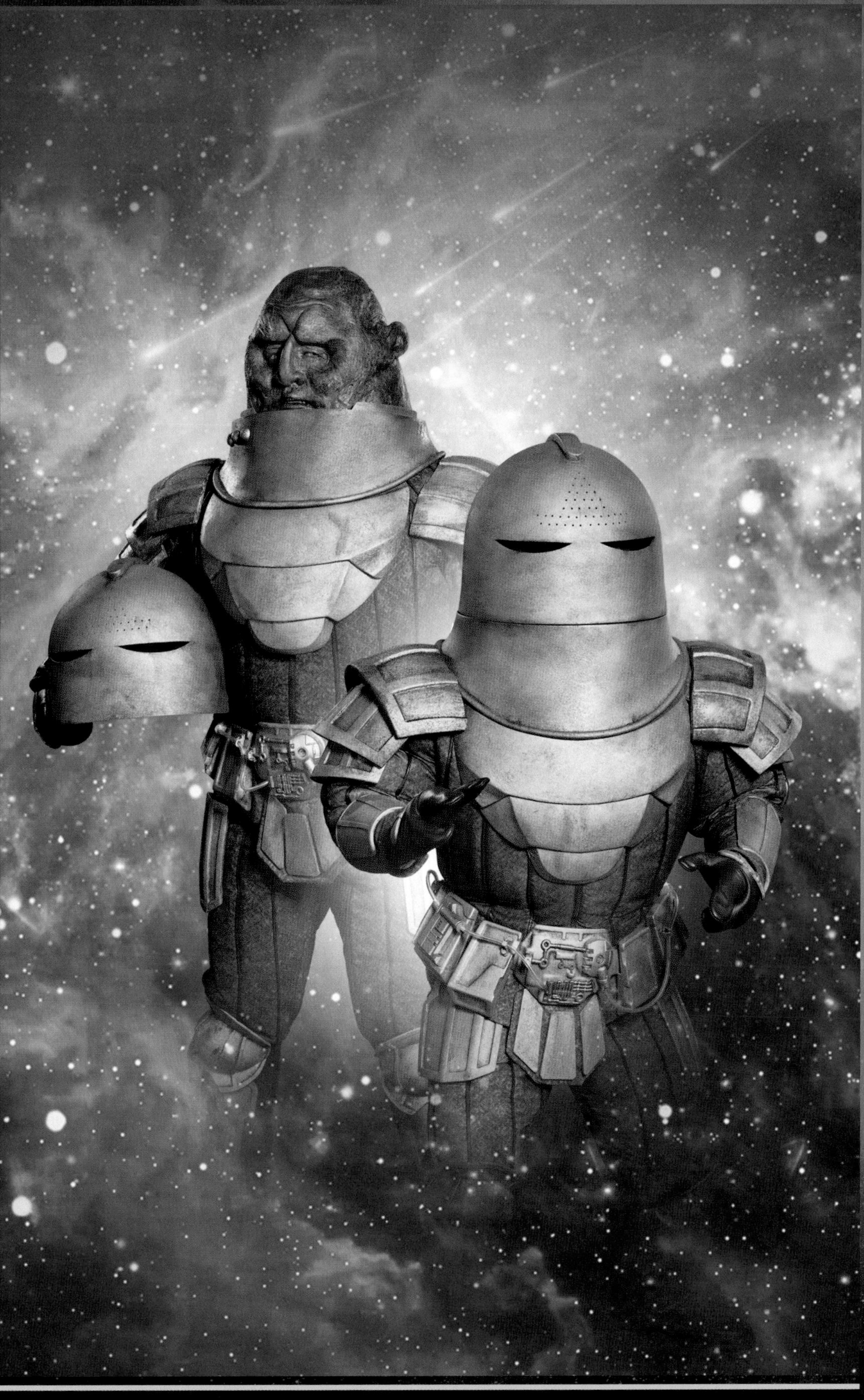

ISSUE #1 COVER B • ANDREW LEUNG

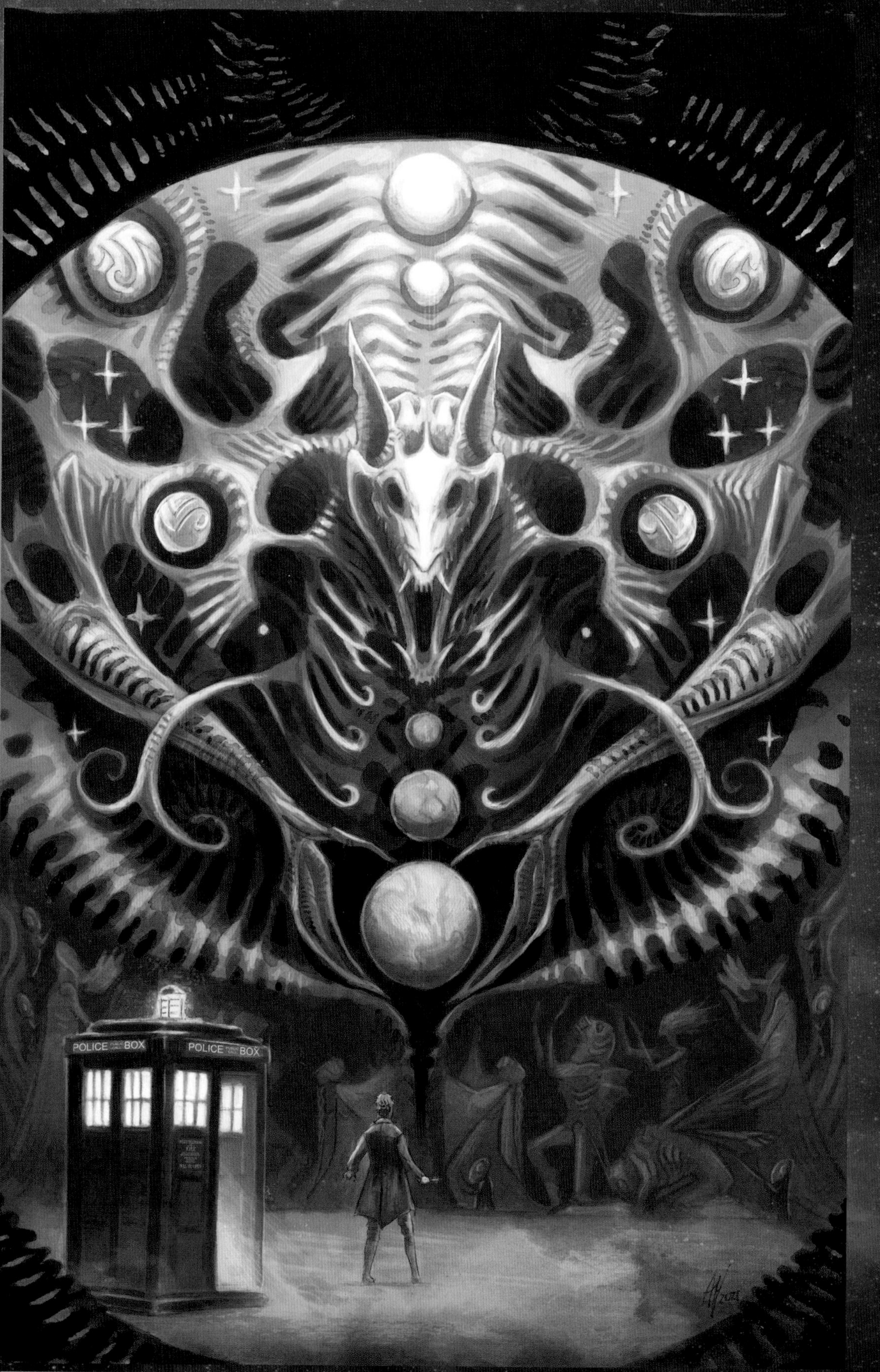

POLICE BOX
POLICE BOX

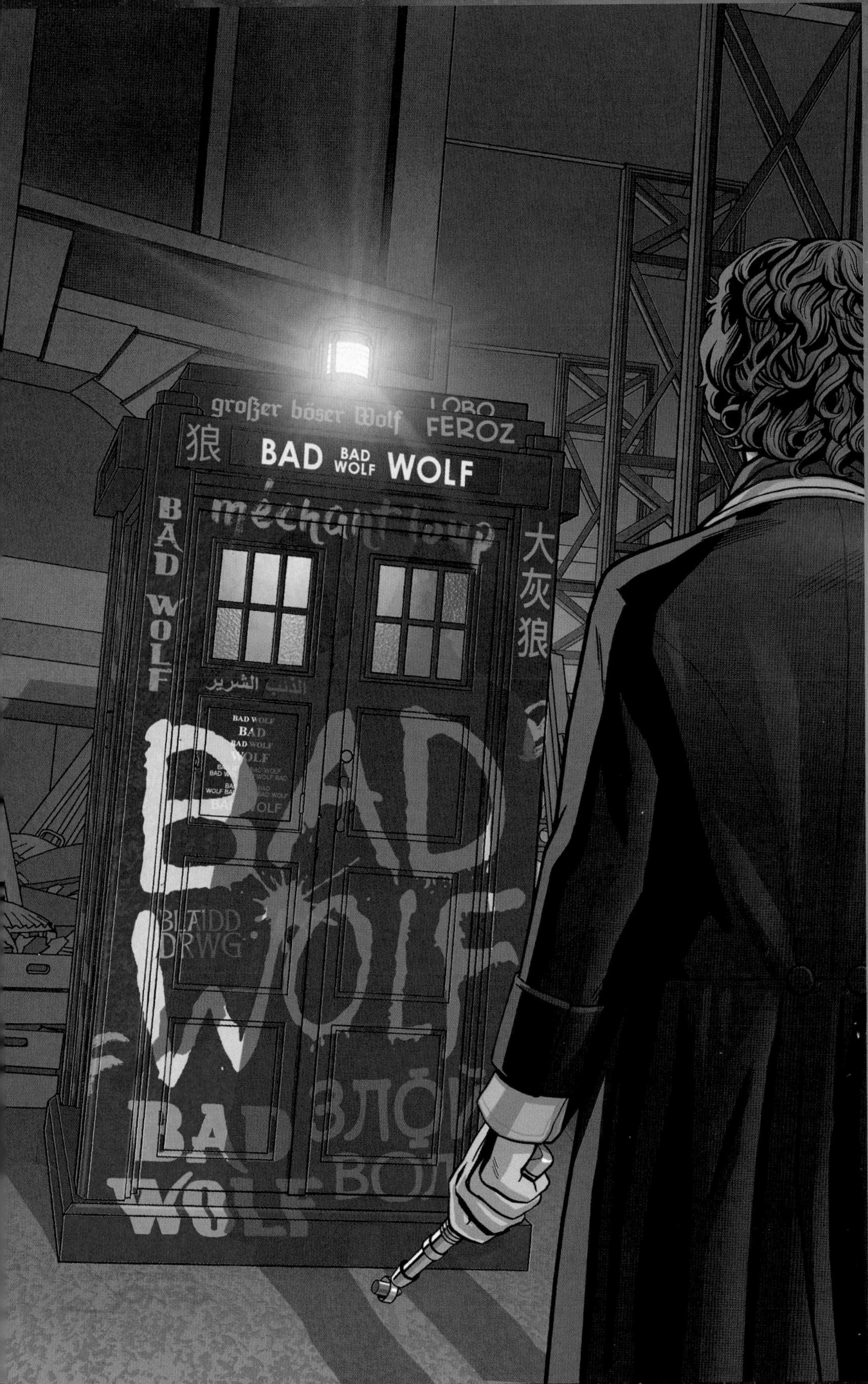
großer böser Wolf
LOBO FEROZ
狼
BAD BAD WOLF WOLF
méchant loup
BAD WOLF
大灰狼
الذئب الشرير
BAD WOLF
BLAIDD DRWG
BAD WOLF
ЗЛОЙ

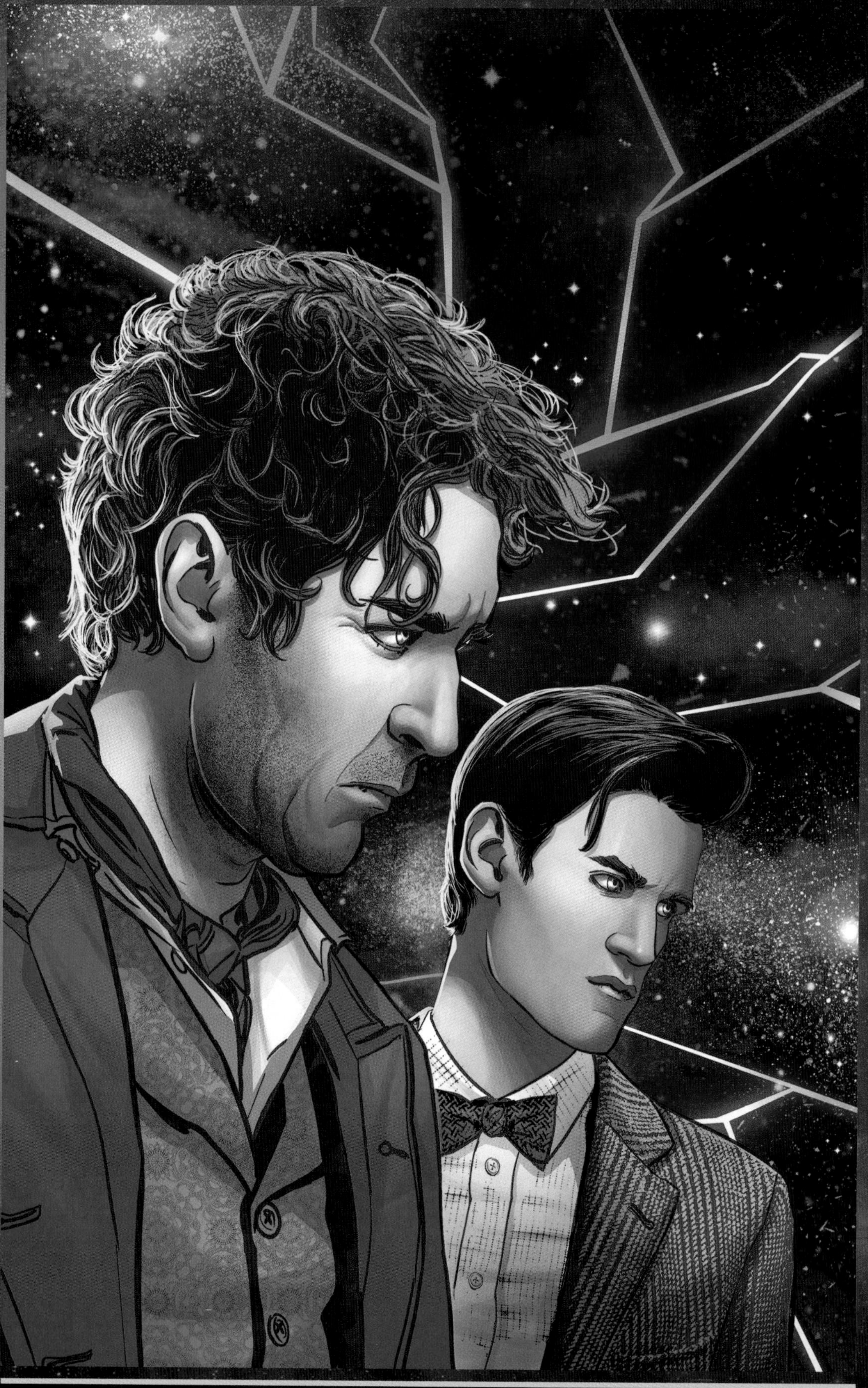

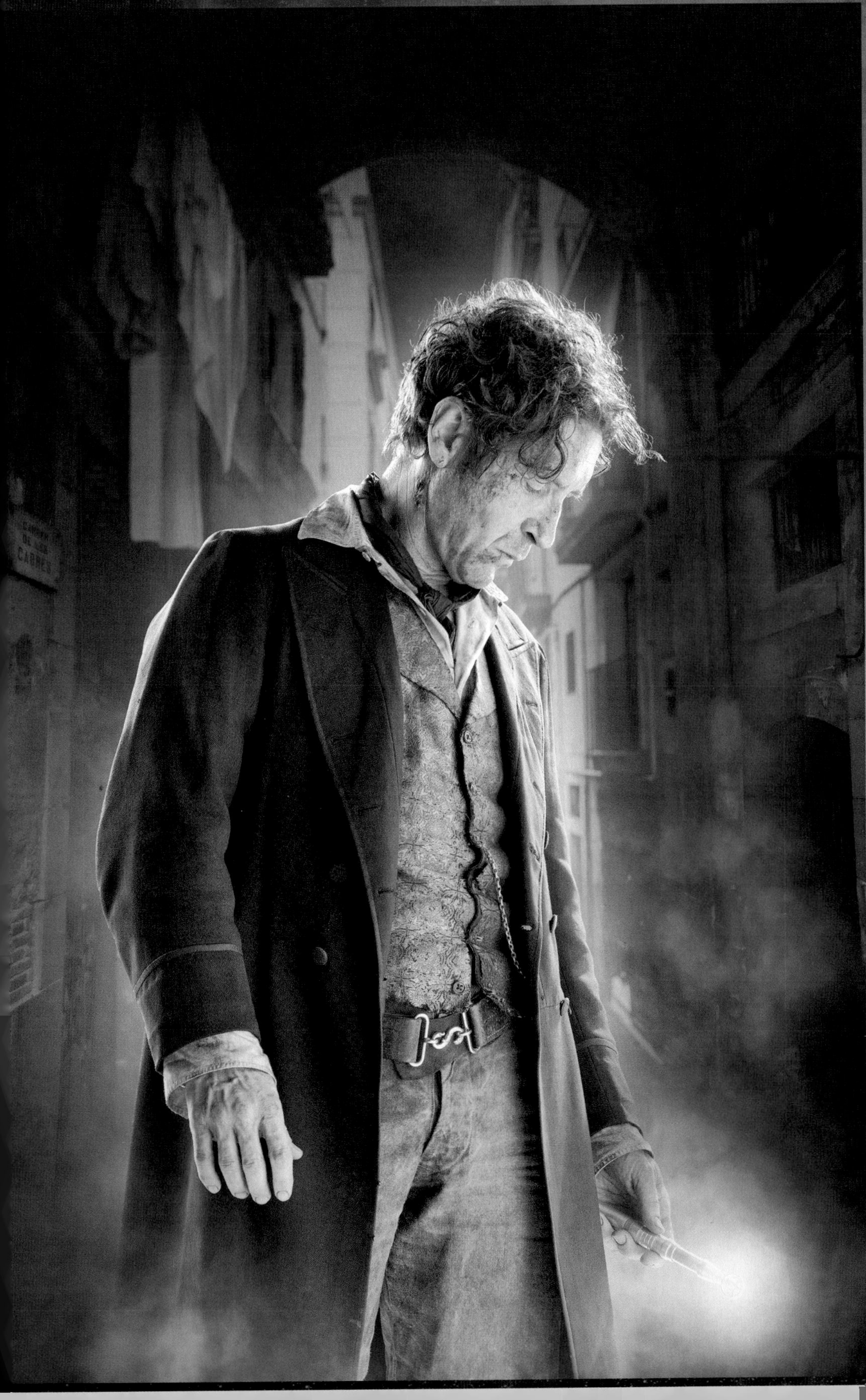

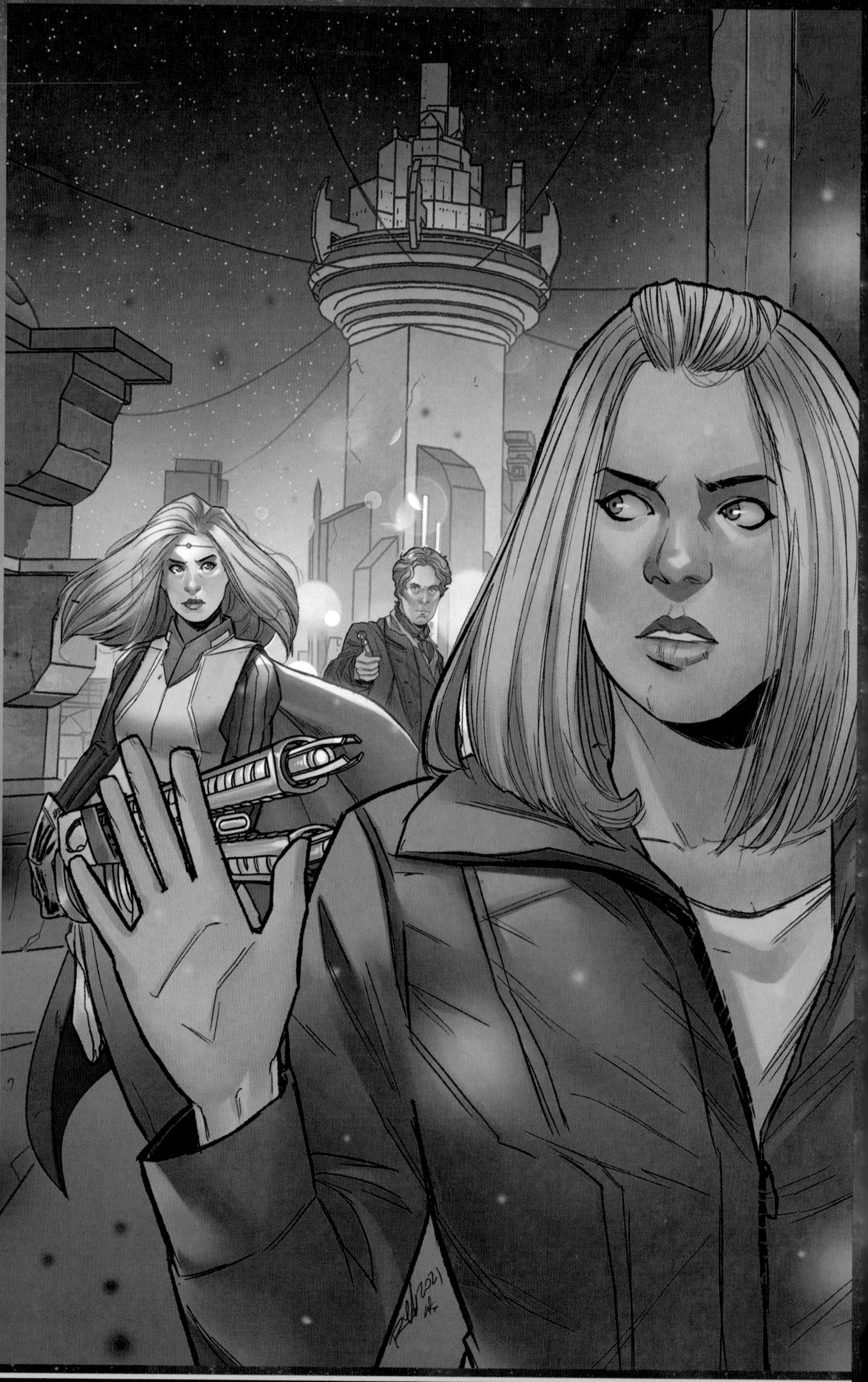

ISSUE #2 COVER C • ROBERTA INGRANATA & WARNIA K. SAHADEWA

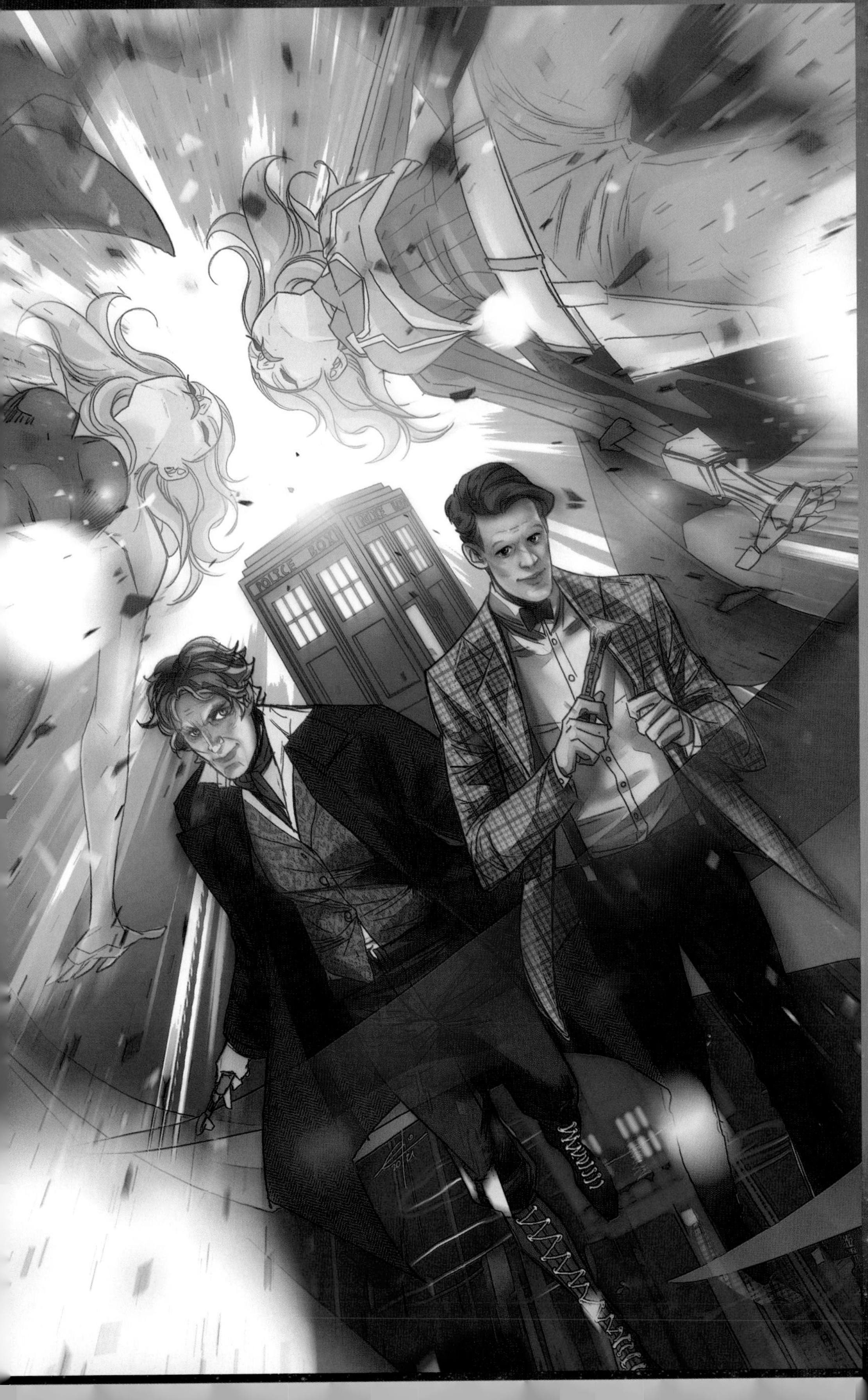
POLICE BOX

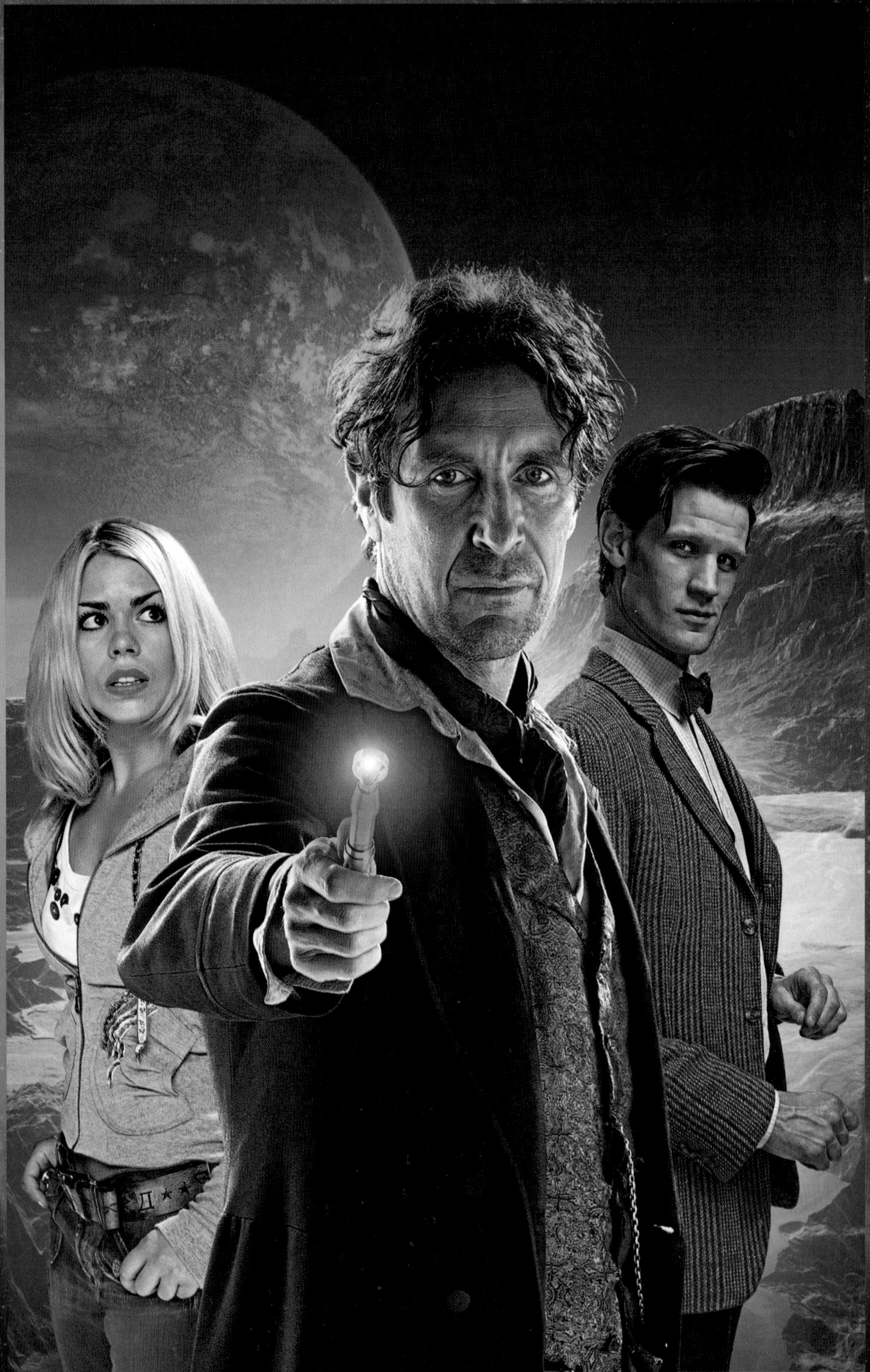

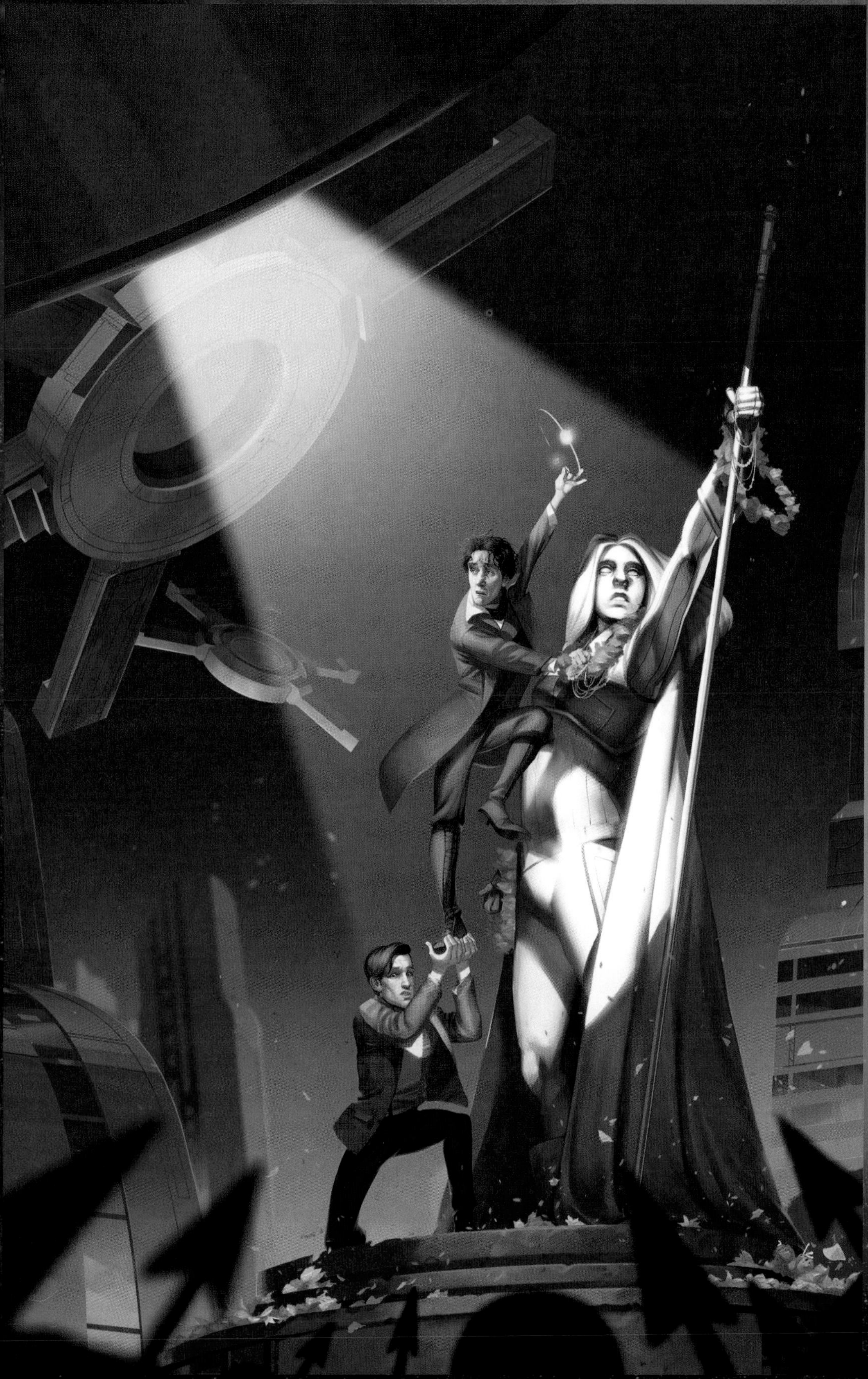

ISSUE #3 COVER C • VV GLASS

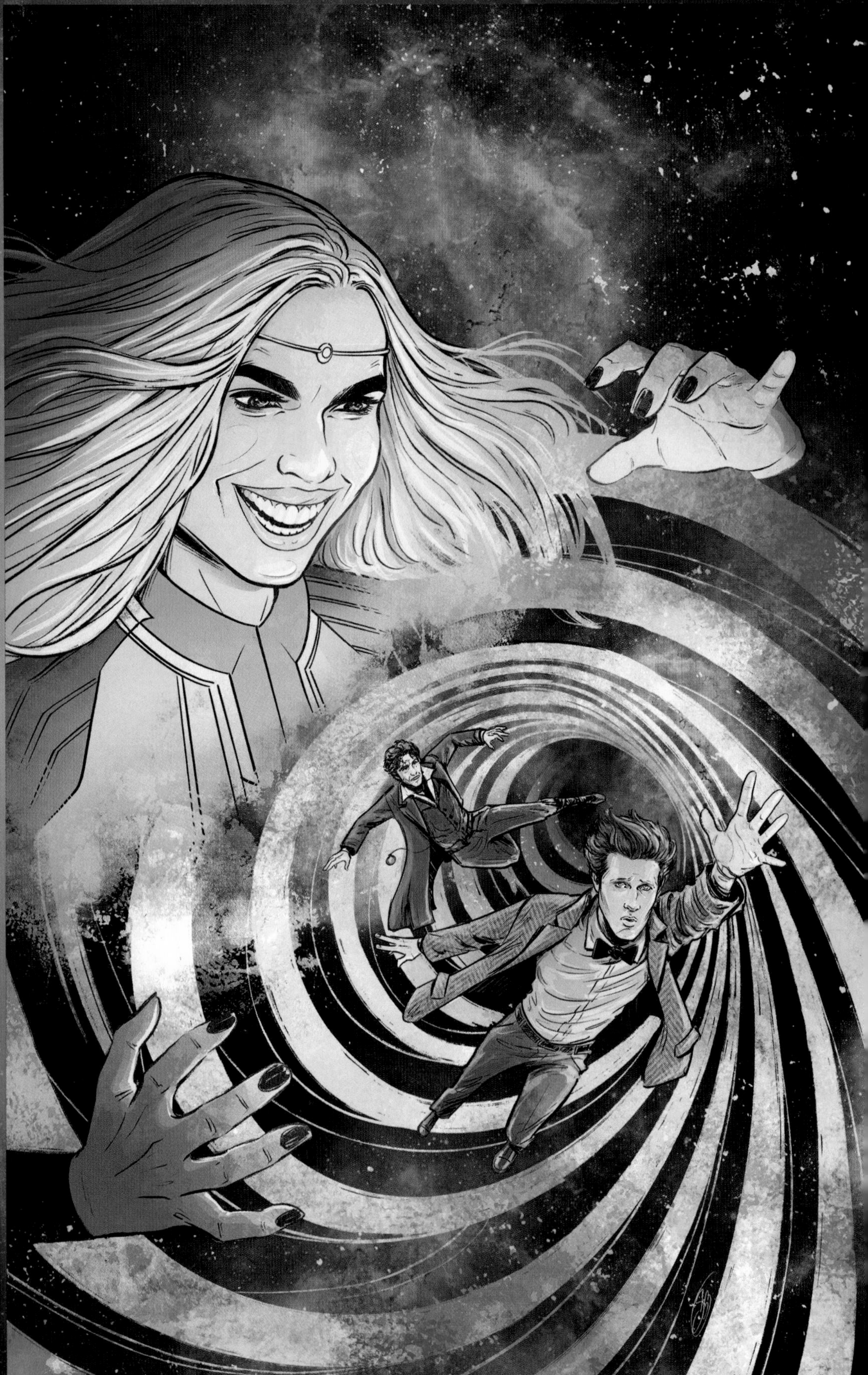

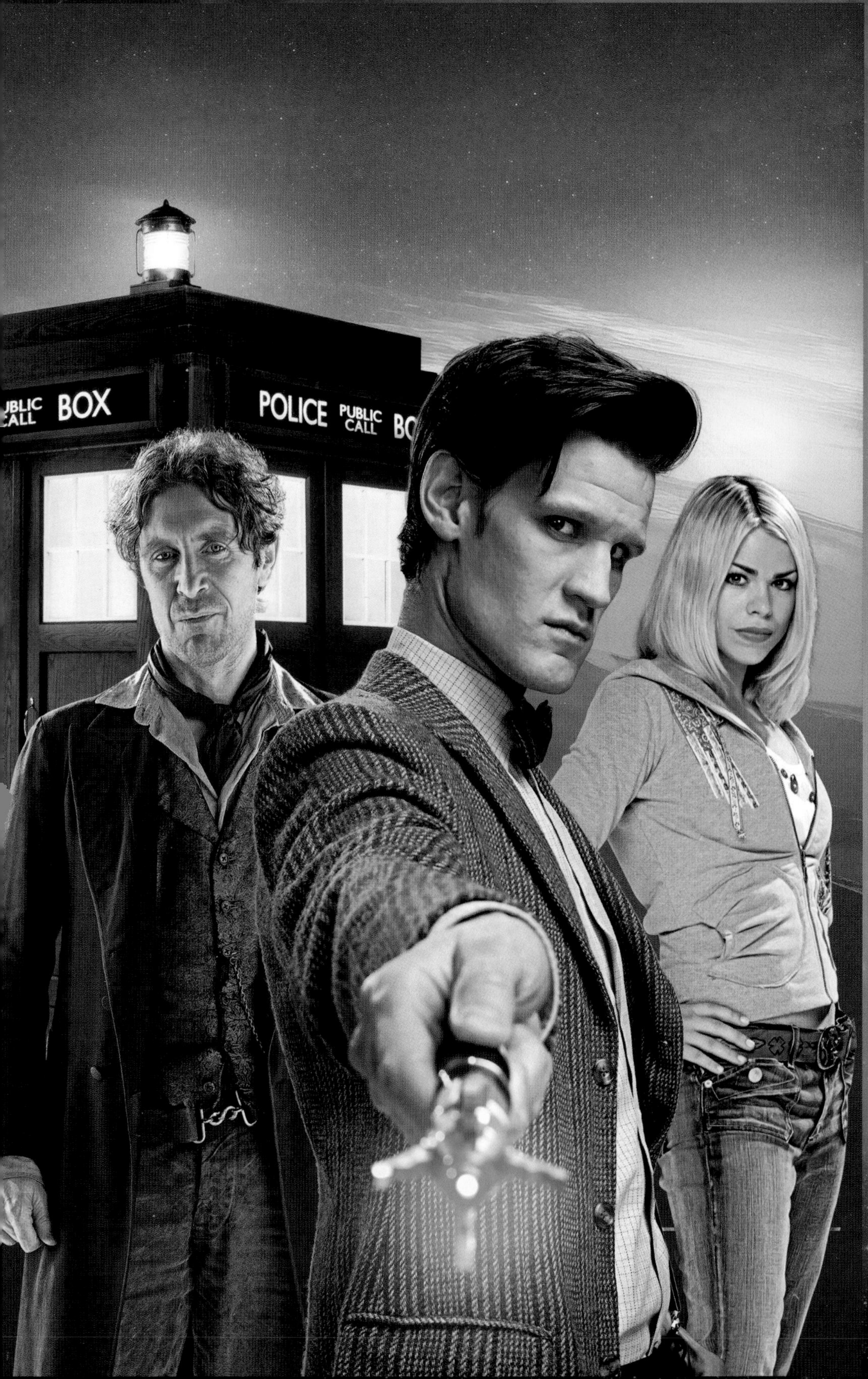

PUBLIC CALL BOX
POLICE PUBLIC CALL BO

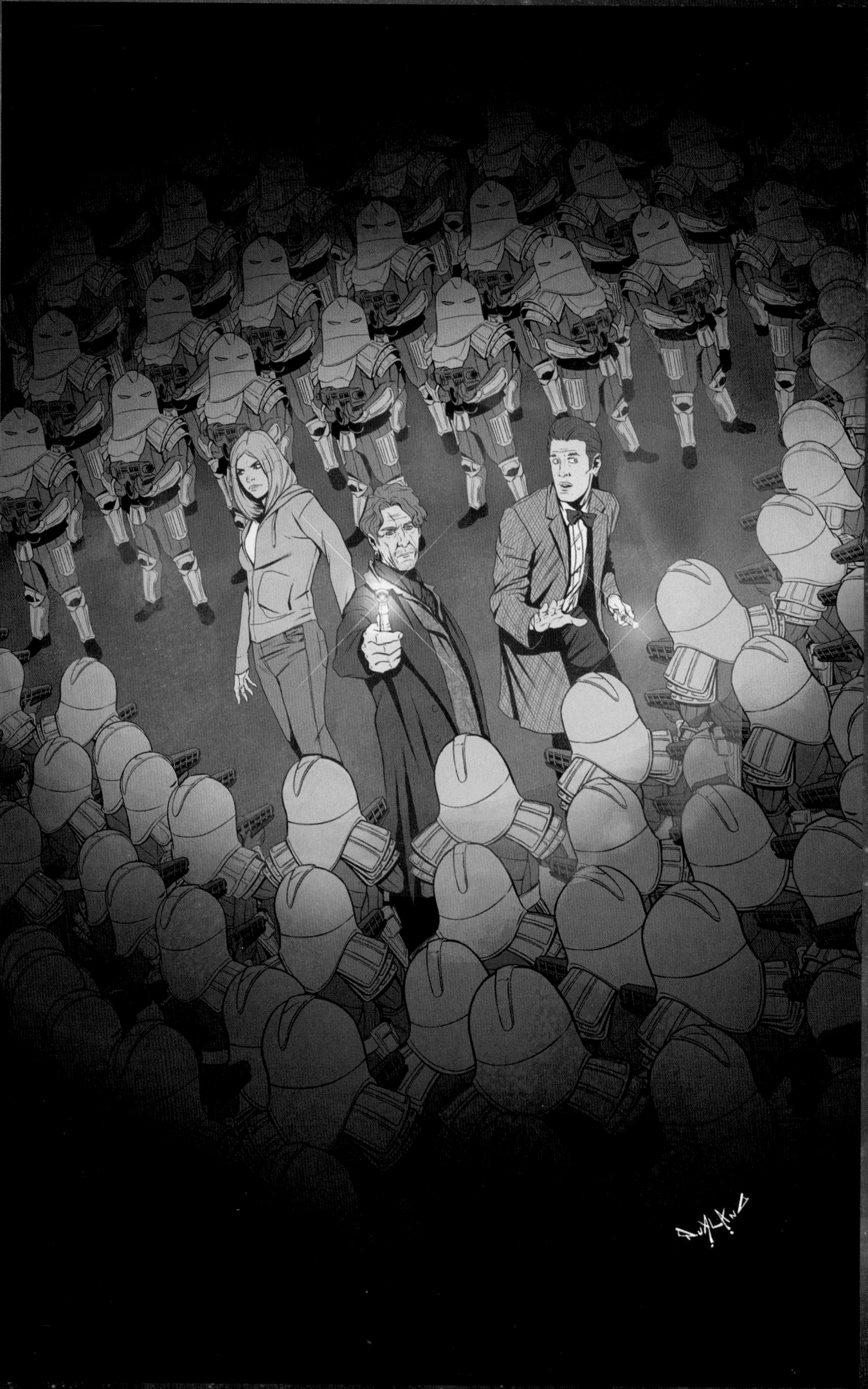

The Art Process
Creating Doctor Who

LAYOUTS AND INKS BY ROBERTA INGRANATA
COLORS BY WARNIA K. SAHADEWA

Rose has a long and fascinating history with the Doctor. In this opening page, Roberta captures the saga succinctly and skillfully, and picks up our story after Rose's bittersweet last appearance.

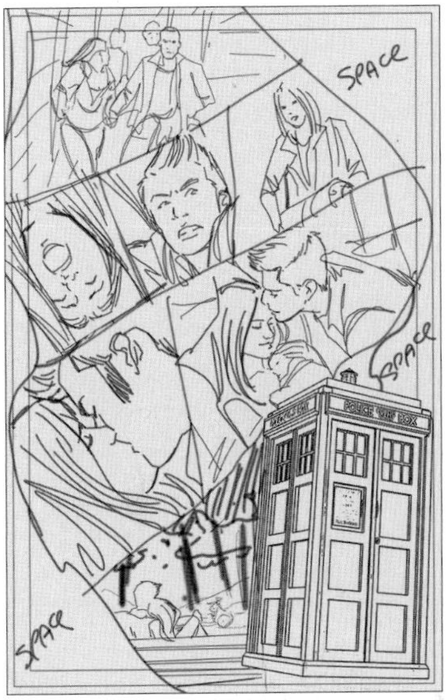
SPACE
SPACE
SPACE

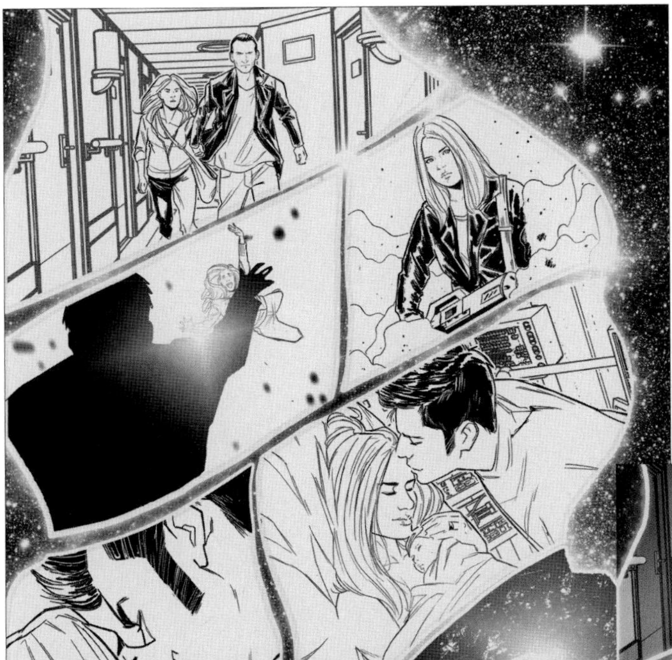

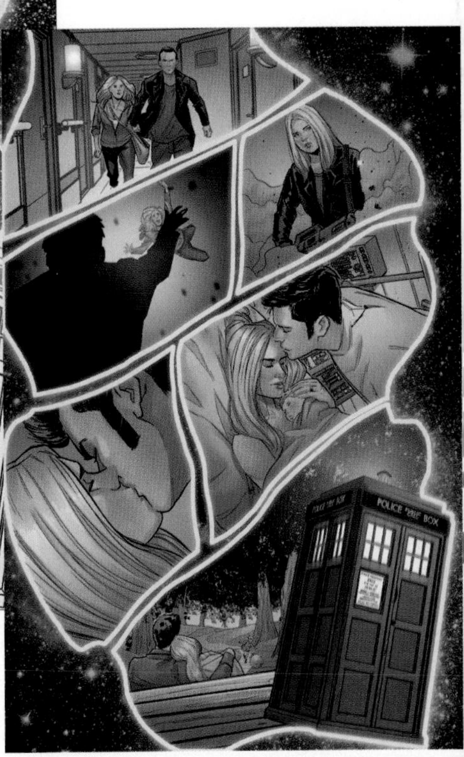

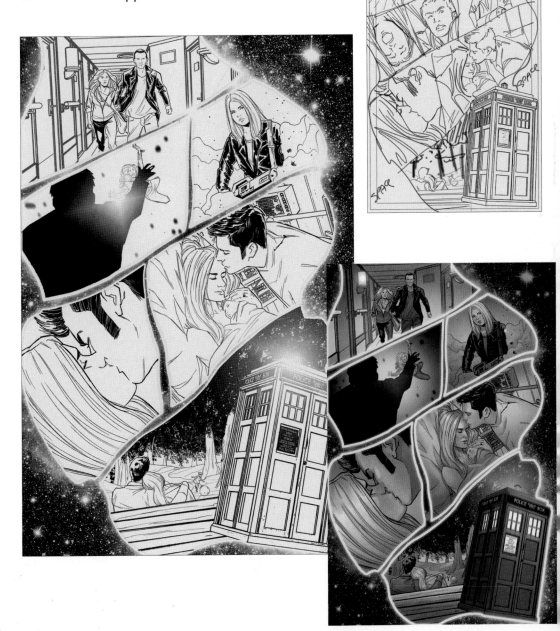

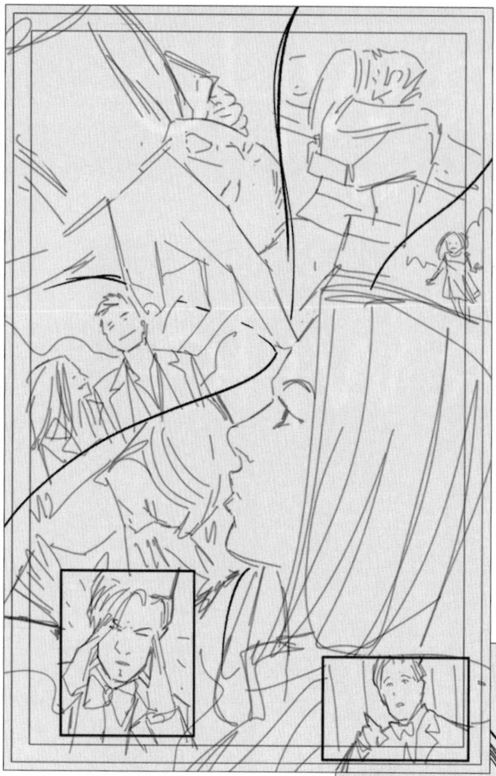

This beautifully designed page offers an insight into the history and plight of the Bad Wolf Empress, an alternate version of Rose Tyler. After a dominating first impression, here we get to see a softer and more intimate side to the character, and how a connection to the Doctor is the gateway to her path of redemption.

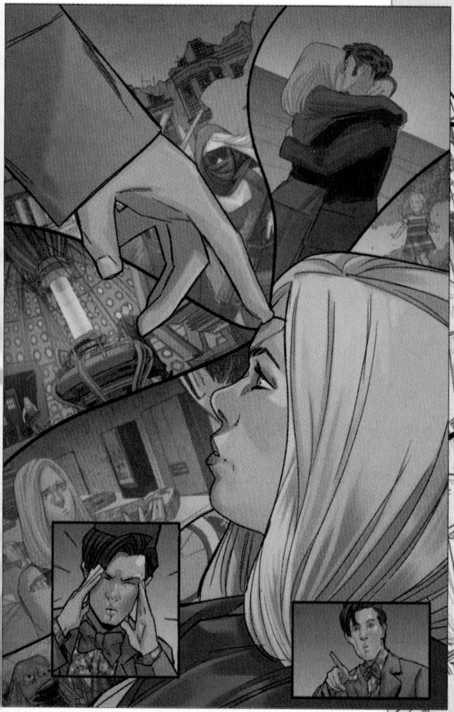

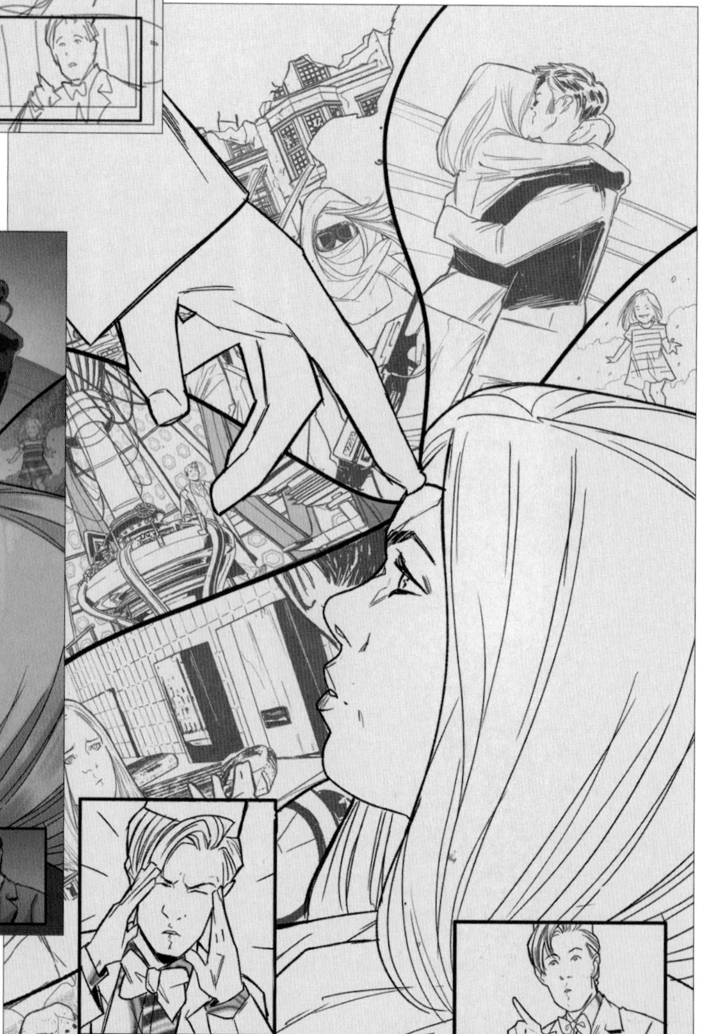

BBC

DOCTOR WHO

COLLECTIO

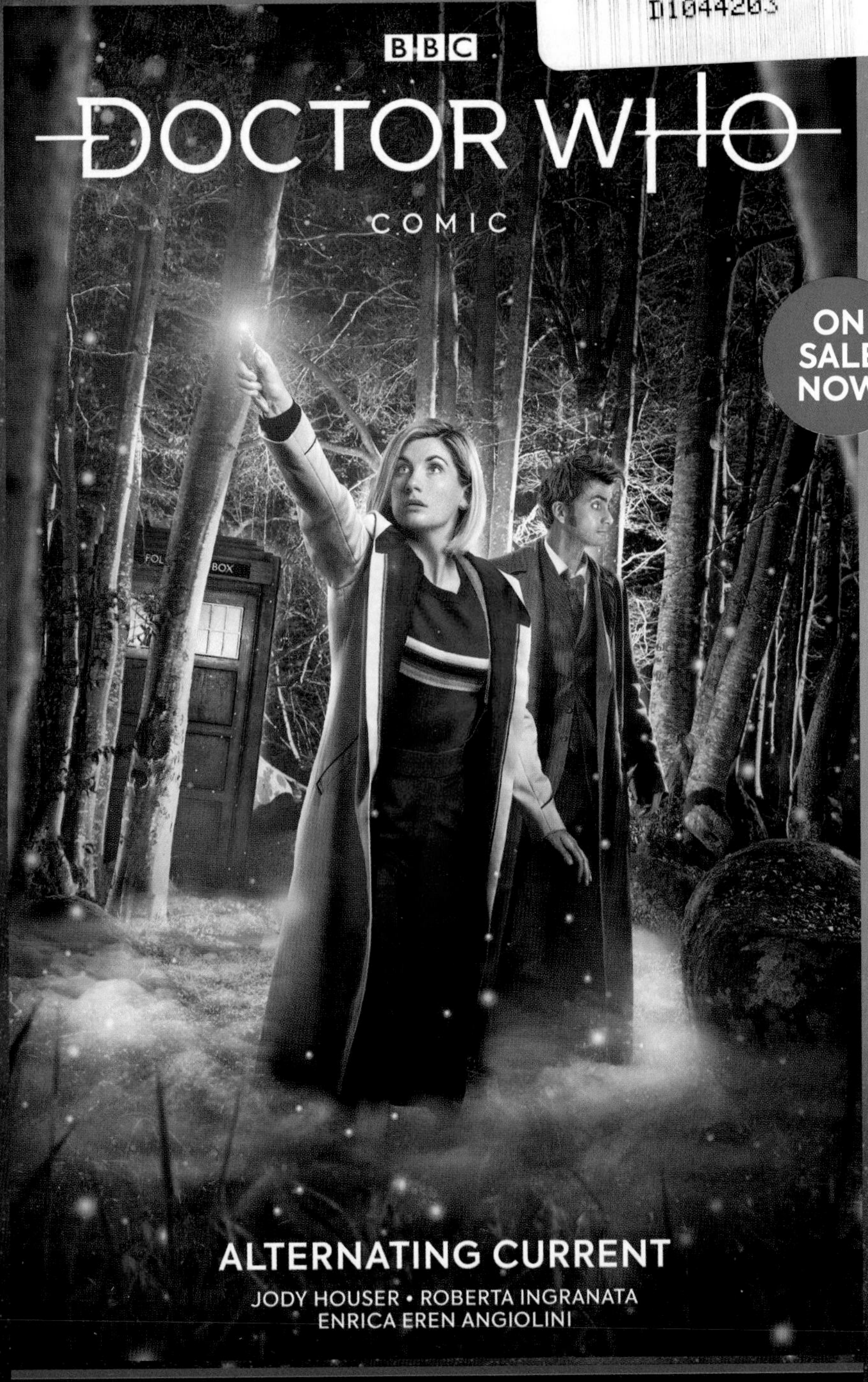
BBC
DOCTOR WHO
COMIC
POLICE BOX
ALTERNATING CURRENT
JODY HOUSER • ROBERTA INGRANATA
ENRICA EREN ANGIOLINI

Cover by ANDREW LEUNG

FROM JODY HOUSER • ROBERTA INGRANATA